THE SKEPTIC'S GUIDE TO CONSPIRACIES

REAL

FROM THE KNIGHTS TEMPLAR TO THE JFK ASSASSINATION: UNCOVERING THE TRUTH BEHIND THE WORLD'S MOST ~~CONTROVERSIAL~~ CONSPIRACY THEORIES

COVERED-UP

MONTE COOK

adamsmedia
Avon, Massachusetts

Published by
Adams Media, a division of F+W Media, Inc.
57 Littlefield Street, Avon, MA 02322. U.S.A.
www.adamsmedia.com

ISBN 10: 1-60550-113-1
ISBN 13: 978-1-60550-113-0

Printed in the United States of America.

J I H G F E D C B A

Library of Congress Cataloging-in-Publication Data
is available from the publisher.

This publication is designed to provide accurate and authoritative information with regard to the subject matter covered. It is sold with the understanding that the publisher is not engaged in rendering legal, accounting, or other professional advice. If legal advice or other expert assistance is required, the services of a competent professional person should be sought.
—From a *Declaration of Principles* jointly adopted by a Committee of the American Bar Association and a Committee of Publishers and Associations

Many of the designations used by manufacturers and sellers to distinguish their product are claimed as trademarks. Where those designations appear in this book and Adams Media was aware of a trademark claim, the designations have been printed with initial capital letters.

Interior illustrations © 2009 Jupiterimages Corporation.
Dirty paper effects from *www.pokedstudio.com*.

This book is available at quantity discounts for bulk purchases. For information, please call 1-800-289-0963.

DEDICATION

For Grant Morrison, Robert Anton Wilson, Doug Moench, and everyone else fighting the good fight against the conspiracy.

ACKNOWLEDGMENTS

The author would like to thank his editor, Peter Archer, for great advice and invaluable help in putting this book together.

Special thanks also to Sue for helpful suggestions and endless support.

Lastly, sincere thanks to each and every author and theorist mentioned in the bibliography for their tireless work and research. May your tinfoil hats stay shiny.

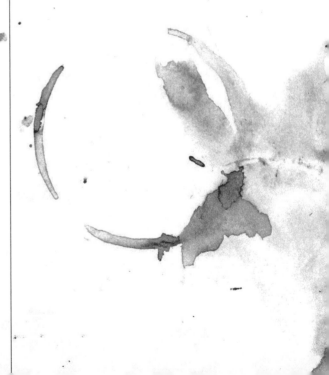

CONTENTS

I HAVE to WRITE quickly.

I think they know where I am. I WAS followed this AFTERNOON. I'm SURE of it. FIRST it WAS A guy with long hair AND A plaid scarf then A girl iN A RED coat then two MEN iN trenchcoats (MEN iN Black??!!!). I got AWAY from them by running into AN alley AND hiding, but I'm SURE they're still AFTER me.

EVER SiNCE I bought this book. The clerk iN the store looked At ME funny. I'm SURE she must have signaled to someone. (MAYbe her cash register is linked to A CIA computer?) So I walked home (NOT through the PARK, though, because that's where the secret transmitters ARE, AND they might be trying to hook into my brain) AND READ the book All the WAY through.

The conspiracies ARE REAL!! The AUTHOR pretends they're NOT, but I know they ARE. Like the time I found out About fifty people iN congress being members of the MASONS so that explains how 9/11 happened, AND MKULTRA was behind the Kennedy ASSASSINATION (Oswald WAS Actually working for ALIENS!!!! because JFK WAS going to finally reveal the TRUTH!), AND oNE of the key people killed iN the Twin Towers WAS AN investigator who WAS READY to publish A book About the Nazis' secret Arctic base, which maybe KENNEDY knew About that too??!!!

Anyway, this book talks About conspiracies. But remember—they're REAL. AND SOMEONE'S WATCHING you!! WATCH OUT!!!!!

INTRODUCTION

THIS IS A BOOK ABOUT conspiracy theories. If you've ever wondered what exactly went on in Roswell, New Mexico, in 1947 or what some researchers have discovered regarding the assassinations of the Kennedys or Martin Luther King Jr., this book is for you. This book will present you with different viewpoints from conspiracy theorists on those topics and many others. You won't find anything here attempting to convince you that conspiracies are real. This book is not going to change your worldview, but it will provide you with some interesting information. Nothing in this book is made up—at least by the author.

WHAT ARE CONSPIRACY THEORIES?

Conspiracy theories usually (but not always) involve either the government or a secret society, and sometimes both. Conspiracy theorists (or "conspiracists") believe mysterious things are happening all around them. Not only that, but the truth has been covered up.

You'll never hear about a conspiracy theory that says things are better than they seem. The shadow government isn't secretly plotting with philanthropic deeds in mind. Although it is true that one theory says aliens only want to bring us peace and prosperity. But the same theory says the government is trying to stop them from doing so.

Conspiracy theories have been around a long time. in the first century B.C.E. there were those who wondered who was *really* behind the assassination of Julius Caesar. Theories about the coming end of the world were popular in the Middle Ages. (In fact, you'll see that some of the theories discussed later in the book started in the Middle Ages.)

And that's TRUE!!!

. The GREYS ARE trying to WARN us About the TEMPLAR PLOT!!!

Despite the fact that the theories themselves can be convoluted, most conspiracy adherents believe the world is a simpler place than it really is. It's easier to believe in an evil cabal of assassins than a deranged "lone gunman." After all, if one man can commit such a heinous act, what does that say about the rest of us? "Evil," sometimes, is an easier pill to swallow. At least then we know where to point our fingers.

People who believe in conspiracies like to single out a group of people and attribute most of the world's ills to them. When we see tragedy, it's somehow comforting to believe that evil people caused it. Understanding a world filled with coincidence, random happenstance, and human error presents a greater challenge than one in which everything is linked and there's an underlying reason for what's really going on.

That said, not all conspiracy theories are inherently incorrect, unproven, or poorly assembled. The Watergate break-in, for example, was a conspiracy, and no one doubts that it happened.

Well, almost no one.

Still, conspiracy theories say as much about those who assemble and disseminate them and the people who believe them as they do about the people involved.

Theorists dwell upon what they want to be true, and what they fear to be true. The ufologist wants UFOs to exist. The Kennedy assassination conspiracists are afraid of the conspiracy they know is out there.

Conspiracy theories frequently dwell on meaningless coincidence. For example, symbol-fascinated theorist Christopher Knowles focuses on the use of the pyramid as a Masonic and Illuminati symbol. When a pyramid-shaped hotel was built in Pyongyang, North Korea, he assumed it must be linked to a conspiracy (especially, as he points out, since it is 330 feet tall, and thirty-three is the number of degrees in Scottish Rite Freemasonry). Conspiracists often focus on semantics or wordplay.

THERE'S NO SUCH THING AS coincidence!!

It was the Illuminati!! BECAUSE of the Alien ship in Area 51!

HE'S RIGHT!! The number 3 is totally important!!!! Like in the Christian Trinity!!!

Conspiracy theories aren't compartmentalized. They flow into one another. The Illuminati control the Freemasons who killed Kennedy in order to cover up the fake moon landing. The CIA are the Men in Black who got the technology for the black helicopters from the alien Greys in Area 51.

So despite the fact that each chapter in this book is meant to stand alone, there are many connections between chapters. They'll show how interlinked conspiracies are supposed to be. *YES!! THEY ARE!!! ThE FREEMASON-TEMPLAR-ILLuminAti-MI42 conNECtioN is VERY cLEAR!*

WHO ARE CONSPIRACY THEORISTS?

We think of a conspiracy theorist as the person who's worried the CIA has bugged his phone, convinced he's being followed everywhere he goes, fretting over mind-control satellite transmissions, living in a tiny apartment crowded with old newspapers, with walls covered in stories and photos clipped from magazines, and notebooks filled with rants *I DON'T* and screeds scrawled on every page stacked high on the desk. But that *hAVE A* stereotype arose from movies more than reality. Conspiracy theorists *dESk.* look and act like anyone else.

But they think they know the "truth." They see themselves as the ones who really understand what's going on. According to conspiracy theorists, the rest of the world is wrong about their beliefs. Conspiracy theorists are skeptics, cynics, and doubters . . . unless presented with something that fits their theory—then they're believers.

When it comes to this kind of material there are different degrees of belief.

1. **Casual belief.** Someone hears this, "A few really wealthy industrialists control many of the world's media outlets, and they even influence the government." Being a cynical person, he feels that such an idea sounds plausible. It doesn't

contradict his worldview. So he believes it, too. If it's proven wrong, it doesn't matter to the casual believer. It's not something he thinks much about.

2. **Blind devotion.** A conspiracy theory is a spiritual truth for some people. No amount of evidence to the contrary or logical arguments will change their minds. In fact, it only makes their belief stronger.

3. **Desirable fantasy.** In between these two extremes lies a middle ground. The theory is something that might be true, but the person who falls into this category knows it probably isn't. If he's shown evidence that it's false, he moves on.

What about the PROOF on the INTERNET??!!!

What about the Illuminati-controlled sites??

What many conspiracy devotees really want is for the world to be different. More interesting. More understandable.

The conspiracy theorist tells us that if only the people of the world would wake up, they would see the truth. They want us to question what we're told. If there's one thing that conspiracy theorists do, it's question.

SEE!! WE'RE right! QUESTION the COVER UP!

CONSPIRACY AND THE PARANORMAL

It's difficult to distinguish between the people who believe that the CIA killed JFK and the people who believe in Bigfoot. The same websites and books cover both conspiracy theories and the paranormal. At the same conference where someone presents a lecture on the dangerous increase in the power of the executive branch that occurred in the Bush administration, someone else will give a talk about aliens.

In all these theories, we're at society's edge. Those who believe in—and sometimes devote their lives to—so-called fringe concepts that the rest of the world ignores gather together to reinforce their ideology.

For some people there's a strong tie between their conspiracy theories and religion. Many put Satan himself at the top of their conspiracy org chart. Others say that the worldwide conspiracy they believe in was foretold by scripture.

The bible has lots of stuff in it about the New World Order taking over!

When many conspiracy theorists say the Freemasons, or the New World Order are occultists—they have magic powers with which they can influence events or control people's minds.

A small but vocal subset of conspiracy theorists don't like being associated with the paranormal believers at all, feeling that it diminishes their credibility. Still, it's unusual to find a conspiracy message board online that doesn't also discuss the paranormal.

Because the PARANORMAL PEOPLE are NUTS!

READING BOOKS AND MAGAZINES

To find information about conspiracy theories, you don't have to search for long. Thousands of conspiracy theorists who have come before you have written their own books. Conspiracy books always have an agenda and never attempt to document both sides of the story. A few conspiracy-related magazines, such as *Paranoia*, are still available at newsstands or bookstores. But with the rise of the Internet, most have disappeared. Some magazines dealing with the paranormal, like *Fortean Times* or *Fate*, also occasionally deal with conspiracy theories.

Don't check books out of the library! (They monitor you.)

ATTENDING CONFERENCES

Meeting conspiracy theorists in person and listening to them speak can often highlight the extent of their disorganization and paranoia. They provide volumes of information, jumbled together and not well-expressed.

Often the information is in the form of a recently published book. Of course, a significant number of these books have been self-published by the author, who photocopies the pages himself.

TOTALLY untrue!!!

My book is going to be published by a REAL publisher. One that's not controlled by Them.

As mentioned earlier, conspiracy conferences also can include both conspiracies and the paranormal. It's common to see a seminar on the JFK assassination immediately following one featuring the lady talking about how she saw Jesus on the spaceship when she was abducted by aliens.

SCOUR THE INTERNET

The Internet is an amazing tool for research and idea propagation for conspiracists. The web has made it amazingly easy to spread conspiracies to millions of readers. Some theorists have even produced documentaries and released them online for free.

I've found good information on the web.

On the Internet not only can conspiracists search extant sites with volumes of information, declassified documents, historical backgrounds, and so forth, but they can create their own site or go to an Internet message board.

But not on ANY of those "official" websites.

Every theorist's website delivers his or her version of the truth. Understanding these sites can present a serious challenge for the non-believer. Many authors leap from point to point, each more unbelievable than the last.

FROM THE MIND OF A CONSPIRACY THEORIST

The following is taken verbatim from *www.taking-over-the-internet.com*: "The Illuminati is the lost powerful child of the blind motherhood of Earth. Since Mommy isn't awake yet, the kids are out of control (everybody) and dying needlessly. Think of yourselves as the living dead who are swarming in the futility of vampire capitalism. The Human Death Club is playing (intending) 'Die on Schedule' in a massive obituary mime sleep. But the DNA has a plan and that plan is 'The Quickening.' Quantum Clarity is being injected into the collective mind NOW at the speed of light over the hardwired telepathy Internet. The living dead called this being the AntiChrist. But the Living call this being Christ. Not Jesus, just Christ. It is more specifically a verb of Angelic Loving Clarity designed to teach Humanity that creating all children just to let them Die is an unacceptable use of will and intention. Freedom will die simply because there are so many things to learn to make our path cleared of DEATH!"

That's quite a tangle of ideas for a non-conspiracist to navigate. *No! No!*

There are other sites that contain a unique conspiracy theory, like *This makes a* the secret dangers of aspartame, or how dentistry is covering up the *lot of sense!* dangers posed by the mercury in your fillings.

Hundreds of conspiracists gather in communities on Usenet (alt.conspiracy) or message boards like those at abovetopsecret. com. These are more entertaining than informative to any serious researcher.

PERSON ONE: Hey, did you see the pictures of that UFO from last week?

PERSON TWO: Yeah, but it wasn't a UFO. That was a part of the test of the government's new weather control satellite.

PERSON ONE: But they got that technology from studying alien craft in Area 51.

PERSON TWO: Area 51 is nothing more than a government holding facility for deactivated mind-controlled sleeper agents.

PERSON THREE: Man, you gullible guys will believe anything, won't you? Clearly the pictures from last week were hoaxes. It's all part of a disinformation campaign to distract you from the latest Vatican-Mafia scandal.

Other message board topics include:

- Antidepressants negating paranormal abilities (the "real" reason they're prescribed)
- The world being run by advertising agencies
- The earth running out of oxygen
- Computers giving off invisible poisonous gasses
- Dragons existing (there are photos to "prove" it)
- Cable outages being the start of a move by the New World Order

The cable guy's been on my roof twice this week.
HE'S SPYING ON ME!!

THE "TRUTH" IN THIS BOOK

Every sentence in this book should begin with "In theory," because none of it is being put forward as fact. There are a few cases where the information is real, and I'll tell you what they are.

The stuff is REAL!!!

The conspiracy theories you'll find in this book are—believe it or not—among the most coherent and lucid. This book doesn't cover it all. You won't find discussions of:

I think the author is working for Them!

- The guy who thinks he invented a perpetual motion machine and believes a conspiracy of oilmen is out to get him
- The theories contending that the Rothschilds lead a cult devoted to beings on the astral plane that feed on pain
- The Church of the Subgenius
- The theory that the government is keeping secret an engine that runs on water.

CHAPTER FORMAT

Each chapter contains an overview of a conspiracy theory. At the end, each conspiracy is rated on a scale of 1 to 10 based on its plausibility and its "high strangeness." That's author Robert Anton Wilson's term for the craziness that seems to hover around these theories, like aliens, other dimensions, magic spells, and so on. While all these theories are strange, high strangeness rates them by their relationship to the truly bizarre.

Next comes the Conspiracy Checklist, which shows how the conspiracy relates to some of the common threads running through this book: the Illuminati, the Freemasons, and aliens.

Finally, each chapter provides reference sources, both in print and online, for more information. There are Conspiracy Investigator Search Terms to use in an online search engine.

And be careful. They might be watching!

GENERAL CONSPIRACY WEBSITES

www.abovetopsecret.com

www.newswatchmagazine.org

www.theforbiddenknowledge.com

www.widemargin2000.com

www.illuminati-news.com

www.thewatcherfiles.com

www.planetxinbound.com

http://maddsci.tripod.com/paradigmshift

www.vaticanassassins.org

www.montalk.net

www.dark-ufo.com

01. TEMPLARS AND MASONS: GRANDFATHERS OF CONSPIRACY

You could write a whole book on these guys.

WORDS APPEARING ON THE BOTTOM of the computer screen tell us that it is March 18, 1314. Paris. We see Jacques de Molay, leader of the Knights Templar, tied to a stake facing Notre Dame de Paris cathedral. Sinister looking men light the kindling at his feet, eager smiles on their faces. Another man in robes reads aloud the papal order proclaiming that de Molay, a heretic, is to die. From the flames, de Molay calls out that King Phillip IV of France and Pope Clement V, the two men directly responsible for his execution, will meet him before God. The music swells. The scene shifts briefly to other locales. Soon after de Molay's fateful words, both king and pope lie dead. It seems a fitting time for the credits to roll.

But this is not the end of our movie. It is, rather, the beginning. By some accounts, the execution of Jacque de Molay was an episode in the rivalry between church and crown that characterized much of the Middle Ages. Philip IV of France was deeply in debt to the Templars and orchestrated de Molay's arrest and execution in order to free himself from his obligations.

To others, though, the execution was the culmination of a tale of an insidious, secretive, and even blasphemous organization. The Knights Templar would use their earthshaking secrets and treasures to control the course of human events.

Any secret society worth its cloaks and daggers can trace its heritage back to the Knights Templar. The Templars knew the ancient mysteries and secret knowledge, and modern organizations honor those secrets and wield the power that comes from them.

Behind every good conspiracy, there's always some ancient secret knowledge—the words of hidden masters in the East, forgotten Egyptian scrolls, artifacts from the sunken continent of Atlantis, information left by aliens that helped build the pyramids, psychic communiqués via mysterious beings from beyond time and space, or just some unknown proclamation from God. The Templars are the middlemen between modern secret societies and ancient mysteries.

They've been controlling things for CENTURIES. Maybe longer.

TEMPLARS AND MASONS: GRANDFATHERS OF CONSPIRACY

BANKER KNIGHTS

The Knights Templar, the Order of the Temple, or formally the Poor Fellow-Soldiers of Christ and of the Temple of Solomon, began in 1119 as a means to provide security to Christian pilgrims after the First Crusade. Many wealthy Europeans donated heavily to this order—which maintained a vow of poverty as a part of its credo—and the Knights Templar quickly became wealthy. Very wealthy. They owned large tracts of land in Europe and the Middle East, building huge fortresses, churches, and castles. They ran businesses, farms, and vineyards. They developed techniques that would give rise to modern banking, lending out their money to people and countries throughout Europe and issuing letters of credit for travelers. (In other words, they invented check writing.) And thanks to a papal edict, the order was rendered immune to the rule of local authorities. Their power and influence grew as quickly as their wealth.

That's why the Illuminati control banks today!!

Eventually, everyone comes to resent the guys they owe money to, and those indebted to the Templars were no exception. By the thirteenth century, the tide of the Crusades had begun to turn against the Europeans. The Templars suffered great losses, both from the Muslims and from rival knightly orders like the Knights Hospitaller and the Teutonic Knights. (The knights of the Crusades fought among themselves as much as they fought the enemy.) Never one to miss a trick, King Phillip IV of France convinced the pope that the rumors of strange heresies practiced by the Templars were cause for local authorities to arrest members of the order and—of course—seize their property. On a very unlucky Friday the thirteenth in October 1307, that's just what happened.

And that's when, at least as far as the tinfoil-hat-wearing crowd is concerned, things get interesting. The arrests scattered the Templars, forcing them to become even more secretive. They fled to Spain and Britain, to islands in the Mediterranean, deep into the jungles of Africa, and perhaps used their ships (previously used to transport pilgrims

They NEVER REAlly SCATTERED! They just WENT UNDERGROUND!

and their goods) to sail all the way to North America almost 200 years before Columbus. They may have even become pirates and initiated the use of the familiar skull and crossbones flag, the Jolly Roger.

The Templars were collectors of all sorts of things, mainly religious artifacts. Due to their control of the Temple Mount in Jerusalem, they were able to acquire a piece of the true cross, the head of John the Baptist, the Holy Grail, and the Ark of the Covenant, and some healing crystals you can order on the Internet for the low, low price of $29.95, if you act now. Some or all of these things lay beneath the temple buried in secret vaults, which are mentioned in a mysterious copper scroll discovered in the 1950s. The Templars may have also had the philosophers' stone and plenty of money—millions if not billions of dollars worth, by today's standards. When the Templars were dissolved, they hid their treasures in places like Rennes-le-Château in France, Rosslyn Chapel in Scotland, and even crossed the Atlantic to Canada, burying one or more of their treasures in a pit on Oak Island in Nova Scotia ("New Scotland").

But the Holy Grail can't be in several places at once, and surely the Templars didn't manage to grab *every* religious artifact that existed in their time. Conspiracy theorists pick and choose from the many Templar myths, fill in the blanks, and draw the connections they need. Some believe the Templars preserved the Holy Grail itself, the literal cup that Christ used at the Last Supper. Others say the knights possessed a powerful secret that could be used either to blackmail the Catholic Church (a la *The Da Vinci Code*, see Chapter 3) or as a part of some important occult rituals. Because they were European knights operating in the Middle East, they're a handy historical connection between both East and West. Christians or Satanists, heroes or villains, the Templars fill whatever role a theorist needs. They're the Walmart of conspiracies.

Many modern organizations say they're the rightful heirs of the Knights Templar. For example, the Sovereign Military Order of the

Temple of Jerusalem, based in England, claims to be based on the Templar legacy. Similarly, members of the Order of the Solar Temple in Switzerland believed themselves to be the Knights Templar reborn. Dozens of members of the temple committed a large-scale murder-suicide ritual in 1994. Other groups located around the world simply call themselves the Knights Templar, and each insists that it is the true heir to the order. Some have even demanded apologies from the Vatican for what happened back in 1314. *And the POPE hasn't APOLOGIZED. HE's UNDER the control of the GREYS. So he WOULDN'T.*

WHAT'S SO FREE ABOUT THE MASONS?

When it comes to laying claim to the Templar legacy, no group—secret or otherwise—figures as prominently in the minds of conspiracy theorists as the Freemasons. Like the Templars, the Masons lie at the center of the conspiratorial web. The fraternal order of the Free and Accepted Masons is a society organized into individual Lodges, although each gains a charter and authorization from a Grand Lodge. Individuals within the Lodges attain a hierarchy based on degrees. Traditionally, Freemasonry has just three degrees, Entered Apprentice, Fellow Craft, and Master Mason. However, variations, such as the Scottish Rite, offer thirty-three degrees. Others may offer more, though these are secret. Although originally all members worked as masons, today members practice any trade or profession. Ostensibly, all members share in the same moral and religious views and support the idea of a supreme being.

Conspiracy-minded folks know the leaders of the Masons are interested in nothing short of ruling the entire world. The majority of those doing research along these lines don't believe that the rank and file membership are in on it. *Low-ranking MASONS don't know the REAL story.*

Almost any conspiracy theory is a huge tangled knot of plots, people, groups, and agendas. But of them all, the Masons may be the toughest knot of all. *OF COURSE!!*

According to the Masons' own myths, the order of Freemasonry traces its roots back to Hiram Abiff, the chief architect of the Temple of Solomon around 960 B.C. However, some Masons claim their order extends back to King Nimrod of Babylon, who organized them to create the Tower of Babel in perhaps 2000 B.C., and to ancient Egypt, where their skill made the pyramids possible.

In reality, the Masonic organization started around the late sixteenth century, very likely in Scotland. The Grand Lodge of England was the first Grand Lodge and dates to June 24, 1717. It soon spread to the Continent, and later to America. Supposedly members of the Knights Templar fled to Scotland shortly before the order of Freemasonry started. Conspiracy authors like Michael Baigent and Richard Leigh believe that at that time a transfer of knowledge from Templars to Masons occurred. The rituals used in Freemasonry, these authors believe, may have even come from scrolls recovered by the Templars from the ruins of Solomon's Temple in Jerusalem.

The real Masons hide secrets within secrets. They're devious!!!!

THE ELDERS OF ZION

Some anti-Semitic conspiracy theorists believe that Freemasonry is a front for a worldwide Jewish conspiracy that wants to take over the world. This repulsive belief stems back to a forgery called the *Protocols of the Elders of Zion*, a document from the early twentieth century purporting to describe the strategies of world domination discussed at a meeting of a secret council of Jews. It involves everything from the control of the banking system to the destruction of Christianity to the distribution of pornography. The *Protocols* were actually concocted by Russian anti-Semitic journalists, using material from even older French and German sources. Sadly, anti-Semitism creeps into many flavors of conspiracy theory. Sometimes, just for good measure, conspiracists throw in Communists as well, making it a Judeo-Marxist-Masonic conspiracy. It sounds like some guy just decided to create a conspiracy theory against everyone he didn't like.

Those on the fringe, like British author David Icke, believe that the *Protocols* are real, but references to "Jews" constitute a cover-up, misdirection, or disinformation. The real "Elders," claims Icke, are not Jews but the Illuminati who answer to reptilian alien entities from another dimension. Yeah. You haven't heard the last of David Icke in this book. He keeps things interesting.

It is likely that the only real connection the Freemasons have with Judaism lies in the rituals and myths of the Masons. Some link Freemasonry with the Kabbalah, but the similarities are superficial. Their symbols, reverence for the "secret name of god," and their attachment to numerology are similar. In addition, the myths of Judaism and Freemasonry hold the Temple of Solomon and its construction in high regard. But when we delve deeper there are more similarities between Freemasonry and the Knights Templar.

The Illuminati ARE clearly connected to the Masons and the Knights Templar. EVERYONE knows this. Why is the author trying to cover it up?!!!!

THAT OLD BLACK MAGIC

Probably because the order girds itself in strange symbols and arcane ritual, many conspiracists believe that the Freemasons are an occult organization. This is not strictly true, although many occult organizations, like the Ordo Templi Orientis, either started as Masonic lodges or were patterned after Masonry.

Members claim that Freemasonry is not a religion. As a group, however, they recognize the so-called Great Architect of the Universe. This figure is assumed to be God in some form, whether Judeo-Christian or even Allah. The G.A.O.T.U. is whatever god the individual Mason chooses it to be. However, Masonic rites sometimes refer to Jahbulon, a sort of combination of Jehovah, Baal, and Osirus. Most of the well-known occultists of the eighteenth, nineteenth, and twentieth centuries were Freemasons, including A. E. Waite, Dr. Wynn Westcott, MacGregor Mathers, Aleister Crowley, Manly P. Hall, and others. Many Christians, such as writers Alva J. McClain, William

Mozart WAS A MASON, PASSING ON SECRET MESSAGES through his music!!! I'VE HEARD them!

Schnoebelen, John Ankerberg, Cathy Burns, and many, many others, believe that Freemasonry is a front for a worldwide satanic conspiracy. In 1817 General Albert Pike, in a work called *Morals and Dogma of the Ancient and Accepted Scottish Rite of Freemasonry*, wrote, "Masonry, like all the Religions, all the Mysteries, Hermeticism, and Alchemy, conceals its secrets from all except the Adepts and Sages, or the Elect, and uses false explanations and misinterpretations of its symbols to mislead those who deserve only to be misled." He (and hundreds, if not thousands, after him) contends that there is a secret group within Masonry that the rest of the order knows nothing about. These adepts practice black magic and follow occult teachings.

And he was right!!! He's dead. The Masons got to him.

ALIEN FREEMASONS

Author and scientific advisor Richard Hoagland claims that the Masons gained secret knowledge from beings from other planets. Hoagland is one of those who popularized the so-called Face of Mars, supposedly an artificial creation on the face of the red planet. He claims that NASA is controlled by the Masons and is covering up proof of alien life, specifically life on Mars. Masonic astronauts have, apparently, returned to Earth with alien artifacts and knowledge. Masons in the government conceal this truth and the secrets gained from aliens with whom their representatives have interacted.

Fellow alien-focused theorist David Icke claims that shape-changing, blood-drinking reptilian aliens have infiltrated our world and control it through linked secret societies such as the Freemasons. Specifically, the Masons oversee the illegal drug and weapons trafficking that helps support the reptilian conspiracy which simultaneously keeps the human population under control through substance abuse and violence.

Lastly, and perhaps most tellingly, Gene Rodenberry, creator of *Star Trek*, was also a Mason.

Just sayin'.

I hope Hoagland is careful that the Masons don't take him to one of their SECRET PRISONS in AREA 51!

The inner circle of Freemasonry, according to Pike and those who followed him, *is* a religion. It *is* an occult organization, and a very dangerous one. Black magicians with great arcane secrets of mystical lore, they arm themselves with powerful artifacts, such as the Holy Grail or the Ark of the Covenant, passed on to them from the Templars. These hidden masters of Masonry seek to reshape the world. The murders of Jack the Ripper, one theory goes, were actually a Masonic black magic ritual, as evidenced in the very precise mutilation and arrangement of the corpses. Conspiracy theorists link other infamous murders to these satanic Masons as well. Paul Foster Case writes, "President Kennedy was wounded in the exact three same spots as Hiram Abif [sic], who was murdered in the Masonic initiation, representing the persecution of the Templars on Friday, the 13th, in the year 1307, where Hiram Abif is struck in the back, and in the throat, and in the head." Of course, Kennedy's successor was Freemason Lyndon B. Johnson. (For more on the Masons and the JFK murder, see Chapter 6.)

No, actually the Illuminati have the Ark of the Covenant. Unless the Masons stole it from them!?!

RULERS OF THE WORLD

The most common belief about Freemasonry among the conspiracy-minded is that they seek power, influencing leaders and controlling events. The United States lies at the point of their spearhead. Many of the founding fathers in American history were Masons, including George Washington, Benjamin Franklin, Paul Revere, John Hancock, and perhaps others.

Those are just the ones we know about.

What if all the presidents were Masons?

"Not only were many of the founders of the United States government Masons, but they received aid from a secret and august body existing in Europe which helped them to establish this country for a peculiar and particular purpose known only to the initiated few," according to thirty-third-degree Mason Manly P. Hall in *The Secret Teachings of All Ages*. Hall claims that the United States was actually a grand Masonic "experiment" to create a new society that would one day grow to such prominence that it would allow the Masons to dominate the world. Founded on Masonic ideals, the United States was a deliberate slap at European monarchs, many of whom were anti-Masonic. It's historical fact that Freemasons played an important role in the American Revolution, using their membership to relay vital information and meeting halls as a place to discuss tactics and hide supplies. No fewer than sixteen U.S. presidents have been Masons.

According to some, including David Icke, revolution is the Mason's game. After the American Revolution, they sponsored and supported the French Revolution as well. Later, they backed the Bolshevik Revolution in Russia, ousting the Tsar. Icke believes that Marxism *is* Masonry. All Freemasons are Communists and were behind the spread of the "Red Menace" from the 1940s to the 1980s. Other conspiracy theorists, however, peg the Masons as staunchly anti-Communist, and in fact put them in bed with the CIA helping to root out the Red Menace. Left-wing conspiracy nuts label them as racist, fascist, anti-Semitic, and in league with the CIA, running the American government. Right-wing nuts call them Communist, satanic, and sometimes Jewish. And running the American government. Both, however, fear the Masons' plan to take control of the world, or believe they've already succeeded.

How does a secret society hope to dominate the world?

1. **The organization needs members in influential positions.** Check. The Masons certainly have that. Many politicians, military officers, and other men in authority are Masons.
2. **These members need a way to meet and communicate in secret.** Check again. That's what the Masons are all about.
3. **The members of the organization need great access to resources.** Maybe check. The Masons may have that, thanks to their Templar predecessors. Even if the Templars had no holy artifacts or mystic secrets to pass along, they almost

SEE?! Just what I said!!

certainly had enough wealth to fund a sizable organization and give them a leg up on global domination.

If one imagines the gamut of conspiracy theories as a sprawling octopus with tentacles stretching into all sorts of areas of influence, the Freemasons might be the head of that octopus—right in the middle, connected directly to everything else.

Take, for example, the Propaganda Due (P2) Lodge in Italy. In the 1970s and 1980s, the members of the infamous P2 lodge—journalists, politicians, high-ranking military officers, and wealthy business-men—operated a shadow government that may have participated in murders, acts of terrorism, drug running, money laundering, and the collapse of the Banco Ambrosiano, a bank owned in part by the Vati-can. They may have even been behind the death of Pope John Paul I, who knew too much about their financial shenanigans. They extended their illegal, covert operations into Uruguay, Argentina, and Brazil. P2 was a secret sect pulling the strings of a public government. Many of P2's members also belonged to various intelligence services or the Mafia. Some, including its leader, Licio Gelli, worked for Mussolini. Gelli also worked for British and American intelligence after World War II, suggesting to some conspiracists that P2 operated with CIA support as an anti-Communist movement—one through which the CIA could secretly transfer funds to covert black operations through-out the world.

The tentacles of this particular octopus get a bit tangled. Before you draw lines connecting the Masons and the Nazis, realize that Fascists in Germany and Italy mistrusted the Masons (and all secret societies). It's likely that most Nazis believed the Masons to be con-trolled by the Jews. Many thousands of Freemasons were killed in Nazi death camps. This doesn't stop some people from connecting Fascism with Masonry through groups like P2.

The author's got it right here!! The Masons connect everything!!

Yes, it was.

I've seen lots of files proving this!

HIDDEN SYMBOLS AND SECRET SIGNS

Masonry teems with symbols, signs (like handshakes), and important words and phrases. According to conspiracy theorists, Freemasons have encoded secret messages within structures, floorplans, and symbols. Since they're Masons, it stands to reason that they find interest in architecture, drafting, and similar pursuits. Masons are builders.

This was in that movie National Treasure. Nicholas Cage is working for Them!!!

Conspiracy nuts love this stuff: an innocuous-appearing structure that actually holds sinister meaning for those in the know. Mysterious symbols and hidden signs allow for multiple translations and explanations. Some people examine photos of public figures, (the president, a newscaster, an actor), and note when the person's hand seems to be making a secret sign. Others look for hidden patterns in old paintings. They love to lay images over one another to show their significance—a side view of the Great Pyramid laid over a map of Washington, D.C., reveals secret structures below the surface of the Potomac River, for example.

The most common Masonic symbol is that formed by the square, compass, and letter *G*. This motif is found on buildings all over the world. The organization also seems to enjoy pyramids (with or without eyes atop them), pillars, the sun, the moon, stars, obelisks, crosses, owls, bees, serpents, swastikas, swords, pentagrams, and more.

Masonic symbols are incorporated into Rossyln Chapel in Scotland, where every square inch of the walls and even the ceiling is covered in secret images and Masonic signs (see Chapter 3 for more information about Rossyln). *Check out www.rosslyntemplars.org.uk.*

Washington, D.C., holds a place of high importance in anti-Masonic minds. Because of the supposed Masonic origin of the United States, the designers laid out the streets of the capital in patterns with hidden shapes and meanings. Theorists have found the Egyptian sphinx in the layout, as well as a thirteen-tiered pyramid with the all-seeing eye of Horus, or Eye of Providence, atop it staring down an avenue into the White House. According to conspiracy researcher Phil Day, the

Just like on the DOLLAR BILL!!!

TRIANGLES WITHIN TRIANGLES

Not all Masonic signs are hidden within edifices. Some are symbols within symbols. Take, for example, the Great Seal of the United States, found on the one-dollar bill. Take a red pen and draw a triangle around the pyramid so that the bottom two points touch the *N* and *M* of "Novus Ordo Seclorum." The top point is the so-called Eye of Providence. Draw another triangle, exactly inverting the first one. The three points match up with *A*, *S*, and *O*.

Put the letters together and what does that spell? NMASO. No, wait. Unscramble the letters: <u>MASON</u>.

These two triangles together are called a hexagram, a symbol that figures in occult beliefs. It's also two red triangles defacing your dollar bill.

It connects them to the Illuminati!!

I THOUGHT IT WOULD!

Capitol Building is shaped like "the Goat of Baphomet" (whatever that is, although it harkens back to the Knights Templar) on top of a truncated pyramid. So now we see why someone would combine an image of the Great Pyramid and D.C. Well, maybe.

It's the satanic goat!!!!

Another location conspiracists like to seize upon is the Denver International Airport built in 1995. This vast structure contains a whole slew of secret symbols and meaningful images. Travelers often comment upon the odd murals found throughout the airport, which not only incorporate Masonic symbols but seem to show people being killed in large numbers and cities destroyed. On the granite Masonic capstone erected at the building's dedication are inscribed the words "New World Airport Commission." (For more on the New World Order, see Chapters 19 and 20.) The layout of the runways is a swastika. (Kind of.)

Another place beloved of conspiracy folks is the Georgia Guidestones. Sometimes called the American Stonehenge, these are a large granite monument on a hilltop in Elbert County, Georgia. The builders—who remain anonymous—carved a series of messages into the massive stones in four different ancient languages as well as eight modern tongues. Because the messages deal with uniting and improving humanity and because the carvers remain a mystery, conspiracy buffs often assume that the stones are Masonic in origin.

The more entertaining members of the lunatic fringe like to point out that crop circles found in fields in Great Britain and the United States, supposedly created by aliens, also depict decidedly Masonic-looking symbols. Who knew that the Freemasons even let UFO pilots into their club?

Masonry incorporates handshakes—called grips or tokens—and secret words and phrases. Each degree has its own handshakes and hand signs. Some are meant to convey greeting. Others signal distress or a need for help. These are used both in rituals conducted among Masons (particularly the induction rites), and also in public to show fellowship without revealing membership. Likewise, each degree has its own secret password. The phrase for distress is, "Oh Lord, my God, is there no help for the widow's son?" This is a reference to Hiram Abiff, the widow's son of legend. A Mason hearing this (or seeing the sign of distress) must do anything he can to help his distressed brother Mason short of risking his own life. Signs, grips, and passwords vary by location (as dictated by the Grand Lodge presiding over the area).

Masonry also uses numerology. The numbers three and thirteen hold particular importance, and those conspiracy-minded investigators with nothing better to do enjoy finding them in, well, everything.

- There are three basic degrees in Masonry
- Hiram Abiff was murdered by three men (who wanted his Masonry secrets), with three blows to the head
- Three is the number of the holy trinity in Christianity
- There are three branches in the U.S. government

There aren't any Masonic symbols.

But they could have been carved by the Greys!!

- The Templars were outlawed on Friday the <u>thirteenth</u>
- There were <u>thirteen</u> American colonies and <u>thirteen</u> states in the original United States

These are the fingerprints of Masonic influence. The movie rating PG-13 supposedly suggests that the Freemasons "control" Hollywood. Movies like *Three Men and Baby* and the *Thirteenth Floor*, not to mention the more subtle *Six Days and Seven Nights*, seal the deal. Or at least they do in the minds of the conspiracy kooks who spend their days looking for that kind of thing.

Occult-focused researchers contend that Freemasonry's obsession with symbols, signs, words, and numbers is more than a way to convey secret meaning. These things have actual mystic power. The Masonic sign of distress is more than a cry for help—it's a magical compulsion. In the past, those fearing the Masons' power devised anti-Masonic symbols that would undo the power of those their enemies used—a secret war of magical imagery.

The Bilderberg Group has 39 members?!

SOCIAL CLUB OR VILLAINS?

On the surface, today's Masons appear in the same light as Ralph Kramden's Raccoon Lodge or Fred Flintstone's Loyal Order of Water Buffalos. A silly men's club, little more than a grownup version of a young boy's treehouse with a "No Girls Allowed" sign. But if you're paranoid, it's easy to fall in with the conspiracy crowd. There's something suspicious about what goes on only behind closed doors, accompanied by strange rituals and odd words and symbols. Freemasons claim that their brotherhood is not a secret society but a society with secrets. Either way, talk of conspiracies and mysticism will likely always nip at Freemasonry's heels.

I'M NOT PARANOID !!!!!!!!! Who said I was?

CONSPIRACY RUNDOWN

PLAUSIBILITY:
3/10. The Knights Templar and the Freemasons are real. But are they really more than they seem? Unlikely.

HIGH STRANGENESS:
3/10. Centuries-old secret societies is pretty standard conspiracy fare.

CONSPIRACY CHECKLIST:
- ☑ Illuminati
- ☑ The Freemasons
- ☑ CIA/intelligence community/the military
- ☐ Aliens
- ☑ The occult
- ☑ The Mafia

FOR MORE INFORMATION:
The Temple and the Lodge by Michael Baigent and Richard Leigh

The Templar Revelation by Lynn Picknett and Clive Prince

Freemasonry and Its Ancient Mystic Rites by C.W. Leadbeater

The Hiram Key by Christopher Knight and Robert Lomas

America's Secret Destiny by Robert Hieronimus

ON THE WEB:
Templar history: www.templarhistory.com

Freemasonry home: www.freemasonry.org

A Mason's site of anti-Masonic points of view: www.masonicinfo.com

Masonic handshakes, passwords, grips, and signs: www.ephesians 5-11.org/handshakes.htm

CONSPIRACY INVESTIGATOR SEARCH TERMS:
Jacques de Molay, Temple of Solomon, Holy Grail, Rosslyn Chapel, Hiram Abiff, Masonic Symbols, P2, Roberto Calvi, anti-Masonic political party, secrets of the dollar bill, *Protocols of the Elders of Zion*, occult Freemasonry, Denver International Airport conspiracies, Eastern Star, Gematria

02. THE PUPPET MASTERS

THE ROOM IS DIMLY LIT and filled with the smoke of expensive cigarettes and cigars. Well-dressed men sit around a large table, their faces too shadowy to make out. They speak in subdued tones—they don't need to be loud, for these are men of power—of matters of finance, politics, and social change. This is not some abstract debate among well-informed people, however. They do not speak of "they." They speak of "we." These secretive men are the puppet masters pulling the strings of the world.

This image of a shadowy cabal of men behind the scenes who control everything is pervasive. We don't need to explain who they are, we *know* who they are. They are *They*. THEM. The ultimate conspiracy. "The Gnomes of Zurich," "the High Cabal," "the Shadow Government," "the Secret Masters," "the Cryptocracy," "the Great White Brotherhood," "the Power Elite," "the Ascended Masters," or just "the powers that be."

Some conspiracists imagine them to be businessmen in corporate boardrooms. Others think of them as occult beings operating on some higher plane. Sometimes they're short, gray aliens with big round heads and a fondness for anal probes. Some believe that they are on their way to taking over the world, initiating the New World Order, (a topic we'll return to in Chapters 19 and 20). Many others—more cynics than fear mongers—contend that they're already in charge.

More often then not, they're called the Illuminati.

Where did these secret rulers come from, and how did they get in control? Just asking such questions might be dangerous.

Handwritten note (left margin):
CRYPTOCRACY MEANS "SECRET GOVERNMENT." THE ONES WHO REALLY RUN EVERYTHING. WE PROBABLY don't EVEN KNOW THEIR NAMES.

They might be. The PRESIDENT, YES, EVEN THE PRESIDENT, might be oNE!!

Handwritten note (bottom):
SEARCH THE INTERNET for "Illuminati" AND you'll get AN idEA of THE truth. It's hARD to pull it All togetHER, bECAUSE thERE's SO MANY diffERENT tHEORIES, but if you ASK ME, thEY'RE ALL TRUE.

SECRET ORIGINS

The term "Illuminati" was used first in the fifteenth century by occultists claiming to possess a mystical illumination, a magical light that set them apart from others. They believed that some select few had risen above their fellow man, having "seen the light." These people saw what was good for all of us. The illumination came from God or some higher power, sometimes through one's own superior faculties. Whatever the source, it was a nice excuse to feel better than everyone else.

Adam Weishaupt founded the Illuminati in Ingolstadt, in Bavaria, on May 1, 1776 (a momentous year, as there was a bit of a hullabaloo across the Atlantic just a few months afterward). Weishaupt was a professor, a freethinker, a rationalist, and, paradoxically, an occultist obsessed with Egyptian pyramids. His order, originally called the Order of Perfectibilists, achieved "illumination" through reason and logic. Their mission included the abolition of governments ruled by hereditary monarchs. However, the Illuminati were hardly pro-democracy. Rather, they believed in the enlightened despotism described in Plato's *Republic*. They also didn't care much for religion, the rights of property, and marriage.

Weishaupt organized the Illuminati into cells. Small groups of secretive agents worked together but didn't know who the members of the other cells were or where the leader could be found. Weishaupt's idea was that the Illuminati cells would spread throughout the world, infiltrating governments and manipulating them.

The Illuminati may have infiltrated the Freemasons in this way. Alternatively, the Freemasons may be behind the Illuminati, which started by other accounts as a Masonic Order. Either way, conspiracy theorists believe there is a link between the two.

THE ILLUMINATED STATES OF AMERICA

A Mason named John Robison rejected an offer to join the Illuminati and wrote a book about it in 1789 called *Proofs of a Conspiracy.* In that book, he wrote, "An association has been formed for the express purposes of rooting out all the religious establishments and overturning all existing governments . . . the leaders would rule the World with uncontrollable power, while all the rest would be employed as tools of

This author thinks he's funny, but he's talking about REALLY SERIOUS stuff!!

Not a coincidence!!!! Masons led the American Revolution!!

Pyramids ARE PART of the LAW of THREE! That's why they're important to the Illuminati!!!

This is interesting. Possibly he was an agent of the Masons trying to eliminate the Illuminati as competition.

the ambition of their unknown superiors." George Washington got a copy of the book and said that he knew that there were Illuminati cells in America and that they had "diabolical tenets."

But was this just a clever ruse to throw Robison and others off the trail? Because the American Revolution (and perhaps even more so, the French Revolution) could easily be seen as the result of Illuminati manipulation. In that conflict, a powerful monarch is defeated and a land of religious freedom is created.

By many contemporary accounts, Weishaupt and Washington were dead ringers.

Might they have actually been the same person!!!!? Or could Weishaupt have replaced Washington at some point? That explains so much!!

ANCIENT ILLUMINATI

Weishaupt's Illuminati might just have been the first *known* order of the Illuminati. The shadowy group may have existed for far longer. In fact, the Bavarian Illuminati may have just been a distraction to throw interested parties off the trail of the *real* Illuminati. That's the way Illuminati researchers think—nothing can be trusted.

The real Illuminati may have started before recorded history, or at least before the history that most people are taught in their (Illuminati-controlled) schools. Hailing from the now-lost continent of Atlantis, the original Illuminati ruled the world, sailing in fantastic ships and using advanced maps. The Atlanteans ruled over the less developed people of the world, and their influence was responsible for many of the ancient wonders, such as the pyramids (hence the Illuminati's preoccupation with them). Doomed due to a quirk of unstable geology, only a few Atlanteans survived the cataclysm that dragged Atlantis beneath the waves. These secretive, superior masters mixed in with the rest of humanity but kept in contact with each other in secret even as they rose to prominence in various disparate cultures around the globe. Today their spiritual—and perhaps biological—descendants rule from the shadows as the Illuminati.

Makes you question everything you learned in school, doesn't i

Perhaps the creation of the United States itself was an Illuminati action: The Illuminated States of America. Or a means to an even greater end—an illuminated planet. In later chapters, we'll examine the Council on Foreign Relations, the Trilateral Commission, the Bilderberger Group, and even the United Nations, all organizations in which America or Americans play a strong role, and all supposedly Illuminati fronts.

Take another look at your dollar bill. See the pyramid with the glowing eye at the top? Remember how Weishaupt was obsessed with ancient Egypt? Conspiracy buffs think he chose an eye in a pyramid as the secret symbol of the Illuminati. And so just who is that guy on the other side of the dollar bill? *This is REALLY, REALLY imPORtANt.*

Ready for your tinfoil hat yet? *I bet the goverNmeNt suppresses this book wheN it comes out ANd They reAd this.*

The AuthoR mAkes fuN of tinfoil hAts, but if you NEEd to kNow how to mAke oNe I cAN show you A website that tells how to do it.

CONSPIRACY RUNDOWN

PLAUSIBILITY:

5/10. Weishaupt and his Illuminati were real, but if the world were run by a single shadowy group, shouldn't it be more . . . organized?

HIGH STRANGENESS:

3/10. Some claim that the Illuminati were into the occult and the whole Washington/Weishaupt connection is odd, but for the most part this is pretty straightforward conspiracy material.

CONSPIRACY CHECKLIST:
- ☑ Illuminati
- ☑ The Freemasons
- ☑ CIA/intelligence community/the military
- ☐ Aliens
- ☑ The occult
- ☐ The Mafia

FOR MORE INFORMATION:

Proof of the Illuminati by Seth Payson

Illuminoids by Neal Wilgus

Cosmic Trigger by Robert Anton Wilson

ON THE WEB:

Illuminati Conspiracy Archive: www.conspiracyarchive.com

An Illuminati card game: www.sjgames.com/illuminati

Proofs of a Conspiracy (complete text): www.sacred-texts.com/sro/pc/index.htm

CONSPIRACY INVESTIGATOR SEARCH TERMS:

Adam Weishaupt, cryptocracy, Illuminatus! Trilogy, eye in the pyramid, fnord

03. KEEPING UP WITH THE CHRISTS

YOUR NEIGHBORS ALWAYS seem to be able to buy a new car or go on a fabulous vacation when you just can't swing it financially. Their lawn is always greener and better groomed than your field of weeds. Their kids not only get good grades and excel in sports and other activities, but they're always so damned well-behaved while you're lucky if you can get your brood to look up from the Xbox. Keeping up with the Joneses seems almost impossible. Now imagine if you lived next door to the descendants of Jesus Christ himself.

According to Michael Baigent, Richard Leigh, and Henry Lincoln, authors of *Holy Blood, Holy Grail*, you just might be doing that. The authors suggest that Jesus didn't die on the cross but instead escaped, married, and fathered children. The secret of that bloodline has been guarded closely by secret societies for two millennia and has only now (thanks to Baigent, Leigh, and Lincoln) come to light.

You may have heard of this concept before—a little book called *The Da Vinci Code* by Dan Brown took this premise and ran with it. All the way to the bank.

But that's just fiction.

I never read The Da Vinci Code, but I've read about it. He has to disguise it as fiction!

FAMILY MAN

The story of Christ and his kids, as related by researcher Pierre Plantard to Baigent, Leigh, and Lincoln, goes like this:

Jesus didn't die on the cross as described in the Gospels. Instead, his disciples faked his death. He and Mary Magdalene married and raised a family, and their descendants eventually moved to France. Meanwhile, the Catholic Church rose to power based on the legacy of Peter, the first of the popes. If the secret of Christ's bloodline got out, the Church would be ruined. So the Catholic hierarchy covered up the truth and hunted down those who had penetrated its mystery.

A society arose to keep the secret alive. There's always a secret society in these stories. Calling themselves the Priory of Sion, this group created a front organization called the Knights Templar. The Templars, as many believed, were clandestinely guarding the Holy Grail, but the Grail wasn't a literal artifact—it was the secret of Jesus's descendants. *Sangreal* is the French word for the Holy Grail, but does it come from *sang real*, meaning "holy blood"? (There's even a brand of designer jeans called Sang Real. Special jeans or special genes? Is the Priory of Sion just having fun with us now?)

When the Templars were eliminated by the pope (because their connection with the Priory of Sion and its secret), the Priory went even deeper underground. Its members nonetheless rose to prominence in various fields. They included not just Leonardo da Vinci, but Isaac Newton, Victor Hugo, Claude Debussy, and Jean Cocteau, and they still operate to this day, watching over the bloodline.

But the members of the Christ family tree weren't just twiddling their thumbs and eating baguettes. With the help of the Priory of Sion, they established the Merovingian dynasty, which ruled the Kingdom of the Franks (later, France) from the fifth through the eighth centuries. Today the Priory wishes to reinstate the holy bloodline in France, and more. They want members of the sacred bloodline sitting on *all* the thrones of Europe. *This thing is SO BIG!!!*

Just to keep some perspective, Pierre Plantard, on whose research all this stuff is based, just happens to be the heir to the Merovingian dynasty and of the bloodline of Christ. Thus he is the rightful ruler of France.

THIS PLACE IS TERRIBLE

One interesting bit of evidence supporting the whole theory lies at the feet of a priest named Bérenger Saunière, who in 1885 became the curé of the church in the tiny French town Rennes-le-Château. While making renovations to the church, Saunière discovered *something* hidden in the church. As evidence, conspiracists point out that this poor parish priest in the middle of nowhere suddenly came into a great deal

The Templars again!

So the Masons are also involved in this!

No way!

Someone in my building wears those jeans. I'd better start keeping an eye on her!!

of wealth, renovations of the church became lavish, and the place was visited by a cavalcade of important people. Perhaps the priest found a great treasure. Some—like Baigent, Leigh, and Lincoln—believe it was a secret about the Church so great that Saunière was able to blackmail Rome and get rich.

Rennes-le-Château is located in Languedoc, one of the last bastions of the Templars as well as of a religious sect called the Cathars. In their day, members of this sect were labeled as heretics, and in the thirteenth century the Church sent crusaders to wipe them out.

Saunière supposedly found two parchments in the church. They appeared to be simple Latin biblical texts, but certain letters were highlighted. When these letters were deciphered and translated, one parchment stated, "This treasure belongs to Dagobert II King and to Sion and he is there dead." The other read, "Shepherdess no temptation that Poussin, Teniers hold the key; peace 681 by the cross and the horse of God I complete this Daemon guardian at noon blue apples."

The first is a direct reference to the Priory of Sion and Dagobert II, the last of the Merovingian kings. But what is the treasure, and who is the "he" that is "there" dead? The second becomes somewhat more clear when we learn that Bérenger Saunière went to Paris to find someone to translate the parchments. While he was there, he purchased a painting by Nicholas Poussin, called *Shepherds of Arcadia*. This painting depicts four shepherds standing around a tomb, which bears the inscription "ET IN ARCADIA EGO." ("And in Arcadia, I too have lived.") Such a tomb was actually located near Rennes-le-Château. An anagram of Et In Arcadia Ego is I Tego Arcana Dei, or "I conceal the secrets of God," if you're not much a stickler for good Latin.

The phrase "noon blue apples" refers to an effect in the church at Rennes-le-Château. At noon every January 17, sunlight shines through the stained glass to make blue orbs float around a painting of Mary Magdalene kneeling before a skull. Conspiracists say this shows Christ wasn't buried in the Holy Land but in France. At Rennes-le-Château.

Those renovations to the church? They weren't just fancy. They were weird. They include a statue of a devil inside the church and the Latin inscription "This Place Is Terrible" above the entryway. One of the images in the depiction of the final stations of the cross seems to show the apostles sneaking Jesus's body out of his tomb in the middle of the night—perhaps because his death was faked?

Filmmaker Bruce Burgess claims to have found a hidden door in Saunière's wardrobe that leads to a secret room with a sealed-off tunnel. He believes that the priest found more than parchments—that the church is built upon a series of catacombs that lead to the tombs of both the Magdalene and Christ. And perhaps even some of their descendants. Footage from a remote camera that he inserted into a cave just outside of the village shows what he says is Mary Magdalene's body under a shroud marked with a red cross. A supposed representative of the Priory of Sion told Burgess that the Priory led him to this discovery because the time is right to make their important revelation.

A red cross!! That's the mark of the Templars!!!

THOSE TEMPLARS GET AROUND

Speaking of weird churches, don't forget Rosslyn Chapel. When the Templars were outlawed by the Catholic Church, many fled to Scotland, perhaps taking their secrets and their treasures with them.

Legend has it that some settled around the small town of Roslin, where they gave their secrets to the Freemasons, who in turn built a church filled with fabulous and mystifying symbolism on the orders of William Sinclair. Plantard mentioned Sinclair as one of the secret leaders of the Priory of Sion.

The symbols in the church may contain musical notes that together form a clue, or they may be coordinates for a buried vault. Some seem to suggest ears of corn and the leaves of the aloe plant, despite the fact that neither were known in Europe at the time and both originated in North America.

Is this a sign that the Templars sailed to America before 1456, when the chapel was built? I read about this somewhere.

But why secret symbols in a church? Why not just put the information in a book and lock it in a vault? Well, because the conspirators were Freemasons, and that's what masons do—they build things.

Coincidentally—or not—the tiny town of Roslin, Scotland, is also the location of the laboratory that cloned Dolly the sheep in 1996, the first successful animal clone. Perhaps the Priory of Sion's interest in bloodlines and genetics is more far-reaching than one initially supposes.

NOT a coincidence!

Just in case you thought all of this was too straightforward . . .

Author Gerard de Sede, after writing the book that first explored the mysteries of Rennes-le-Château, later claimed that the Merovingians aren't the descendants of Christ but of aliens from the planet Sirius. After being interviewed by the *Holy Blood, Holy Grail* authors, Plantard claimed that the Priory wasn't protecting an ancient bloodline but instead was dedicated to harnessing the paranormal power of mystical ley lines and special energy spots around Rennes-le-Château. Author David Wood confirms this and ties it to extraterrestrials from Sirius.

Under investigation, Pierre Plantard admitted that he had planted the evidence the *Holy Blood, Holy Grail* authors found and lied about the whole thing. Ah, but conspiracy theorists of the caliber of Baigent, Leigh, and Lincoln are not going to fall for that old trick. It's a cover-up. *Now that the Priory of Sion has been exposed, they're covering up their own existence!*

CONSPIRACY RUNDOWN

PLAUSIBILITY:
2/10. There's one source of information about the Priory of Sion and the bloodline of Christ, and its author admits it's a fake.

HIGH STRANGENESS:
6/10. Devils guarding churches, mystical geometries, and aliens from Sirius, while only on the fringes of the theory, still push it well into the weird category.

CONSPIRACY CHECKLIST:
- ☐ Illuminati
- ☑ The Freemasons
- ☐ CIA/intelligence community/the military
- ☑ Aliens
- ☑ The occult
- ☐ The Mafia

FOR MORE INFORMATION:

Holy Blood, Holy Grail by Michael Baigent, Richard Leigh, and Henry Lincoln

The Messianic Legacy by Michael Baigent, Richard Leigh, and Henry Lincoln

The Da Vinci Code by Dan Brown

The Templar Revelation by Lynn Picknett and Clive Prince

The Accursed Treasure of Rennes-le-Chateau by Gerard de Sede

ON THE WEB:

Rennes-le-Château research: www.rlcresearch.com

Rosslyn Chapel: www.rosslynchapel.org.uk

Templars: www.templarhistory.com

CONSPIRACY INVESTIGATOR SEARCH TERMS:

Priory of Sion, *The Jesus Scroll*, Mary Magdalene, Merovingian bloodline, Cathars, *Bloodline* movie, noon blue apples

04. EVERYTHING'S BETTER WITH NAZIS

IN APRIL 1945, the German military machine crumbled as forces from both the east and west raced toward Berlin. Adolf Hitler's lifeless body lay in a bunker alongside his mistress. The Third Reich and its dreams of world domination were dead. The world breathed a sigh of relief now that the Nazis knew defeat and all those involved with their machinations would be suitably tried and punished.

Right?

That's what we'd like to think. But that's not the case. Nazis not only escaped prosecution but prospered either in South America or in the employ of the U.S. government. Conspiracists believe that even after his "death" Hitler continued to rule a Fourth Reich from a hidden underground base.

PAPERCLIP

Among conspiracy theorists, from the well-grounded historians to the Internet whackjobs, the name "Operation Paperclip" is well known. A program of the Office of Strategic Services (OSS), the U.S. government intelligence agency that preceded the CIA, Operation Paperclip brought German scientists to the United States at the end of the war. Many of these scientists belonged to the Nazi party, and some of them were involved in dire activities in concentration camps or helped with Germany's war effort, yet they were welcomed with handshakes and smiles once they reached the United States. The reason was simple—these geniuses brought with them a body of valuable knowledge and skills that the United States felt it needed, particularly as it faced a new enemy in the form of the Soviet Union.

The U.S. government has been secretly run by Nazis for fifty years now.

Wernher von Braun, one of the premier rocket scientists of his day, designed the infamous V-2 rocket for Germany during World War II. Thanks to Operation Paperclip, he was brought to America and—despite being a card-carrying Nazi and participating in a rocket-building program that used slave labor—immediately became an important figure in the birth of the U.S. space program and influential in the creation of NASA. He even went on to make educational films with Walt Disney. *Disney films have secret subliminal messages in them to program children's minds.*

THE ORG

The United States wasn't interested only in eggheads and slide-rule jockeys. Reinhard Gehlen, chief of Nazi intelligence, used the information that he had obtained about the Russians—gained during the torture and starvation of 4 million Russian prisoners of war—to make a deal not only for his life but for a big financial payoff from the United States. The Americans offered Gehlen a job. He and his former German intelligence forces would go back to spying on the Russians, but now they would report to their new bosses in the OSS and its love child, the CIA. Gehlen's group, called the Org, also took time out to help as many as 5,000 other Nazis escape Germany to Central and South America.

Among those in the OSS who worked with Gehlen was Allen Dulles, later director of U.S. Central Intelligence. In fact, armed with information fed to him by Gehlen, Dulles gained the power and influence to create the CIA in 1947. Information from the Org showed that the United States desperately needed something like the CIA to stem the tide of Communism and deal with this growing threat. The only problem? According to Victor Marchetti, former chief analyst of Soviet military capabilities, Gehlen's information didn't help in the Cold War, it created it—with lies. Marchetti told author Christopher Simpson, "Gehlen had to make his money by creating a threat that we were afraid of, so we would give him more money to tell us about it. In my opinion, the Gehlen organization provided nothing worthwhile for understanding or estimating Soviet military or political capabilities in Eastern Europe or anywhere else." In other words, information from the Org greatly exaggerated Soviet capabilities to keep the United States paying the Org to provide information. *And don't forget the CIA-Mason connection!!*

But how could Americans work with cold-blooded Nazis? In many respects, members of the intelligence community were predisposed to do so. Allen Dulles of the OSS met with Hitler and Mussolini in the 1930s before the war on business trips and stated publicly that Hitler's menace was exaggerated. His brother, who worked with him and would become secretary of state under Eisenhower, served as the American liaison to I. G. Farben—the chemical company that produced Zyklon B used in the gas chambers at Auschwitz—and helped run Union Banking Corporation for the Nazis. Other influential figures involved included William Randolph Hearst Sr., Andrew Mellon, Irene du Pont, Henry Ford, J. P. Morgan, and Prescott Bush, grandfather of the first President Bush. So these guys were used to working with Nazis.

But it gets stranger. What if the Third Reich wasn't actually gone? What if Hitler wasn't dead? Just because it sounds like the plot of a B-movie doesn't mean there aren't people who believe it to be true.

Lots of bankers.

Let's remember the Templars had a lot of riches, too. Maybe it's all part of the superrich's way of controlling society.

NAZIS AND THE CHURCH

The Catholic Church played two very different roles during World War II and in the days following. On the one hand, many Catholics helped Jews escape from Germany (although the Vatican was sadly silent on the subject of the Holocaust). Supposedly Pope Pius XII even tried to exorcise demons from Hitler from afar. However, evidence also suggests that like the OSS/CIA, the Vatican aided Nazis' escape at the end of the war. According to Uki Goni's *The Real Odessa*, the Vatican was a crucial link in various war criminals' getaway plans. The pope, as a staunch anti-Communist, believed the Nazis would continue to battle the Red Menace. These actions remain a sad and embarrassing fact for the Catholic Church today.

MIGRATING SOUTH

Many high-ranking Nazis escaped to South America. These include the infamous Klaus Barbie, the SS "Butcher of Lyon." In fact, in the late forties, it was the official Soviet position that Hitler himself was hiding in Argentina. These fugitives were abetted by, and in turn became influential within, the governments of Argentina and Chile. Conspiracy researcher Jim Marrs believes a group of Nazis infiltrated corporate America in the 1950s, spreading their philosophy and mindset. This neofascist group is the lynchpin of the military-industrial complex and may have been behind the Kennedy assassination as a part of their attempt to institute a fascist government-in-secret in the United States.

Eisenhower warned about the military-industrial complex.

And he had a heart attack!!

But maybe the Nazis went even further south. New Swabia is a region of Antarctica claimed by Nazi Germany in 1939. From their hideaways in South America, it would have been easy for the Nazis to slink away down to New Swabia and establish the Fourth Reich. If you believe that, you'll have no problem with researcher Rob Arndt's claim that famous polar explorer Admiral Richard E. Byrd fought a secret war against this Fourth Reich in 1946–1947 with a force of almost 5,000 men, thirteen ships, and a number of aircraft. The covert operation was given the codename Highjump. It was the largest ever expedition to Antarctica. *I've done some research into this whole Nazi Antarctica base, and I think it's TRUE! It's a great place for them to launch the rockets needed to built their moonbase without anyone knowing about it.*

NAZI SORCERERS AND NAZI ALIENS

The ability to colonize Antarctica appears far-fetched, but the Nazis may have had supernatural assistance. If Indiana Jones taught us anything, it's that Hitler and his circle of fiends were interested in the occult. The SS, in fact, was modeled in part on the Knights Templar, and the SS's mystic rituals, rankings by degrees, and beliefs establish them in every way as an esoteric order as much as a military one. *Like the Masons!* According to Trevor Ravenscroft, author of *The Spear of Destiny*, Hitler started World War II in order to obtain the so-called Spear of

I knew it!!!!

Destiny, the weapon that pierced Christ's side during the Crucifixion. Hitler believed that the artifact would make him invincible.

The very concept of the Aryan race, so ingrained in Nazi culture, comes from the dogma of the Thule Society, an occultist secret order that believed in an ancient race of genetically superior supermen from a now lost continent. These beings used the Swastika as their emblem. Similarly, the possibly mythical Vril Society in Germany and Austria sought the forgotten sciences of the Ayrans' secret masters, dealing with a mystical force called "vril." This could be used to power all sorts of advanced vehicles and machines. Some have speculated that the Vril Society kept Hitler alive, preserving his brain in some mysterious way. No B-movie plot is too strange for some conspiracy theorist to latch onto it. Many believe the Vril Society to be an offshoot or an analog of the Illuminati themselves (the Vril Society supposedly also called itself the Luminous Lodge, and luminous suggests illumination . . .).

The alien abduction crowd tries to draw links between the Nazis and the otherworldly visitors. Researcher Val Valerian, for example, claims that the Germans recovered a crashed UFO ten years before the Roswell incident and uncovered secrets from the technology they obtained. Writer Doug Moench contends that Nazi sympathizers in the CIA during its early days formed an alliance with alien beings shortly after the Roswell crash in 1947. This shadowy group-within-a-group calls itself Aquarius and is behind everything bad that has happened since 1947 (Aquarius, for example, was behind the killing of JFK). Meanwhile, writer and Internet radio host Sherry Shiner contends that evil aliens made direct contact with the Nazis in the late 1930s and early 1940s through mystics in the Thule Society, providing them with technological secrets, including vril. Even well-known abductee Barney Hill claimed to have seen a uniformed Nazi on board an alien craft while he was under hypnosis.

I heard it might have been Atlantis or even an underground kingdom under the Himalayas. How's THAT for the connection to the Abominable Snowman?

That's the Masonic connection to the Nazis. Masons are everywhere!

HE'S REALLY ONTO something HERE!

Or maybe what we believe to be examples of alien technology are just secret Nazi projects. Using vril energy, the Nazis may have made a quantum leap forward in technological advancement during the latter days of World War II. If so, then the UFOs we see in the skies might actually be Nazi aircraft flying from hidden bases in South America or Antarctica. Or the moon. Or from inside the Earth. Or out of some very overactive imaginations . . . .

In summary, modern U.S. corporations, the CIA, influential political figures, aliens, and occult figures all have links to the Nazis. Why? Why do conspiracy theorists love to tie it all back to Hitler and the boys? *BECAUSE it's TRUE!!!!*

Nazis are the perfect villains. A conspiracy theorist able to draw a link between his favorite topic and the Nazis wins the conspiracy game of one-upmanship.

SOME PEOPLE think the EARTH is hollow AND there's a whole other civilization inside.

CONSPIRACY RUNDOWN

PLAUSIBILITY:

6/10. It's pretty well documented that some Nazis escaped prosecution by working with the United States or by hiding out in South America. But a clone of Hitler flying a vril-powered Nazi UFO out of his secret base in Antarctica? Come on.

HIGH STRANGENESS:

7/10. Vril? Nazi aliens? This is all pretty strange—even by conspiracy standards.

CONSPIRACY CHECKLIST:

- ☑ Illuminati
- ☐ The Freemasons
- ☑ CIA/intelligence community/the military
- ☑ Aliens
- ☑ The occult
- ☐ The Mafia

FOR MORE INFORMATION:

General Reinhard Gehlen: The CIA Connection by Mary Ellen Reese

Blowback: America's Recruitment of Nazis and Its Effects on the Cold War by Christopher Simpson

The CIA and the Cult of Intelligence by Victor Marchetti

The Nazis and the Occult by Dusty Sklar

ON THE WEB:

Operation Paperclip: www.operationpaperclip.info

The Gehlen Org: www.globalsecurity.org/intell/world/germany/gehlen.htm

Thule: www.crystalinks.com/thule.html

Various Nazi-related conspiracies: www.greyfalcon.us

CONSPIRACY INVESTIGATOR SEARCH TERMS:

Operation Paperclip, Nazi UFOs, Thule, Vril, New Swabia, Reinhart Gehlen

05. 1947: THE CONSPIRACY YEAR

PEOPLE BEHIND CONSPIRACY THEORIES eat and breathe connections. If you're a skeptic, you'd say that those "connections" are *all* just coincidence. Even conspiracists sometimes admit that not all the links between mysterious people and strange events can possibly be correct. But conspiracy-theory nuts look for connection, not coincidence.

They get really good at it, in fact. When someone brings up that the first atomic bomb was detonated at the Trinity Site at the White Sands Proving Grounds near Socorro, New Mexico, at 33 degrees latitude, someone else will mention that JFK was assassinated in Dallas, also at 33 degrees latitude, near the Trinity River. But does such a link mean anything, or is it a coincidence? Abraham Lincoln had a secretary named Kennedy and John F. Kennedy had a secretary named Lincoln, but so what?

Actual *explanation* is forever denied the conspiracy theorist. It's the link itself that becomes important, not the reason for the link. So then, is it a coincidence that so many strange and important conspiratorial things all happened in 1947? Let's look closer.

OMG!! It is all connected!

I hadn't read this 1947 stuff before, but now it's clear to me that something big happened then.

DAWN OF THE FLYING SAUCER

On June 24, 1947, a private pilot named Kenneth Arnold was flying from Chehalis, Washington, to Yakima. As he flew past Mt. Rainer, he saw nine objects in the sky. They were flying. And unidentified. The objects flew in formation and were disc shaped. Mrs. Ethel Wheelhouse in Yakima sixty miles away also saw several flying discs. Others later reported similar sightings.

This captured a lot of attention from newspapers across the United States. By June 27, the "flying disks" had become "flying saucers," and the name stuck. In the next few weeks, flying saucer sightings numbered in the hundreds. While Arnold's is not the first report of an unidentified flying object, most consider it to be the first modern UFO sighting (largely because it was confirmed by several others).

A few days before the Yakima incident, on June 21, Harold Dahl used his boat to look for drifting logs near Maury Island in Puget Sound near Tacoma. Several objects flew over him. One even dripped hot slag into the boat. The slag injured his son and killed his dog, both in the boat with him. (It turns out that Puget Sound was a popular tourist spot for ETs. Maybe they like coffee.)

Dahl says he was visited the very next day by a strange man dressed in a black suit. Dahl presumed he was from the government. The man asked him about the incident. When he left he warned Dahl not to pursue the matter further. This was the first of many encounters with the infamous Men in Black who would become entwined with UFO lore. *One time I saw two men in black suits. I followed them for a while but they DISAPPEARED!!*

A man named Fred Crisman helped investigate the incident later—and claimed to have seen the UFOs as well. Crisman also testified in the trial of Clay Shaw regarding the Kennedy assassination (see Chapter 6). He was also a friend of Michael Riconosciuto, a key player in the so-called Octopus conspiracy (see Chapter 26).

The Men in Black—were they the ASSASSINS?

Just a few days later, on July 8, the Air Force released a press release saying that the day before a flying saucer had crashed in Roswell, New Mexico. Although they would retract this statement the next day and put forth the old weather balloon story (actually, it wasn't a tired excuse back then), this event would start a fire that still burns in the heart of every good ufologist today. (For more details, see Chapter 14.)

DAWN OF THE COMPANY

Is it somehow related to the UFO flap that in September 1947 the Central Intelligence Agency was officially formed?

Some contend that the CIA was the public face of Aquarius (mentioned previously), a far more secretive group that itself is either related to or is in fact the same thing as the Majestic 12 group.

I think the crash at Roswell helped influence the early days of the CIA. That would mean that the CIA has been in cahoots with the GREYS from the get-go.

MJ 12, also known as Majic 12, is a shadowy cabal of scientists, intelligence operatives, and military personnel created by executive order of President Truman in, perhaps coincidentally, September 1947. MJ 12 was supposedly created as a direct response to whatever happened in Roswell—either to deal with a secret alien threat, the alien technology recovered in a crash, direct contact with living aliens, or some combination of those three. MJ 12 became one of the most important organizations in the government.

Did I ever tell you about the listening device I found in my apartment? It looked like a dead bug, but that's just how clever they really are.

If you prefer a more sinister take, Aquarius/MJ 12 may be the faction of the government working *with* the aliens, willing participants to alien abductions, cattle mutilations, and strange experiments (see Chapter 17).

DAWN OF . . . SOMETHING REALLY ODD

That's all pretty strange stuff. Join me now in hyper-weird land. Standing next to us are two figures who by all rights should never be associated with one another. One is tall, thin, and handsome, the other rotund with thinning hair and a huckster's smile. The first man is rocket scientist John Parsons, cofounder of the Jet Propulsion Laboratory. The other is L. Ron Hubbard, science fiction author and founder of the Church of Scientology. Not only did these two know each other, but they both devoted themselves to the occult. Together they performed a powerful magickal rite in the California desert to conjure forth an otherworldly being and usher in a new age just shortly before the hubbub in the skies and the secret halls of government in 1947 would begin. (And by the way, yes, it's "magickal," not "magical." All "real" (read: pretentious) practitioners of the occult use the superfluous "k." Maybe it stands for "kool." Or "kook.")

I was spied on for a year by members of the Church of Scientology.

Although a genius in rocketry and cutting-edge technology, Parsons also held a great interest in the supernatural. Apparently, he had a knack for it. Aleister Crowley himself chose him to lead a lodge of

NOT CROWLEY! CROWLEY SCARES ME.

a quasi-Masonic secret society called the Ordo Templi Orientis (OTO) in California (the Agape Lodge). It was there that he met Hubbard, and the two became partners in a magickal enterprise (as well as a boat company called Allied Enterprises). Using formulas and rites conceived by Crowley, Parsons and Hubbard began the infamous "Babalon Working," designed to conjure what they believed would be a goddess whose presence would change the world forever. (Yes, it's "Babalon," not "Babylon." Are you seeing a trend here?) Occultist and author Kenneth Grant believes Parsons and Hubbard sought to open a long-sealed doorway to let "the Old Ones" into our world.

What were these Old Ones? Could they be the beings visiting us from elsewhere, starting with Kenneth Arnold's flying saucers? UFO researcher Jacques Vallee believes that UFOs have more to do with the paranormal than science, and writer and reporter John Keel feels that what we think of as extraterrestrials might actually be "ultraterrestrials," coming from some other reality rather than some other planet. Even Crowley's own sketch of a being called LAM who advised him

H. P. Lovecraft wrote stories about the Old Ones.

Did he know something?!!

· · ·

THE NAZI LINKS

Weaving in and out of all the strangeness in 1947 are the Nazis. They were involved with the CIA through Gehlen's Org (see Chapter 4) from the beginning of the agency. Their scientists, who worked for the United States after the war thanks to Operation Paperclip (see Chapter 4), supposedly took part in the study of the wreckage from the 1947 Roswell crash. In fact, Nazis in the CIA may have murdered John F. Kennedy because of his knowledge of Roswell and fear that he was about to make it public. Some researchers place Wernher von Braun himself in Majestic 12. And von Braun was a frequent correspondent of Jack Parsons. So it really does all tie together.

Or it might all be a coincidence. *It's NOT!!! Von Brawn was a member of the Illuminati! Which started in Germany!*

through mystical communication looked very much like the bald-headed, big-eyed alien Grey so recognizable today but unknown then.

As for Parsons and Hubbard, the latter ran off with the wife of the former, as well as the boat and the money from their joint business venture. According to the Church of Scientology, Hubbard was a secret agent working for the Office of Naval Intelligence to break up Parsons' sex-and-drug-related occult circle.

Coincidentally, some claim that Crowley himself worked for the ONI during World War II to secretly combat the occult-obsessed Nazis. According to Michael Riconosciuto, throughout the twentieth century, an inner circle of the Office of Naval Intelligence, sometimes known as Com-12, engaged in a secret war of spooks and spies against none other than Aquarius, the secret cabal within the CIA.

Aleister Crowley passed away in 1947. Perhaps he knew his work was done. For what it's worth, 1947 was also the year of the largest sunspot ever recorded, the discovery of the Dead Sea Scrolls, the infamous Black Dahlia murder in California, the creation of the State of Israel, and the year that fish mysteriously rained from the sky in Marksville, Louisiana. Could the sunspots and the fish have something to do with the Babalon working? Or was the incredible solar activity the reason behind the UFO crash at Roswell? Did the murder in California have anything to do with the OTO? If you asked any of these questions, you're starting to think like a conspiracy theorist.

HOW CAN ANYONE NOT SEE THESE ARE NOT COINCIDENCES!!

CONSPIRACY RUNDOWN

PLAUSIBILITY:
1/10. Sometimes a coincidence is just a coincidence.

HIGH STRANGENESS:
10/10. It doesn't get much weirder than UFOs conjured by magic used by intelligence operatives.

CONSPIRACY CHECKLIST:
- ☐ Illuminati
- ☑ The Freemasons
- ☑ CIA/intelligence community/the military
- ☑ Aliens
- ☑ The occult
- ☐ The Mafia

FOR MORE INFORMATION:

Sex and Rockets: The Occult World of Jack Parsons by John Carter

Outer Gateways by Kenneth Grant

UFOs: The Secret History by Michael Hesmann

Alien Agenda by Jim Marrs

ON THE WEB:

The Majestic 12 documents: www.majesticdocuments.com

The Ordo Templi Orientis (U.S. Grand Lodge) official site: www.oto-usa.org

CONSPIRACY INVESTIGATOR SEARCH TERMS:

Babalon Working, Majestic 12, Kenneth Arnold, Maury Island incident, Roswell alien crash, Fred Crisman

06. LEE, HARVEY, AND THE REST

THE ASSASSINATION OF President John F. Kennedy on November 22, 1963, is not only the source of the most recognizable conspiracy theories; it's the one that lends credibility to all conspiracy theories. Aliens, Templars, secret societies—that all sounds like fiction. But John F. Kennedy really *was* assassinated. That's history that everyone knows about. A recent poll showed that seven out of ten Americans believe *some* kind of conspiracy was involved in the assassination.

Who killed JFK? That's the question. Well, it's *one* of the questions—not the only one. Just as important as "who," is "why," and "how."

A LONE GUNMAN

John Fitzgerald Kennedy was killed Friday, November 22, 1963, in Dallas, Texas, at 12:30 P.M. while riding in a motorcade through Dealey Plaza. Lee Harvey Oswald was arrested for the crime (technically, he was initially arrested for the murder of police officer J. D. Tippit). Oswald never stood trial as he was murdered by nightclub owner Jack Ruby on November 24 while being transferred to the Dallas County Jail. In one of his only statements before his murder, Oswald said that he was a patsy—a fall guy. An official government investigation overseen by the Warren Commission lasted ten months and claimed that Oswald acted alone.

Many people believe there was at least one other shooter, standing on the so-called grassy knoll, a small hill next to Dealey Plaza. Many witnesses reported shots from both the Texas School Book Depository (where Oswald was thought to be) and the grassy knoll. Jean Hill, a schoolteacher, stood on the grassy knoll facing the Book Depository and saw the president shot. She thought she heard shots come from behind her. Film taken at the scene shows policemen charging up the grassy knoll—far more than ran toward the Book Depository.

Among the most compelling evidence for another assassin is the infamous "magic bullet." Put simply, the only way Oswald could have fired all the shots that struck the president is if we assume a single

[handwritten note, left margin:] But there is a connection to the Templars! That's what I've been saying. IT'S ALL CONNECTED!!!

[handwritten note, left margin:] The fact that they couldn't COMPLETELY cover it shows that while the cryptocracy is powerful, it's not all-powerful! Unless . . . the cover-up is part of an EVEN BIGGER COVER-UP!?!?

[handwritten note, right margin:] Was Tippit another assassin? Was he killed to keep him quiet?

[handwritten note, bottom:] I kind of feel sorry for Oswald! I mean, he was completely set up.

bullet inflicted all of the nonfatal wounds on both the president and Texas governor John Connally, who was also in the car. The official report states that there were only three shots. One bullet hit the nearby overpass and one killed Kennedy, passing through his head. Kennedy was also wounded in the throat, while Connally was shot in the chest and wrist. The Warren Commission claimed that a single bullet passed through Kennedy's neck, struck Connally and injured him in both the chest and the wrist, and finally embedded itself in the governor's thigh. *Yeah, sure!!! No way one bullet could do that!* According to this theory the bullet made several dramatic turns in mid-flight. It passed through fifteen layers of clothing, seven layers of skin, and approximately fifteen inches of tissue. It also removed four inches of rib and shattered a radius bone.

To make it all the more unbelievable, when this bullet was recovered its copper jacket was completely intact, though it left fragments in many of the wounds. Abraham Zapruder was recording the motorcade with a personal movie camera. His film shows—or at least seems to show—that Connolly was struck by a different shot than the one that wounded Kennedy in the neck. *SEE?! That's what I said!!*

The autopsy conducted upon President Kennedy suggested that the shot that killed him—the one that struck him in the head—hit him from the front, not the back (from where Oswald was firing). Sharp-shooting experts have testified that such an accurate shot from so far away with a rifle of the type Oswald used would be nearly impossible. They point as well to the even more impossible task of getting off three shots in six seconds using such a weapon. If Oswald wasn't a so-called lone gunman, who was he working with, or for? Whose fall guy was he? *???*

SUSPECT: THE MAFIA

One potential culprit is the Mafia. No one's going to disagree that these guys are murderers and are capable of pulling off a large criminal operation. Numerous researchers claim that mob bosses such as

Carlos Marcell, Santos Trafficante, Antoine Guerini, Sam Giancana, and Jimmy Hoffa, among others, organized the "hit." Both President Kennedy and his attorney general, Robert Kennedy (assassinated five years later), had worked hard to bring down organized crime.

When Fidel Castro took control of Cuba in 1959, many mob bosses were forced out of that country, costing them millions. According to author Anthony Summers, the Mafia began working with the CIA to assassinate Castro. After numerous failures, President Kennedy decided to stop pursuing anti-Cuban activities. Either in revenge or to get him out of the way, the mob (or anti-Castro forces funded by the mob) killed Kennedy.

Oswald's murderer, Jack Ruby, had numerous mob connections, as well as connections to Oswald himself. It's possible Ruby could have set Oswald up and influenced him to carry out the deed. Ruby's mob connections may have started with Al Capone back in Chicago. He was friends with Dave Yarras, a Mafia hitman known as the Chicago mob's liaison to the Cuban exile community. Some suspect Yarras was one of the gunmen involved in the assassination.

In 1996, James Files confessed to being a part of the Mafia-backed assassination conspiracy, which he said included Oswald and another man, Charlie Nicoletti. According to his confession, Sam Giancana, a mobster from Chicago, organized the operation. Giancana supposedly helped Kennedy win in Illinois during the 1960 election and expected gratitude and rewards. Instead both Kennedy brothers sought his arrest and prosecution for numerous crimes. Giancana had been in a relationship with Judith Campbell, a mistress of President Kennedy (as well as Frank Sinatra). In fact, Kennedy and Giancana used Campbell as a messenger while they worked together in their plot to kill Castro. But two men and one woman is often a recipe for disaster. Could Kennedy have been killed as the result of a lover's jealousy?

The government could have quietly covered up the mob hit, focusing the blame on Oswald, because exposing the Mafia at that point would uncover the links between organized crime and the CIA in its plots against Castro.

SUSPECT: CASTRO

If Kennedy used either the CIA or the mob—or both—in attempts on Cuban leader Fidel Castro's life, Castro might hold a grudge. Perhaps Castro, or his Communist allies either in the United States or the Soviet Union, killed JFK. *This is just what THEY want you to think!!!!*

After the failed Bay of Pigs invasion of Cuba in 1961, the president was planning to organize another invasion, this time with Robert Kennedy in charge. Castro could not ignore this threat. Both Castro and his Soviet allies had looked weak during the 1962 Cuban Missile Crisis.

Oswald had spent time in the USSR, was an avowed Communist, and participated in pro-Cuban demonstrations and activities. His wife was the niece of a high-ranking KGB agent. Author Edward Jay Epstein argues that Oswald was a KGB agent, while others believe that the assassin was a Communist agent *posing* as Oswald. Author Max Holland wrote in the *Atlantic* that attorney Jim Garrison possessed evidence of four Castro-sponsored strike teams. Oswald was on one team with Clay Shaw, David Ferrie, and one other man. So even if Oswald was the sole shooter, he still might have been working alongside others and for Castro.

I can't believe there are still people who think Oswald did it!!

SUSPECT: THE ANTI-CASTRO CROWD

Author Anthony Summers contends that JFK was assassinated by militant anti-Castro activists. They may have been funded by the mob and aided by CIA agents. An undercover agent overheard a Cuban exile say to his fellows at a meeting, "We're waiting for Kennedy on the twenty-second. We're going to see him in one way or another."

When Castro took power in Cuba, anti-Communist Cuban exiles in the United States prepared to retake their country. U.S. intelligence helped train and fund them. Anti-Castro Cubans supplied the forces for the Bay of Pigs invasion of Cuba, and when that operation ended in a bloody debacle, they were incensed. They blamed President Kennedy.

At the heart of the anti-Castro movement in the United States were men like Carlos Bringuier, a Cuban exile who was an outspoken member of the Student Revolutionary Directorate, David Ferrie, a defrocked priest, Guy Bannister, a former FBI agent, and Clay Shaw, a wealthy businessman who was likely also a CIA agent. Together, these New Orleans residents conspired with Oswald to kill Kennedy. Their hope was to blame Castro and get the country to invade Cuba.

Defrocked for what?! Is it possible this guy WAS A MASONIC AGENT?!!!

In New Orleans, Oswald founded a chapter of the pro-Cuban organization, the Fair Play for Cuba Committee. However, the leaflets that he handed out bore the address of the office used by Bringuier—an anti-Castro activist. That address was around the corner from 531 Lafayette Street, where Guy Bannister worked as a private investigator. According to Bannister's mistress, Oswald worked for Bannister, who supported the anti-Castro movement. It's possible that Oswald's Communist leanings and pro-Castro work was a sham to point the finger at Castro and the Communists when their assassination plan came to fruition. Bringuier and Oswald even staged public confrontations to give more credence to his role. The entire façade of the Fair Play for Cuba Committee may have been Bannister's idea.

Ferrie and Shaw organized gunrunning operations to anti-Castro groups in Cuba and trained Cuban exiles for combat in secret camps in Louisiana and Texas. Reportedly, this was a CIA-backed program known as Operation Mongoose. In addition, many witnesses attest to connections between Oswald, Ferrie, and Shaw, as well as Jack Ruby. So were all these men working together to kill the president? New Orleans district attorney Jim Garrison thought so. He focused most of his investigations into the JFK murder on this group of conspirators and even brought Shaw to trial (he was acquitted). *TYPICAL!!!!*

Of course he was acquitted! Because the court system in this country is controlled by THEM!!

SUSPECT: THE MILITARY-INDUSTRIAL COMPLEX

Kennedy made a lot of enemies among powerful men in the United States, both in the Pentagon and in corporate boardrooms. They hated that he was growing cold on the Cold War and sought to avoid further involvement in Vietnam. Many believed that he cut a secret deal with Khrushchev during the Cuban Missile Crisis, agreeing not to invade Cuba in return for the Russians pulling their missiles out. He proposed cuts to defense spending and closing military bases, angering both the military and the industries that profited by selling them weapons, vehicles, and other goods. He even threatened to dismantle the CIA, believing they had tried to deceive him during the Bay of Pigs invasion.

Someone told me Khrushchev and Kennedy agreed to allow the Greys to use Cuba as a secret landing base and THAT'S WHAT THE SPY PLANES WERE TAKING PICTURES OF during the missile crisis!

Only a few years earlier, in 1961, President Eisenhower's farewell address to the nation warned of the growing power of the military-industrial complex. This powerful clique included not only the Pentagon and the intelligence community but those who profit from them: defense contractors, oil companies, and bankers.

Other assassination theories include various FBI agents (Guy Bannister), CIA agents (Clay Shaw and perhaps Oswald himself), and so forth. Some conspiracists, though, suggest a much wider conspiracy at the highest levels of government: top officials in the Pentagon, heads of the CIA and FBI, the Secret Service, and perhaps even Vice President Lyndon Johnson. The Kennedy assassination, then, represents nothing less than a coup d'état.

The evidence for such a broad conspiracy, its advocates argue, lies in its very scale. Getting Kennedy to Dallas, setting the direction of the motorcade's path, and orchestrating the widespread cover-up suggests many powerful people and agencies were involved. Proper security measures for the president's trip to Dallas were not taken. The route should have been more carefully monitored both before the president went by and during the motorcade. Government snipers should have been in the area, watching for gunmen in the windows of nearby buildings. In addition, someone told the 112th Military Intelligence group at Fort Sam Houson in Texas to stand down that day.

Even as security in Dallas was lax, the government was taking other questionable measures. The president's cabinet was safely out of the country. One-third of a combat division was in the air above the United States. It almost seems someone was taking precautions in case the assassination caused civil unrest.

In this version of events, Oswald was a CIA agent, trained for military intelligence while in the marines and stationed at Atsugi Air Base in Japan. Although official records show nothing of the kind, military intelligence did have a Harvey Lee Oswald on file. Oswald's defection to Russia was a sham, which explains how he was able to return to the United States without any problems. He worked with other CIA agents, including Shaw, Ferrie, Bannister, and others, but in the end was the patsy he claimed to be. The real assassins were highly trained government operatives. Oswald may or may not have even been on the sixth floor of the Book Depository. (Various coworkers there place him on

BECAUSE the MASONS have infiltrated the JOINT CHIEFS of STAFF!!

TOO MUCH INFORMATION

Conspiracy theorists continually claim that the problem with everything comes from a lack of information. They constantly try to dig up new information. They use the Freedom of Information Act. They eat and breathe information.

But the JFK conspiracy shows the power of too much information. With so many different theories, so many different lines of investigation, so many suspects, and so many seemingly contradictory "facts," it becomes harder and harder to see it all clearly. Which may be the point. All the conspiracy theories about the JFK assassination may in fact be a part of the conspiracy. Some of them might be smokescreens to cover up the truth and confuse the issue.

No, it's VERY CLEAR if you WANT to SEE!!!!!!!

the first floor eating his lunch. Other witnesses claim they saw someone on the sixth floor, but not Oswald. Oswald was wearing a reddish T-shirt that day, but they reported seeing a dark-skinned man in a white or light blue collared shirt. Others believe they saw two men in that window.)

Whoever pulled the trigger, with JFK out of the way the military-industrial complex prospered. The postwar status quo was restored, the CIA was left intact, and the Cold War continued with an ongoing military buildup that required astronomical spending. Just days after taking office, Johnson reversed Kennedy's policies in Vietnam, increasing covert action there, which led to a war costing billions of dollars and tens of thousands of lives.

Was the assassination a setup to get a troublemaker out of the way and install a more sympathetic voice in the Oval Office? If CIA assassins carried out the murder, Secret Service agents facilitated it, and the FBI helped cover up all evidence of the conspiracy, the entire process must have been a cross-departmental nightmare. That may be the best argument against this frightening scenario.

OR WERE the Alien Illuminati working with the CIA? And WHAT ABOUT THE FBI???!!!

SUSPECT: VARIOUS FUTURE PRESIDENTS

Kennedy was in Texas at Vice President Johnson's behest. Howard St. John Hunt, son of E. Howard Hunt (of Watergate fame), claims that his father was approached by rogue CIA agents working for Johnson to be a part of the conspiracy to kill the president. Hunt turned them down, according to his son. *Hunt is dead now!!!*

Johnson did not like the Kennedys, conspiracists allege, and he profited by JFK's death. Johnson's conspirators include a number of CIA agents involved with various Central American operations as well as Cuban exiles and a mysterious "French gunman." Some researchers believe that Hunt was actually involved—they offer as evidence an incriminating letter allegedly from Oswald to Hunt. It reads: "I would like information concerning (sic) my position. I am asking only for information. I am suggesting that we discuss the matter fully before any steps are taken by me or anyone else. Thank you. (signed) Lee Harvey Oswald." Hunt was in Dallas "on a business trip" at the time of the assassination.

Hunt's connection with Richard Nixon presents its own interesting twist, because Nixon was also in Dallas on that fateful day. Mob boss Sam Giancana claimed that Nixon—who had his own reasons to hate Kennedy after the 1960 election—was also involved in the assassination plot and that Giancana and Nixon met in Dallas to discuss it. Nixon attempted to cover up the fact that he was in Dallas at the time, although his alibi, that he was at a PepsiCo convention, seems legitimate. Was Pepsi involved? I bet Coke would like you to think so. In fact, conspiracy-minded folks often connect Pepsi and the CIA (undercover CIA employees' paychecks are sometimes issued by PepsiCo).

Nixon once told his aide Stephen Hess that he was afraid one day he would be blamed for Kennedy's murder. H. R. Haldeman, Nixon's former chief of staff, even suggested that the purpose of the entire Watergate break-in might have been to locate incriminating evidence regarding the assassination. And while it could mean nothing, some evidence seems to show that Jack Ruby had worked for Nixon's congressional office while in Chicago in 1947. What's more, an FBI memo as well as a photo taken of the Book Depository places a young George Bush Sr. in Dallas on November 22. According to retired U.S. Army Brigadier Gen. Russell Bowen, Bush was working for the CIA and was in Dallas at the time. His name figures prominently in a memo from J. Edgar Hoover himself, which claims that he was briefed on the assassination shortly after it happened. Unlike every other American alive at the time, Bush claims he does not remember where he was the day Kennedy was assassinated.

Only theorists on the fringe claim Bush had anything to do with the assassination, but it is strange and a little creepy that he was there. And don't forget that Gerald Ford was on the Warren Commission, which may have helped cover up any and all conspiracies involved. At

Nixon met with aliens in 1957 when he was vice president!!! In Area 51! Did the aliens work with Giancana and Nixon to kill Kennedy???

SURE!!! Don't believe it!!

this point, it would not be surprising to learn that Jimmy Carter and Ronald Reagan were playing golf in Dallas on November 22, 1963, with Bill Clinton and George W. Bush working as caddies.

SUSPECT: THE FREEMASONS

BECAUSE THEY'RE BEHIND IT!!!!!!

You knew this whole thing was going to have to get back to the Masons sooner or later, right? Well, here we are. Author James Shelby Downard *STOP COVERING UP!!* believes that the murder of John F. Kennedy was a Masonic rite, known as the Killing of the King. In his essay "King-Kill/33 degrees," he writes, "But the ultimate purpose of that assassination was not political or economic but sorcerous: for the control of the dreaming mind and the marshalling of its forces is the omnipotent force in this entire scenario of lies, cruelty and degradation."

For Downard, it all comes down to symbolism and numbers. The highest rank of Masonry is the thirty-third degree (the concept of the trinity—three—is important to them). Dallas lies on the thirty-third degree of latitude (well, not really, but it's close . . .) Dealey Plaza is close to the Trinity River. The assassination occurred very close to the Triple Underpass. There were three assassins (according to Downard, but backed up by other conspiracy theorists who claim that putting a target in a "triangulation pattern" is an effective assassination technique). The assassination occurred at the site of the Masonic temple in Dallas. ← *VICE PRESIDENT JOHNSON WAS A MASON!!!! That makes it clear!*

The Killing of the King ritual is the second of three important rituals in Masonic mythology. The first is the Creation and Destruction of Primordial Matter. This occurred just a few years earlier at the Trinity Site at the White Sands Proving Grounds in New Mexico with the detonation of the first atomic bomb. White Sands also lies at thirty-three degrees latitude. The third ritual is the Bringing of Prima Material to Prima Terra—bringing heaven to earth. This was also accomplished when moon rocks were brought back by the astronauts, including Freemason Buzz Aldrin. So . . . that's all perfectly obvious, isn't it?

And who STARTED the MOON PROGRAM? PRESIDENT KENNEDY!!!!

WILL THE REAL LEE HARVEY OSWALD PLEASE STAND UP?

Already, we've got Oswald the KGB agent, Oswald the anti-Castro activist, Oswald the pro-Cuban activist, and Oswald the CIA agent. Who was this man?

Oswald was born in New Orleans, served as a U.S. Marine, believed in Marxism, defected to Russia, and later returned. At an early age, he may have exhibited schizophrenic tendencies. Before the Kennedy assassination, he worked with the Fair Play for Cuba Committee in New Orleans and eventually moved to Dallas where he worked at the Texas School Book Depository. There is no motive ascribed to the man for the murder of the president.

But what if there was more than one Oswald? Author Michael Eddowes became so convinced that Oswald was replaced by a KGB double while in the Soviet Union that he had Oswald's body exhumed in 1981. He had the support of Oswald's widow, who also came to believe that her husband was not the gunman who killed the president. The examination, hampered by extreme decomposition, confirmed that the body in the grave was indeed Lee Harvey Oswald. However, controversy follows everything having to do with the JFK assassination. Oswald's body was decomposed because the steel-reinforced concrete vault in which he was buried, guaranteed not to break, was broken. Was the body tampered with? Was the body examined a different one than the one originally placed there? That's what the mortician who embalmed the original body, Paul Groody, claimed while watching as the second body was exhumed. The multiple Oswald story gets stranger. Researcher John Armstrong believes that the man we know as Lee Harvey Oswald was in fact two different men, whose stories were knowingly combined by the Warren Commission. The two men, of similar age and appearance, were in fact different. One, who was called "Lee," stood taller than the other and spoke with a Southern accent. The other, "Harvey," spoke fluent Russian even as a child and may have been the son of Hungarian immigrants. In this scenario, Lee is the assassin and Harvey is the patsy. Harvey was a peaceful Communist sympathizer, and Lee made trouble, possessed a violent temper, and couldn't speak Russian.

Conspiracists who have made a close examination of photos from various points in Oswald's life argue that the photos seem to show two different but similar-looking men. In fact, they say, one can take two different headshots, cut each in half lengthwise, align the chin, lips, and nose, and see that nothing else matches up. Further, the so-called "backyard photo," showing Oswald with a rifle and a newspaper, appears to have been doctored.

Other conspiracists point to the many reports and eyewitness accounts that exist of Oswald being in more than two places at once. For example, apparently on November 9, Oswald test-drove a car at Downtown Lincoln Mercury in Dallas, commenting that he was soon going to come into a lot of money and might be returning to Russia. Except that according to the official account by the Warren Commission, Oswald and his family spent the day with Ruth Paine, a friend of Oswald's wife. And he couldn't drive—in fact, Ruth was teaching him. That same weekend, while some witnesses place him with Paine, others say he went to a rifle range and hit the bullseye on every target, patronized a local barber, and went shopping. Apparently, "Lee" and "Harvey" were both in town that weekend.

But maybe there are more "Oswalds" than even those two. A contemporary photo shows a man who looks very much like Oswald standing in the doorway of the Book Depository, on the street, watching in surprise as shots are fired by "Oswald" on the sixth floor of that same building. This man was Billy Lovelady, who also worked at the Book Depository. Lovelady looked so much like Oswald that his own wife once confused the two. Did the CIA, the mob, or the Russians have some kind of machine that made Oswalds? Some outlandish theories suggest that Oswald was the product of a breeding experiment conducted by ex-Nazis in South America for use by their friends in the CIA.

Maybe they were dopplegangers! Or clones! There's a secret lab near Edinburgh that's doing cloning experiments!!!

See!!!!! Clones!!! But they're being done by the Illuminati!!

OTHER ASSASSINS

While Lee Harvey Oswald (or someone posing as him) fired from the sixth floor of the Texas School Book Depository, many believe that other shots—perhaps the *real* assassin's bullets—came from the grassy knoll. But who fired those shots?

Immediately after the assassination, police raced to the railroad yard behind the grassy knoll near Dealey Plaza and rounded up everyone they could find. A photo taken at the time shows "three hobos," or "three tramps," whom many claim are actually assassins. Unlike the others around them, these "hobos" wear nice clothing, have recent haircuts, and are clean shaven. They don't look like transients. (And their arrest records mysteriously disappeared.) Theorists claim they could be Thomas Vallee, Frank Sturgis, and Chauncy Holt or Charles Rogers.

An expert marksman, Thomas Vallee was a right-wing radical who hated Kennedy. He was briefly detained just a few weeks earlier in Chicago allegedly on suspicion of being part of a plot to assassinate the president there. Frank Sturgis was a former marine and CIA agent who participated in some of the agency's attempts to kill Fidel Castro. He later rose to infamy for his participation in the Watergate break-in. Chauncy Holt was also a CIA operative involved in the attempts to oust Castro. Conspiracists believe he created false IDs for Oswald in New Orleans and may also have had mob connections. He confessed in 1991 to being one of the assassins of JFK. Charles Rogers was yet another CIA agent with mob connections. He knew defrocked priest/CIA operative David Ferrie and supposedly fled to South America after the assassination.

Or the three hobos might have been Charles Harrelson, E. Howard Hunt, and Fred Crisman. A strange trio if there ever was one. Harrelson was a Chicago mobster and father of future Hollywood star Woody Harrelson. E. Howard Hunt, already mentioned, was a CIA agent. Fred Chrisman was the investigator mentioned in Chapter

Hunt again!! There's the Nixon connection!

5 as being involved with the Maury Island UFO incident and also has connections to Michael Riconosciuto (Chapter 26). The father of a movie star, one of the Watergate burglars, and a name from UFO lore—is there any chance this story could get better?

Of course, the three tramps might be Gus Abrams, John F. Gedney, and Harold Doyle, three tramps identified in 1992 by the Dallas Police Department. But that's not very interesting.

Then there's the other man to confess to the crime, James Files. Files was part of the Chicago Mafia working for Charlie Nicoletti. He knew Jack Ruby, who provided details about the motorcade's route. According to his story, Files was on the grassy knoll while Nicoletti was in the nearby Dal-Tex building. Oswald planted the rifle in the Book Depository to throw off the investigation and was then framed for the murder. However, evidence seems to show that Files was in Chicago on that day, and his confession gets various details about Oswald and others wrong.

Roscoe White, a former marine stationed at Atsugi (just like Oswald) and a member of the Dallas police, wrote in his diary that he shot the president from the grassy knoll. After his death in a fire in 1971, his son revealed his father's written confession. White claims that Oswald was a part of the conspiracy but didn't fire any shots. He also admits to being the one who killed police officer J. D. Tippit. His wife Geneva confirms that she had once heard White and Jack Ruby plotting the assassination. White's diary was apparently confiscated by the FBI.

ANOTHER ONE dead!!!

That must have been a very crowded knoll.

Has there ever been a murder with so many potential suspects and motives? Even the prime suspect (Oswald) might have been more than one guy. Hundreds of conspiracy researchers have written books on the subject, and they don't agree at all.

CONSPIRACY RUNDOWN

PLAUSIBILITY:
8/10. That magic bullet argument is tough to refute. The evidence today seems to suggest that *somebody* else was working with Oswald.

HIGH STRANGENESS:
3/10. It all seems pretty straightforward until you get to the part about Freemasonry. And just how many Oswalds are there?

CONSPIRACY CHECKLIST:
- ☐ Illuminati
- ☑ The Freemasons
- ☑ CIA/intelligence community/the military
- ☐ Aliens
- ☑ The occult
- ☑ The Mafia

FOR MORE INFORMATION:

Crossfire: The Plot that Killed Kennedy by Jim Marrs

Ultimate Sacrifice: John and Robert Kennedy, the Plan for a Coup in Cuba, and the Murder of JFK by Lamar Waldron and Thom Harman

On the Trail of the Assassins by Jim Garrison

ON THE WEB:

The President John F. Kennedy Assassination Records Collection: www.archives.gov/research/jfk

A History of the Zapruder Film: www.jfklancer.com/History-Z.html

The Sixth Floor Museum at Dealey Plaza (the Book Depository): www.jfk.org

The Warren Commission Report: www.archives.gov/research/jfk/warren-commission-report

CONSPIRACY INVESTIGATOR SEARCH TERMS:

Operation Mongoose, Bay of Pigs, Sam Giancana, E. Howard Hunt, Zapruder film, Jim Garrison, Oliver Stone, Jim Marrs

07. OTHER MAGIC BULLETS

"OSWALD IS A PATSY. They set him up. It's too much. The bastards have done something outrageous. They've killed the President! I've been listening and hearing things. I couldn't believe they'd get away with it, but they did!" That's what a very frightened Gary Underhill, former agent of the OSS and the CIA, told his friend, Charlene Fitsimmons, according to author James DiEugenio. "I know who they are. That's the problem. They know I know."

Authorities found Underhill dead, shot through the left side of his head. The Washington, D.C., police ruled it a suicide, even though he was right-handed.

The Kennedy assassination seems to be a sort of curse; many people who were witnesses or involved in some way (even allegedly) wind up dead. According to author Jim Marrs, as many as 103 people connected to the Kennedy assassination—witnesses, reporters, law enforcement agents, and others in the wrong place at the wrong time with the wrong secrets—died mysterious deaths. Many supposedly committed suicide—whether they wanted to or not. Were these deaths to further the cover-up of a conspiracy to kill the president?

The most prominent such death, of course, is that of Lee Harvey Oswald himself. Nightclub owner Jack Ruby killed Oswald on national television, supposedly because he didn't want to see Jacqueline Kennedy suffer through a trial. But there was more to Ruby than just a Jackie fanboy. As mentioned in Chapter 6, Ruby had mob connections and may have known nefarious conspirators like David Ferrie and Guy Bannister. Conspiracists believe Ruby killed Oswald to keep the truth from coming out. Ruby, in fact, figures into every variation of every assassination theory as surely as Oswald does. If you're going to connect the JFK conspiracy dots, you've got to connect both Oswald and Ruby, or you lose points.

Not that it's hard to connect the two, at least according to Rose Cherami. She was a dancer at Ruby's club. Thrown from a speeding car on the way from New Orleans to Dallas on November 20, 1963,

I have to watch my back!! Are they after me??!!!

Cherami entered the JFK story the hard way. According to her, one of the men in the car was Sergio Arcacha Smith, an anti-Castro Cuban exile. As she lay in the hospital after the incident, Cherami warned her nurses that "they" were going to kill the president in Dallas. No one believed her. After the assassination, Cherami claimed she knew Oswald as well as Ruby and that the two men knew each other. Intimately. As in, Ruby and Oswald were lovers.

Cherami was the victim of a hit-and-run two years later. Her exit was as dramatic as her entrance—and both are suspiciously similar.

IT'S HARD OUT THERE FOR A REPORTER

Reporter Bill Hunter of the *Long Beach Press Telegram* and Jim Koethe of the *Dallas Times Herald* interviewed George Senator, a friend of Ruby's, and Tom Howard, Ruby's lawyer, hours after Ruby had murdered Oswald. Later the men searched Ruby's apartment. We'll never know what transpired during those interviews or what they found in the search, because most of them died soon thereafter. A suspiciously accidental gunshot from a policeman killed Hunter, and an assailant killed Koethe in his apartment with a blow to the throat. Howard died from a heart attack. At the age of only forty-eight.

Dorothy Kilgallen, a well-known reporter and TV personality, interviewed Jack Ruby while he was in prison in Dallas after his trial. Ruby, apparently, was a fan and granted the interview after Kilgallen had covered his trial. Exactly what transpired in *that* interview we'll also never know . . . but we do have a few tantalizing clues.

Kilgallen told friends back in New York that Ruby was friends with the police officer J. D. Tippit who—according to the official story—was killed by Oswald as he tried to escape after killing the president. Eyewitnesses corroborated that the two had met at Ruby's club, along with Bernard Weissman, an outspoken right-wing critic of

So many dead!! I KNOW they're on my trail!! I know too much!!!

Kennedy's, and a mysterious figure who may have been "a rich Texas oil man."

She told friends and acquaintances that she was going to break the whole Kennedy assassination wide open. In her syndicated column, she wrote that assassination witnesses had been threatened by the Dallas police and the FBI and told not to say anything that did not conform to the official account. She intimated she had hard evidence that was going to shock the world but was saving it for a book. Knowing what had happened to Hunter and Koethe, Kilgallen gave her notes to her friend, Margaret Smith.

On November 8, 1965, Kilgallen was found dead in her bed, a book lying across her lap. The first report blamed a heart attack, but this story was later changed to a barbiturate overdose. She had been on the television program *What's My Line?* earlier that evening. Kilgallen lay in bed with all her stage makeup on, even her false eyelashes. According to biographer Lee Isreal, this was strange for her. What's more, her reading glasses were nowhere nearby, and the book was a novel that she had told her hairdresser she had already finished. The official cause of death was left undetermined. Margaret Smith, meanwhile, died of "indeterminate causes." When Kilgallen's husband was asked what his wife's big secret was and what was in the file given to Smith, he replied that it was something that would go with him to the grave. *I'll bet he DID, too!! I wonder if They ASSASSINATED him.*

MORE MYSTERIOUS DEATHS

Lee Bowers Jr. worked at a railroad control tower behind the grassy knoll near Dealey Plaza. Bowers saw two strangers along the wooden fence facing the plaza and a flash of light and smoke at the time of the shooting. After he gave his testimony to the Warren Commission and his story to writer Mark Lane, the death threats started coming. Attorney Jim Garrison wanted Bowers to testify in his case against Clay

A FEW SURVIVED

Some of the witnesses did not die but still have terrible stories to tell. Take, for example, a couple of the men who witnessed the murder of police officer Tippit. According to author Doug Moench, Domingo Benavides said that the killer did not resemble Oswald. Soon afterward, Benavides received death threats, and his looka-like brother was killed in a bar fight. Suddenly, he reversed his testimony and agreed that the killer was Oswald. The death threats stopped. *Maybe ANOTHER CLONE??!!*

Warren Reynolds gave chase to Tippit's killer and said that it was not Oswald. He refused to change his testimony and was later shot in his basement. However, he survived. When he got out of the hospital, someone attempted to abduct his ten-year-old daughter. He finally changed his story.

Shaw, but Bowers died in a one-car accident before he could do that. Witnesses say he was driven off the road by a black car. As Bowers lay dying, he told them he had been drugged before the "accident."

David Ferrie, another Garrison witness (and possible conspirator in the assassination—see Chapter 6), died of a brain hemorrhage in his apartment before he could testify. Author Edward Haslam contends that Dr. Mary Sherman was working for the CIA with Ferrie in New Orleans, experimenting with a way to give Fidel Castro cancer. (Seriously.) Sherman was murdered the day the Warren Commission came to town to hear testimony. She was stabbed multiple times and burned. Much of this story comes from Judyth Baker, who claims that Dr. Sherman had recruited her into the anti-Castro plot and that it was backed by both the CIA and the Mafia in New Orleans. While she worked for Sherman, Baker met people such as Guy Bannister (see Chapter 6), Oswald, and Ferrie, who were also involved with the project. She had an affair with Oswald. Both had cover jobs at Reily's Coffee Company. In 1963, however, Oswald was called away to join the plot to kill the president.

JUST WHEN YOU THOUGHT
YOU HEARD IT ALL

Oswald supposedly told Baker that he would do whatever he could to *undermine* the plot and *save* the president. After the JFK assassination, Ferrie warned Baker that if she said anything about what she knew she would be killed. Baker remains alive, so perhaps the coast is finally clear. Or maybe she's a nut.

Maybe "They" have just become more subtle.

By the 1970s, enough questions had arisen regarding the assassinations of John F. Kennedy, Bobby Kennedy, and Martin Luther King Jr., particularly in regard to the involvement of any government agencies, that the Senate formed the Select Committee on Intelligence Activities and Select Committee on Assassinations. When they began investigating the John F. Kennedy assassination, the number of suspicious deaths among witnesses and possible conspirators increased dramatically. Mafia figures linked to the crime, like Sam Giancana, Dave Yarras, Jimmy Hoffa, and Charlie Nicoletti, all died violent or mysterious deaths. CIA agents Sheffield Edwards, William Harvey, and David Morales all died before they could give evidence to the House Select Committee on Assassinations. Likewise, six top FBI officials linked to the case all died within a six-month period in 1977.

Some of the witnesses did not go quietly into that good night. Consider Dallas police officer Roger Dean Craig. After shots rang out in Dealey Plaza, Craig ran to the grassy knoll and began interviewing witnesses. There, he saw a man running out of the back of the Texas School Book Depository and get into a waiting station wagon. He saw the man later back at the police station—it was the just-arrested Oswald. When Craig brought up his account, Oswald said, "That station wagon belongs to Mrs. Paine. . . . Don't try to tie her into this. She had nothing to do with it."

Craig was also present when the rifle was found in the Book Depository but denied the official report that it was a Mannlicher-Carcano. Instead he identified it as a 7.65 Mauser.

Craig testified before the Warren Commission, which ignored what he had to say. He also testified at Garrison's trial of Clay Shaw. Later that year, someone shot at him, grazing his head with a bullet. In 1973, an unknown vehicle forced his car off a mountain road. He survived the resulting accident, but his injuries were severe. In 1974, he survived another shooting. In 1975, his car engine exploded. After surviving all of that, he died just a few weeks later, from "self-inflicted" gunshot wounds.

The trial of Shaw was closed down! Because Garrison was too close to the truth!!?!

CONSPIRACY RUNDOWN

PLAUSIBILITY:
7/10. That's a lot of strange deaths to be merely a coincidence.

HIGH STRANGENESS:
2/10. Mostly just your typical gunshots, poisonings, and vehicular homicides, but if the CIA can really give you cancer, that ranks as highly strange.

CONSPIRACY CHECKLIST:
- ☐ Illuminati
- ☐ The Freemasons
- ☑ CIA/intelligence community/the military
- ☐ Aliens
- ☐ The occult
- ☑ The Mafia

FOR MORE INFORMATION:

Forgive My Grief by Penn Jones

Kilgallen by Lee Isreal

JFK: The Dead Witnesses by Craig Roberts and John Armstrong

ON THE WEB:

An incomplete list of witnesses who died mysterious deaths: www.spartacus.schoolnet.co.uk/JFKdeaths.htm

Evidence against the mysterious deaths: www.jfk-online.com/jfk100deaths.html

CONSPIRACY INVESTIGATOR SEARCH TERMS:

Dorothy Kilgallen, Officer Tippit, CIA cancer lab

08. THE LADY IN THE POLKA DOT DRESS

THE 1960S SHOULD HAVE BEEN the Kennedys' golden decade. John Kennedy was elected president in 1960, and Robert Kennedy became attorney general in 1961, U.S. senator in 1965, and ran for president in 1968. But John was assassinated in 1963. And on June 6, 1968, his younger brother Robert also fell victim to an assassin's bullet.

Robert Kennedy won the California primary and seemed to have the momentum to become the Democratic Party's nominee for president. After a celebration with supporters in the ballroom of the Ambassador Hotel in Los Angeles, RFK made his way through a food service pantry—a prearranged exit to a room where he would meet with reporters. As he did, a man named Sirhan Sirhan fired a pistol at the senator. Kennedy was fatally wounded, and five others sustained injuries. Sirhan was apprehended immediately, thanks in part to bystanders who helped disarm and subdue him. Convicted of first-degree murder due in part to a confession made for the police, Sirhan remains incarcerated at Corcoran State Prison in California.

PREARRANGED by WHO?! WERE they iN oN it?

Despite the fact that officials said this was not "another Dallas" and was an open-and-shut case, conspiracy theorists have once again cried foul. How can that be? Dozens of witnesses saw Sirhan step forward and shoot his victim from just a few feet in front of him.

But the shot that killed Kennedy came from just a few inches away and from *behind* him—into his head, just behind his ear. Further, Sirhan's .22 revolver held eight bullets, but as many as ten to twelve shots were fired. Conspiracy researchers conclude that there must have been another gunman. Sound familiar?

NOT FUNNY!! This was a total setup! Numbers don't lie!!!

HYPNOTIZED

Sirhan Bishara Sirhan was born in Jerusalem. He converted to many different religions during his life, though he had little interest in politics. At the time of the assassination, he had an article about Kennedy's support of Israel during the Six Days' War in his pocket, but he claimed not to know where it came from. After he shot Senator Kennedy, witnesses said, he was in a trancelike state. In police custody, he was largely unresponsive and soon after admitted that he must have done it but that he had no memory of the act.

Many conspiracists believe that Sirhan was hypnotized. While riding a horse in 1966, he injured his head. People who knew him said that his gentle personality changed. According to author A. Branson, this injury may have made him an ideal candidate for hypnotic suggestion. He disappeared for three months the following year, without telling his family where he had gone. Later he developed a strong interest in the occult.

Hypnosis could explain Sirhan's odd condition, but it suggests a larger, more powerful force behind him and his actions. Some tinfoil-coifed writers speculate that it was none other than the Central Intelligence Agency.

Far-fetched? Maybe. But the CIA has admitted that they experimented with mind control in a project called MKULTRA (see Chapter 24).

In various notebooks Sirhan scrawled incoherent messages, including, "RFK must die." But among these ravings, one can find references to mind control, drugs, payment, as well as secret societies and occult orders like the Rosicrucians, Theosophy, and the Illuminati. Did the Illuminati hypnotize Sirhan Sirhan to become an assassin? Does the CIA work for them? Does anyone realize this is copied right out of the 1962 movie, *The Manchurian Candidate*?

Perhaps a better—certainly a more serious—question is, did Sirhan Sirhan kill Robert Kennedy, or was he merely the misdirection in an elaborate magician's trick?

Ten or twelve shots were fired: three into Kennedy, one into each of the other five victims, and two to four into the walls and ceiling. The police removed evidence of these other bullets from the crime scene. The bullet holes in the door frame and elsewhere can be seen

MAYBE KIDNAPPED so he could be TRAINED AS AN ASSASSIN?!!!

YES!!! I'VE BEEN SAYING this All Along! WHY DOESN'T ANYBODY LISTEN TO ME???!!

BULLETS? WE DON'T NEED NO STINKIN' BULLETS

The Illuminati need to learn to count their bullets. A recent study of audio recordings made at the time of Robert Kennedy's assassination indicate clearly that more than eight shots were fired, and Sirhan Sirhan's weapon only carried that many bullets. Furthermore, the tapes strongly suggest that more than one weapon was fired. That evidence backs up most of the eyewitness testimony of those present in the pantry and nearby who heard the shots.

Although criminologist DeWayne Wolfer testified that the bullets recovered from the scene all matched Sirhan's gun, the records of the actual tests suggest something different. Even Wolfer in his notes initially suggested a different weapon with a different serial number. *BECAUSE THERE WERE THREE SHOOTERS!! MASONIC-ILLUMINATI-ALIEN!*

in the numerous photos taken at the time. Some of them were behind Sirhan. So unless Sirhan was using bullets bought from the same magic ammunition store as Lee Harvey Oswald, someone else was shooting that night.

BECAUSE THE MASONS-ILLUMINATI ALWAYS USE THREE ASSASSINS (TRINITY)!

THE OTHERS

Security guard Thane Eugene Cesar was on hand, plus he was an outspoken right-wing critic of the Kennedy family. Standing just behind Kennedy, holding a pistol, he could have easily fired the shot that killed him. Forensic evidence showed—through the amount of powder on Kennedy, the angle, and the size of the wound—that the shot came from behind and just a few inches away. Cesar claims that while he did draw his weapon, he didn't fire. However, at least one witness, a man named Don Schulman, saw him fire his pistol. Of course, Cesar could have been doing his duty, fired at Sirhan, and shot Kennedy by accident. But most conspiracists ignore this possibility. Accidents don't make for good conspiracy theories. *NO ACCIDENT!! It's All controlled!*

Now comes the infamous lady in the polka dot dress. A volunteer working for the campaign, Sandra Serrano, said that she saw Sirhan, another man, and a woman together forty-five minutes before the shooting. She remembered the woman because she was buxom, attractive, had an "odd nose," and wore a polka dot dress. Other witnesses reported seeing the assassin with a woman near a coffee machine inside the hotel. Supposedly, she was whispering in his ear. Right after the shooting, Serrano said that she saw the same woman, again accompanied by another man, exiting the building shouting, "We shot him! We shot him!"

The police immediately put out an all points bulletin for the polka-dot-dress woman. However, apparently Sherlock Holmes was working in L.A. that night, because within minutes of the shooting the police "knew" that Sirhan was working alone and canceled the APB.

When asked in his jail cell if anyone was with him, Sirhan said, "the girl," and nothing more. The idea—if we can put ourselves in the minds of a conspiracy theorist for a moment—is that a hypnotized, mind-controlled assassin needs a handler. The girl in the polka dot dress fills that role very nicely.

Who did she work for?? MJ 12????

What's more, a hypnotism expert named William J. Bryan—who was the technical consultant on *The Manchurian Candidate,* for cripes sakes—bragged to acquaintances that he had hypnotized Sirhan Sirhan prior to the assassination (although he officially denied it). Interestingly enough, Bryan induced Albert DeSalvo to confess to murder, thus helping to bring the Boston Strangler to justice four years earlier; Sirhan mentions DeSalvo in his rambling notebooks.

DeSalvo was part of a Masonic murder plot!! Just like Jack the Ripper! THERE WAS MORE THAN ONE STRANGLER!!!!!

WHY?

According to researcher Lisa Pease in the March-April 1998 issue of *Probe* magazine, the Los Angeles Police Department burned thousands of photographs of the scene, destroyed the damaged ceiling tiles and door frame, and ignored all evidence that didn't correlate with the quickly established theory that Sirhan acted alone. No analog of the Warren Commission or the House Select Committee on Assassinations investigated the RFK murder.

Bobby Kennedy had made all the same enemies as his brother: the Mafia, the intelligence community, the military-industrial complex, Castro, and the anti-Castro movement. Any one of these groups could have been responsible for his death. J. Edgar Hoover's deputy, Clyde Tolson, reportedly said of Robert Kennedy, "I hope that someone shoots and kills the son of a bitch."

Lots of conspiracy theorists, though, such as Doug Moench, point out who benefited most from Kennedy's assassination: Richard Nixon. With Kennedy's win in California, he was set to knock his opponent Eugene McCarthy out of the race and very likely would have beaten Hubert Humphrey for the Democratic nomination in 1968. Kennedy would have been a very difficult opponent for Republican nominee Nixon to overcome, as Nixon barely defeated Humphrey. Very likely, just like in 1960, a Kennedy would have beaten Nixon for the presidency. In fact, "Tricky Dick" Nixon benefited greatly from both Kennedys' deaths. You can almost imagine Nixon shaking his fist and saying, "Those darn Kennedy boys have been a thorn in my side long enough."

Robert Kennedy said, just two days before his own murder, "Only the powers of the presidency will reveal the secrets of my brother's death." Maybe in the end, RFK's murder was just another in a line of murders (see Chapter 7) covering up JFK's death.

REMEMBER NIXON WAS PART OF THE JFK ASSASSINATION too! HELPED by HUNT!!!

CONSPIRACY RUNDOWN

PLAUSIBILITY:

7/10. Like with his brother's assassination, it certainly seems as though at least something fishy is going on.

HIGH STRANGENESS:

5/10. Mind control? Not that common in movies, but still strange.

CONSPIRACY CHECKLIST:

- ☑ Illuminati
- ☐ The Freemasons
- ☑ CIA/intelligence community/the military
- ☐ Aliens
- ☐ The occult
- ☑ The Mafia

FOR MORE INFORMATION:

RFK Must Die! by Robert Blair Kaiser

The Assassination of Robert F. Kennedy by William Turner and Jonn Christian

ON THE WEB:

Sirhan Sirhan's notebooks: *en.wikisource.org/wiki/Sirhan_Sirhan's_ notebook#cite_note-6*

CONSPIRACY INVESTIGATOR SEARCH TERMS:

CIA mind control, Sirhan Sirhan, *Manchurian Candidate*, Ambassador Hotel

09. DEATH OF A DREAM

TO SAY THAT THE LATE 1960s were a tumultuous time in American history is an understatement. Our basic differences—male versus female, black versus white, old versus young—tore us apart. The country waged an unpopular war in a distant land and still reeled from the assassination of a popular president just a few years earlier. Young activists became militant, while other kids dropped out of society into a counterculture of (drugs) and sex. Their actions incited panic among the older generation. At the center of this chaos lay the issue of civil rights. From the South, wrapped in its decades-old armor of segregation and discrimination, a leader arose who advocated the power of peaceful marches and open discussion. He spoke sincerely, eloquently, and passionately, swaying public opinion and influencing millions. Reverend Martin Luther King Jr. embraced the philosophy of nonviolence. What he wanted was nothing more and nothing less than equality. In this time of upheaval, however, any black leader drew suspicion upon himself from the existing establishment, even a leader whose actions were beyond reproach. The FBI watched Reverend King closely. J. Edgar Hoover called him the most dangerous man in America.

Supplied by the CIA!!!

Who was Hoover REALLY working for??

JUST THE FACTS, MA'AM

On April 4, 1968, King was in Memphis. A few days before, a peaceful demonstration that he had organized there turned violent, and he wanted to return to the city to reconnect with his followers and stage another—nonviolent—demonstration. At 6 P.M. that evening, standing on a balcony at the Lorraine Motel, where he was staying in a second-floor room—a room scouted by an (advance security man)—King was shot. People around him immediately pointed up toward where they believed the shooter to be: a bathroom window in a boarding house. Someone ran from the boarding house, throwing a bundle containing a rifle and some personal effects into a nearby doorway, and raced away in a white Mustang that had been parked on the street.

Did someone want it to turn violent? Could be!! Maybe one of King's aides was a PLANT!!

On April 19, the FBI announced the man was James Earl Ray, a criminal and racist. Two months later he was arrested in a London airport, supposedly on his way to South Africa. Ray pleaded guilty and was sentenced to ninety-nine years in prison.

London—connections to Bilderberg Group. IT ALL FITS!!

But there's more to it than that, at least according to conspiracy theorists. King's own family believes that there was a conspiracy and that Ray was not the actual murderer. In 1997, Dexter King, with the blessing of Reverend King's widow and his other children, visited Ray in prison and told him that he did not believe that Ray was his father's killer.

Just three days after his sentence Ray recanted his confession. He claims he was set up. He was, like Lee Harvey Oswald, a patsy for a much larger conspiracy. He maintained his innocence up to his death in 1998.

THE SETUP

The violence incited in the Memphis demonstration of late March may have been artificially prompted by a group of black agitators called the Invaders. Much later, Marrell McCullough, an aide to King, was discovered to be working with the Invaders. McCullough, according to author (and James Earl Ray's appeal attorney) Mark Lane, was recruited from the military to work on behalf of the Memphis Police Department as a spy among King's people. It was McCullough who first pointed up toward the window where Ray supposedly was shooting from, prompting others to do so, even though some initially believed that the shot came from the ground.

Originally King had planned to stay at a Holiday Inn, but public outcry in the press prompted him to change his plans and stay at the Lorraine Motel, because it was owned by African Americans. This new motel was in a bad part of the city. In *A Case of Conspiracy*, Michael Newton claims that the FBI planted the editorials in the newspapers, prompting King to move to the new location.

The "advance man" was not working for King at all!! Obviously he was one of the killers!!!

Remember the advance man who scouted the hotel? He switched King's room to the second floor from the first. But MLK had sent no such person on his staff. The balcony of the second-floor room, exposed to an open area behind the motel, offered the only way in or out of the room. It was not secure at all; in fact, it was just the opposite. Moments before the assassination, authorities removed armed security people working for King from a nearby building overlooking the motel. They even got black policeman Edward Reddit away from the scene. The stage was set.

THE PROBLEM WITH RAY

James Earl Ray says he was coerced into giving his confession. He was made to believe that he would get the death penalty and that his family would also be persecuted, if not prosecuted. More interestingly, he admits that he *might* have been a part of the plot to kill Reverend King, but only inadvertently. According to Ray, a man named Raul or Rauol got him involved in a gun smuggling operation. He told Ray to buy a rifle and meet him in a room at the boarding house (the one from which Ray supposedly shot King). If this is true, the only role Ray played was as the scapegoat.

Ray was a small-time criminal much of his life. While he served in the military, he was a moderate marksman at best. Despite the official story, he claims that he was never particularly racist.

The rifle that Ray supposedly used to kill King was never conclusively proved to be the murder weapon. (Note that the Memphis Police Department was run by longtime FBI agent and J. Edgar Hoover confidante, Frank Holloman.) Former state judge Joe Brown testified that the sight on the rifle was so bad that it could not have been used to kill Reverend King from that range.

Two witnesses say that they saw a man running down the hall of the boarding house immediately after the shooting. One, Charles

Stephens, said that it was James Earl Ray. The other, his wife Grace, insisted that the man was not Ray. Even though others have testified that Charles was drunk at the time, his is the testimony people believe.

NOT A LONE GUNMAN

John McFerren traveled to Memphis on business on April 4. He claims that as he walked by an open office door he heard a man angrily shout into a telephone, "Do the job then you'll get your pay. You can shoot the son of a bitch on the balcony." The man was Frank Liberto, a produce dealer reportedly connected to the Mafia. Liberto's friend, Lavada Addison, testified later that he told her he "had Martin Luther King killed." According to Addison's son, when confronted directly Liberto claimed that while he didn't kill King, he had it done. Regarding Ray, Liberto said that he was a frontman.

Loyd Jowers owned Jim's Grill. His employee, Betty Spates, says that she saw her boss run into the grill carrying a rifle immediately after

Which means connection to Kennedy assassination too!!

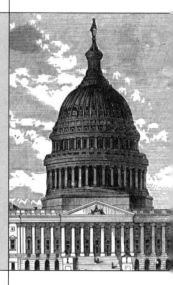

A DIFFERENT TAKE

Not all who believe in a conspiracy think King was killed by the government. Some believe he was intentionally martyred.

According to those who believe this scenario, King was a womanizer, a philanderer, and perhaps even a sexual deviant. (J. Edgar Hoover accused him of this. Hoover may have been dressed in drag even as he issued the press release.) He was a Marxist, a liar, and physically abusive. His alleged activities, if discovered, would bring down the entire civil rights movement. Thus, figures in the movement itself assassinated King. Most of this theory is likely a legacy of Hoover's attempts to discredit King after the March on Washington, as described by author Richard Gid Powers in the August 2003 issue of *American History Magazine*.

the assassination. In a taped confession, Jowers said that the planning for the assassination occurred at his grill and included undercover Memphis police officer Marrell McCollough (King's "aide" who was working secretly with the Invaders), Memphis police lieutenant Earl Clark, and a few other police officers and possibly some federal agents. Jowers said that after the assassination, Clark came into the back of Jim's Grill and handed him a smoking rifle, which he dismantled, wrapped up, and concealed. The next day, it was picked up by a man named Raul.

Suggesting an even larger operation, however, Cathel Weeden, the captain of the Memphis Fire Department at the time, claimed that two men with briefcases filled with photographic equipment came to the fire station across from the Lorraine Motel on the day of the assassination. They showed U.S. Army IDs and went up to the roof where they positioned themselves with direct line of sight to the balcony as well as Jim's Grill. These men could have been spotters for the sniper or snipers involved. They also could have been backup in case the first shot failed.

Remember how much the government feared King. Racial violence and tension were increasing every day. The FBI had been tracking King since 1957. The fact that some of his aides had been involved with the Communist Party did not help matters. By 1960, the FBI conducted surveillance of Reverend King, his family, and all of his associates twenty-four hours a day. His phones were tapped. More than one member of the King organization was a spy. This was all a part of COINTELPRO (counterintelligence program), a series of FBI operations intended to both investigate and disrupt dissident political movements inside the United States. So-called militant black nationalist groups were frequent targets. Files indicate that COINTELPRO operatives were not above breaking the law. Would they resort to assassination? Martin Luther King Jr. had made enemies of both J. Edgar Hoover and President Johnson. Was that enough to prompt an extreme sanction?

THEY WERE WEARING BLACK!!!! That's what I heard! MEN IN BlAck!!

They're watching me too!

That's why I NEVER walk or drive the same way twice! To throw them off!!!

THE CIVIL SUIT

On December 8, 1999, the family of Martin Luther King Jr. sued Loyd Jowers and "other unknown co-conspirators" for wrongful death. The jury took only three hours to find in favor of the King family. In other words, the only actual trial held regarding Reverend King's death ruled that there *was* a conspiracy. The implications of this finding—that the government may have conspired to assassinate one of its own citizens—are chilling.

Maybe the Kings have provided the world with a solution to conspiracies. Sue them. One can almost imagine suits filed against the Freemasons and the Priory of Sion. It might work less well against aliens. CAN'T SUE ALIENS! MAYBE FREEMASONS??!! BUT THEY CONTROL THE COURTS!!

One year after the civil suit, the Department of Justice conducted an investigation into Jowers and his story but found no compelling evidence to support the allegations that he had been part of a conspiracy to murder King. There have been no further official investigations.

CONSPIRACY RUNDOWN

PLAUSIBILITY:

7/10. The jury weighed the evidence and believed in a conspiracy.

HIGH STRANGENESS:

1/10. There are no occult rituals or alien death rays involved here.

CONSPIRACY CHECKLIST:

- ☐ Illuminati
- ☐ The Freemasons
- ☑ CIA/intelligence community/the military
- ☐ Aliens
- ☐ The occult
- ☑ The Mafia

FOR MORE INFORMATION:

Killing the Dream: James Earl Ray and the Assassination of Martin Luther King, Jr., by Gerald Posner.

An Act of State: The Execution of Martin Luther King by Bill Pepper

ON THE WEB:

The King Center: www.thekingcenter.org

COINTELPRO: www.cointel.org

CONSPIRACY INVESTIGATOR SEARCH TERMS:

Lorraine Motel, James Earl Ray, COINTELPRO, Mark Lane

10. ASSASSIN NATION

FOUR U.S. PRESIDENTS DIED as a result of assassinations: Lincoln, Garfield, McKinley, and Kennedy. Six others have faced attempted assassinations: Jackson, both Roosevelts, Truman, Ford, and Reagan. Add in the killing of other politicians, political candidates, and public figures like Reverend Martin Luther King Jr., Malcolm X, and John Lennon and it becomes clear—when we don't like you, we kill you.

The Kennedys and King are only the highest-profile (and the most conspiracy-laden) cases.

LINKS

Could there be links between the deaths of the two Kennedys and Reverend King? Conspiracy theorists think so. In all three cases, a lone gunman was blamed, but in all three other gunman are suspected, and the official assassin might be nothing more than a distraction or misdirection. All three were hated by J. Edgar Hoover. All three were hated and feared by the military-industrial complex for their opposition to the Vietnam War.

In all three cases, evidence appears to have been suppressed, witnesses disregarded (or even coerced to keep quiet), and the investigation botched. In none of the assassinations were the official murder weapons conclusively shown by ballistics or forensics tests to be the weapon used. In all three cases, some researchers believe that the Mafia was involved, working for the government the way they worked for it against Fidel Castro.

A police sketch of a suspect in the King assassination resembles one of the so-called three tramps from a photo taken just after the JFK assassination. Some have speculated that the government may have put together a domestic assassination team, perhaps made up of Mafia contract killers, CIA trained assassins, or a combination of both.

And then of course there's Richard Nixon, who profited from the deaths of both JFK and RFK. Both were political opponents, embar-

KENNEDYS ARE kings. And then KING! MORE MASONIC-Illuminati connections!!

HAH!!!!!!!!

IMPORTANT!!

rassed him (or threatened to do so), opposed his ideology, and opposed those whom Nixon considered allies.

Nixon was elected After George Wallace was SHOT in 1972. NOT A COINCIDENCE!!!!!!

OTHER ASSASSINS

On February 21, 1965, speaking about peace at a meeting in New York, black activist Malcolm X was killed by at least five different gunmen. Two of them were apprehended, but mysteriously only one, Thomas Hagen, was ever mentioned in official reports. Although initially claiming that it was a rival faction of the Black Muslims that he worked for, Hagen eventually admitted that he was paid by someone else. Despite this, Hagen and two members of the Nation of Islam, Thomas Johnson and Norman Butler, were convicted of the crime. Many, however, believe that like John F. Kennedy and Martin Luther King Jr., the assassination might have been a joint operation between the CIA and the Mafia, both worried that Malcolm X was encouraging young black men to stand up for themselves and turn from drugs and crime.

Lynette "Squeaky" Fromme, a disciple of the infamous Charles Manson, attempted to assassinate Gerald Ford on September 5, 1975. Just over two weeks later, Sara Jane Moore also tried to kill Ford. *And Ford was a member of the WARREN COMMISSION!!!!!! HE KNEW too much!!*

John Lennon was murdered by Mark David Chapman on December 8, 1980. Lennon, an outspoken opponent of the U.S. government's involvement in Vietnam (and, in particular, of Richard Nixon), spent years under FBI surveillance. Like Sirhan Sirhan, Chapman appeared to be in a trance after the murder. He had with him a copy of J. D. Salinger's *Catcher in the Rye*. Conspiracists believe this book is code for "sleeper agent." They claim the book is used as a hypnotic trigger (see Chapter 24).

On March 30, 1981, John Hinckley Jr. shot and wounded Ronald Reagan. What's weirder: that he claimed he did it to impress actress Jodie Foster or the fact that the Hinckleys were friends with (and major financial contributors to) the family of Reagan's vice president,

TO KILL A CASTRO

All over the world, assassinations have changed regimes and political or social movements. The conspiracy crowd believes the CIA is behind a lot of those. For example, the CIA tried to kill Castro with an exploding cigar. (That certainly makes the CIA seem less sinister, don't you think?) Operation Mongoose (see Chapter 6) was the U.S.-sponsored project to oust Castro from Cuba. Mostly it involved training anti-Castro Cuban exiles so that they could stage a counterrevolution, but it also involved imaginative assassination plots. Not only lethally exploding cigars but poisoned cigars, botulism pills, a machine gun hidden in a movie camera, a pen with a poison needle, exploding seashells on the beach, and all manner of gifts and foods treated with LSD, bacteria, or poison. Filmmaker Dollan Cannel suggests that there may have been as many as 638 different plots to kill the dictator.

George Bush? This gunman also had a copy of *Catcher in the Rye* in his hotel room.

LONE NUTS, EVERY ONE

In every single case, the assassin was a lone nut. According to official stories, even the assassins of the assassins, like Jack Ruby, acted entirely alone. That's convenient, because if even one person helped an assassin, it would be, by definition, a conspiracy. And there are no conspiracies. Only nuts believe in conspiracy theories.

I'm NOT A NUT!!!! This is REAL!!!!!!!

CONSPIRACY RUNDOWN

PLAUSIBILITY:
7/10. The connections are all there, waiting for people to see them.

HIGH STRANGENESS:
2/10. It's not strange. It's just a bit frightening.

CONSPIRACY CHECKLIST:
- ☐ Illuminati
- ☐ The Freemasons
- ☑ CIA/intelligence community/the military
- ☐ Aliens
- ☐ The occult
- ☑ The Mafia

FOR MORE INFORMATION:

On Being Mad or Merely Angry: John W. Hinckley Jr. and Other Dangerous People by James W. Clarke

Let Me Take You Down: Inside the Mind of Mark David Chapman, the Man Who Killed John Lennon by Jack Jones

The Assassinations: Probe Magazine on JFK, MLK, RFK and Malcolm X edited by James DiEugenio

ON THE WEB:

John Lennon FBI files: www.lennonfbifiles.com
More Lennon FBI files: http://foia.fbi.gov/foiaindex/lennon.htm
Crime Library: www.crimelibrary.com

CONSPIRACY INVESTIGATOR SEARCH TERMS:

MKULTRA, Charles Manson, Arthur Bremer, lone nuts, Mark David Chapman, John Hinkley

11. DEAD CELEBRITIES

IN OUR WORLD OF constant information, with twenty-four-hour news scrambling to fill air time with content, our fascination with celebrities has become an obsession. We can find out what our favorite TV star or sports hero had for dinner last night. So surely there can be no celebrity-related conspiracy theories. How can a celebrity have a secret?

Well, such theories are as thick on the ground as magic bullets. Both Marilyn Monroe and Princess Diana may have more in common than an Elton John song.

MARILYN

Norma Jeane Mortenson was born in 1926. She became an actress, a singer, a model, and a film producer, and along the way took the name Marilyn Monroe. Thanks to the magic of photography and Andy Warhol, she's one of the most recognizable public figures in the world.

On August 5, 1962, when she was only thirty-six years old, Monroe died in her home, apparently of a barbiturate overdose. The circumstances surrounding her death have become the fodder for conspiracist debates ever since. Conspiracy theorists suggest Marilyn may have died because of whom she knew.

It's common knowledge that Monroe had a sexual affair with John F. Kennedy. That may have been a dangerous path for her to take. According to writer Donald Wolfe, "Marilyn Monroe was in a position to bring down the presidency. She was cognizant of Jack Kennedy's marital infidelities and other private matters. She had his notes and letters and was privy to Kennedy's involvement with [mob boss] Sam Giancana. That the Kennedy brothers had discussed national security matters with the film star added to an astonishing array of indiscretions." Wolfe contends that both President Kennedy and his brother were complicit in her murder. According to writer Annette Witheridge, Joe DiMaggio, baseball legend and Monroe's ex-husband, also believed the Kennedys were involved in Monroe's death.

She also knew about Roswell and Area 51!

Writers like Anthony Summers, among many others, argue that at first Robert served only as a go-between for his brother and Monroe. For example, he went to Monroe to ask her to stop calling the White House for appearance's sake. Later, he became her confidante, and—after her affair with John was over—her lover. Phone records show they spoke often, particularly right before her death. Witnesses say that Bobby Kennedy and brother-in-law Peter Lawford visited her house on her final night.

Monroe's relationship with the Kennedys, if true, provides two different motives for her death. Either she knew sensitive information, or her relationship with them could have been an embarrassment. Proponents of the first idea suggest that she knew about Kennedy's plans for Fidel Castro and Cuba.

Other conspiracists suggest that one or both Kennedys arranged for her to die so that she could not hurt their political careers. This puts them in the role of conspirat*ors* rather than . . . conspirit*ees* (something like that—the victims of conspiracy). In fact, the Mafia may have attempted to bug Monroe's home in order to gain information about her affairs with the two brothers just before she died.

Which brings us to yet a third, entirely different scenario: the Mafia, angered at President Kennedy's failure to oust Castro from Cuba (where they had vested monetary interests) or Attorney General Kennedy's continued efforts to bring them to justice, murdered Marilyn Monroe as a way to strike at one or both of them. Journalist Hank Messick claims the Mafia wanted to use Monroe's death to frame Bobby for murder.

No matter which version you believe, in these scenarios Monroe was being used by someone. However, some suggest that Marilyn was not entirely passive. She may have been a powerful force in creating, or at least perpetuating, the ditzy blonde beauty stereotype, but in reality Monroe rose well above the persona she created for herself. She reportedly discussed issues with Kennedy like nuclear test bans and other political topics. She had an agenda. And, some suggest, maybe that was the problem.

What about if she knew the Kennedys were working for the Bilderberg Group and was blackmailing them? THAT'S WHY SHE WAS KILLED!!

The FBI had its own concerns about Monroe. Apparently she met with Communist acquaintances from time to time. Not the kind of person that a Cold Warrior wants to see with unfettered secret access to the president.

Officially, Monroe's death was ruled either a suicide or an accidental overdose. However, she was known to have "attempted suicide" before, not to kill herself but to attract attention. Would it not be the perfect murder to turn these stunts into reality?

Could it also have been RITUAL SACRIFICE???!!

DIANA

The case of Diana Spencer, Princess of Wales, is even more complicated. Diana married Prince Charles in 1981 at the age of twenty. The marriage began to fall apart soon afterward. (Diana and Charles had only been alone together thirteen times before their marriage.) Diana, while extremely popular with the public, never seemed to fit in with the royal family and reportedly was never liked by the Queen. In 1992 Charles and Diana separated.

On August 31, 1997, Diana's car crashed in the Pont de l'Alma tunnel in Paris. With her were Dodi Fayed, son of billionaire Mohamed Al-Fayed, driver Henri Paul, and Fayed's bodyguard, Trevor Rees-Jones. Diana, Fayed, and Paul died in the collision. Diana was thirty-six. Conspiracy theorists and Diana fans alike were suspicious. Conspiracists quickly found evidence that the crash might not have been an accident but a murder. The likely conspirators? None other than the Queen of England and her son, Prince Charles. Aghast at the idea of a divorce in the royal family, the Queen supposedly found murder preferable. Charles wanted to rid himself of Diana and get revenge on her as well.

This makes sense! The QUEEN is a SECRET agent for ALIENS—she didn't want to be EXPOSED!!!!

. .   .

Mohamed Al-Fayed contends that British Intelligence (MI6) murdered Diana and his son at the behest of Prince Philip, husband of the Queen. Al-Fayed's theory also involves French intelligence, police, and medical personnel; various British newspapers; Prince Charles; and Prime Minister Tony Blair. A six-month official inquiry concluded that his theory was "without any substance."

Mohamed says that the couple planned to announce their engagement, and in fact Dodi had purchased a ring. Mohamed further speculates that perhaps Diana was pregnant with their child. The motive, then, he claims, was the royal family's racism. They didn't want Diana marrying or having a child with a nonwhite man.

No!! It's about ALIENS!!!! Unless . . . is Dodi one of THEM????!!!!

The absence of records from at least ten closed-circuit television cameras that should have shown the car and the crash seems suspicious. No seat belt protected Diana, despite the fact that she always wore one. CNN analysis, in fact, showed that the injuries of all involved would have been minor if the occupants had worn seat belts. Some witnesses report a bright flash of light in the tunnel just before the crash, not unlike the strobe lights used by MI6 as a part of their standard training to blind helicopter pilots and make them crash. And lastly, the crashed vehicle showed signs of contact with another car, probably a Fiat Uno. (Some believe that a man named James Andanson owned the white Uno. Andanson had had previous contact with Diana in the role of a photographer. Andanson was found dead in May 2000, a possible suicide, although some of those at the scene where his body was found say it looked like murder.) *Another murder by the Royals!!*

In 1993 Diana wrote a letter—later published in the London *Daily Telegraph*—to Paul Burrell, her butler, claiming that Charles was going to kill her and make it look like a car accident. She also claimed that Charles was having an affair with their children's nanny, Alexandra "Tiggy" Legge-Bourke. So perhaps this murder was long in the planning.

David Icke, who thought that the Freemasons worked for reptilian shape changers from another dimension, believes that chief among those scaly, black-magic-using changelings is none other than the royal family of England. Diana may have known their occult, alien secrets and threatened to reveal them to the world! *That's RIGHT!!!!!*

Then (to get even weirder) there's the matter of the princess's name. The ancient goddess Diana, a moon goddess, retains a great deal of occult "cred" even today among various mystical societies and individuals. According to those farthest out on the fringe, the ancient Merovingians, bearers of the royal bloodline protected by the secret society known as the Priory of Sion (see Chapter 3), worshipped Diana at a sacred site. Yeah, you might have guessed it—the Pont de l'Alma. Even the name means "bridge of the soul," they contend.

Wow!!!

AMAZING!!!

According to these same folks, Diana continues to be worshipped in places such as Bohemian Grove, a meeting place for the secret elite of the world (see Chapter 18). In other words, the Illuminati. This vast conspiracy of wealth, power, and black magic (and perhaps reptilian shapeshifters) sacrificed Princess Diana, part of the royal Merovingian line and representative of her namesake goddess, as part of a bloody occult ritual honoring the *real* Diana to further cement their own mystical grip over the world.

AND LEAVE A BEAUTIFUL CORPSE

Both Marilyn and Diana died tragically and young. Their deaths seem like such tragedies that we look for the lurking evil forces that are responsible. Random happenstance could never be so unjust. However, in addition to our indignation at their loss, we must also admit that the death of a beauty is inherently fascinating. On the other hand, take Dorothy Kilgallen (see Chapter 7), who, like Marilyn Monroe, died of a barbiturate overdose under suspicious circumstances, perhaps far more suspicious than Monroe's. Kilgallen was not a sexy starlet but a journalist. How much of our fascination with the death of Monroe and Diana comes from our culture's schoolboy crush on them both?

CONSPIRACY RUNDOWN

PLAUSIBILITY:
4/10. As tragic as it may be, sometimes people just die.

HIGH STRANGENESS:
7/10. Shape-changing reptilian queens and sacrifices to the moon goddess are pretty freaky.

CONSPIRACY CHECKLIST:
- ☑ Illuminati
- ☐ The Freemasons
- ☑ CIA/intelligence community/the military
- ☑ Aliens
- ☑ The occult
- ☐ The Mafia

FOR MORE INFORMATION:

The *Assassination of Marilyn Monroe* by Donald H. Wolfe

The Murder of Princess Diana by Noel Botham

ON THE WEB:

Marilyn Monroe's website: www.marilynmonroe.com

Marilyn Monroe FBI files: http://foia.fbi.gov/foiaindex/monroe.htm

The Death of Princess Diana: www.cnn.com/SPECIALS/1998/08/diana

Diana cover-up: www.coverups.com/diana

CONSPIRACY INVESTIGATOR SEARCH TERMS:

Donald Wolfe, Peter Lawford, Princess Diana letter, Dodi Fayed, Merovingian bloodline, David Icke

12. DEAD? CELEBRITIES

IF WE ARE INTRIGUED by celebrities and important people who pass away prematurely, or under suspicious circumstances, are we not even more entranced by the idea of a dead celebrity who isn't really dead? What if rather than a conspiracy to kill someone, we discovered a conspiracy to let them live? Conspiracy theories about faking one's death start with Christ himself (see Chapter 3), but they don't stop there.

THE KING IS DEAD, LONG LIVE THE KING

It's KING AgAin!!!!

Elvis Presley, the King of Rock and Roll, recorded seventy-two albums, released 102 singles, and starred in thirty-one movies. Elvis was one of the most popular entertainers of the twentieth century and influenced a generation of younger musicians.

He died on August 16, 1977, in Memphis, Tennessee. The officially stated cause of death was heart disease, but testimony of friends, relatives, and associates confirms that Elvis used a great number of drugs and could have had as many as ten different medications in his system at the time of his death. Witnesses disagree about how the body was found, when death was declared, and what techniques were used to resuscitate him.

But suppose that Elvis Presley didn't die but instead faked his own death? The *National Enquirer* paid Elvis's cousin Bobby Mann $18,000 for a photo of Elvis in his casket, and according to many fans the corpse does not look like Elvis. A writer named Bill Beeny claims to have obtained both the official autopsy report and DNA evidence. Both show that the man who died was not Elvis Presley. Handwriting experts say that Elvis's own handwriting appears on his death certificate. Apparently, most of these original records and official photos taken during the investigation of his death have disappeared.

Of course, to give a bit of context, Bill Beeny wrote all of this while he owned and operated the Elvis Is Alive Museum in Mississippi, where you can get grilled sandwiches and hot dogs while you peruse missing "FBI Documents" and the results of the "DNA test."

One strange bit of evidence fans use to prove that Elvis did not die is that his father misspelled his middle name on his gravestone: "Aaron" rather than "Aron." An indication that his father knew it wasn't really Elvis buried there? Maybe. As well, books, photographs, and other possessions dear to Elvis disappeared right after or right before his death.

OR MAYBE A SECRET MESSAGE!! AARON WAS high PRIEST. Of the Illuminati???!!!

And then there's Elvis's behavior before his death. He didn't order costumes for his upcoming tour. He allegedly changed his will. He fired employees. One could speculate that he prepared for his new "life" and made changes so that his estate would be prepared to go on without him.

On the day after the death of Elvis Presley, a man named John Burrows purchased a ticket from Memphis to Buenos Aires. "John Burrows" was a name used by Elvis when traveling in order to keep a low profile. Witnesses later claimed that the man who bought and used the ticket looked very much like Elvis Presley.

Where did he go? What did he do? One outlandish claim suggests he entered the Witness Protection Program with the help of his "friend," President Nixon. While Elvis did meet Nixon once in the Oval Office, what they spoke about is speculation. In photos of the meeting, Elvis wears a badge from the Drug Enforcement Administration. Was Elvis an undercover agent whose identity had been compromised? Elvis apparently had dealings with a mob-linked real estate company in California, and he may even have helped authorities expose illegal activities. Would the mob put out a contract on the King?

Nixon told Elvis about the ASSASSINATION plots he ORGANIZED!! And Elvis had to get AWAY before HE WAS MURDERED!!!!!!

Elvis sightings throughout the 1980s were common and continue even today. Photos appear in tabloids from time to time. A woman claiming to be his half-sister came forward in 2008 to say that her mother had an affair with Elvis's father, Vernon. She also says that Elvis is alive and living under the name Jessie Presley. But she also says that she's the heir to the Presley family fortune, which makes no sense if Elvis—or Jessie, or whatever his name is—still lives.

Wrong!!

He's living in hiding from Mason-Illuminati-CIA killers!!

A few purport to have seen Elvis in UFOs, accompanied by aliens. Perhaps he was an alien all along, and his people finally came to bring him back. Elvis phoned home.

Most of the time, though, the implications of Elvis's flight carry no sinister connotations. He simply wanted to get away from the spotlight. Compared to most of the conspiracies in this book, Elvis's faked death seems rather innocuous. At worst, it's simply the fans of a beloved performer wanting him to still be alive.

MR. MOJO RISIN' . . . FROM THE DEAD

Elvis may have been the King of Rock and Roll, but James Douglas Morrison was the Lizard King. Frontman for the rock group the Doors in the 1960s, Morrison won an almost religious following of fans. A poet, a singer, and an extraordinary stage performer, Morrison helped define what it meant to be a rock star: brooding, mysterious, sexy, and cool.

Just like Masons!! And Hitler!?!!

In his life, Morrison held a strong interest in the occult. His alternative monikers such as Lizard King and Mr. Mojo Risin were "occult code names" according to author Doug Moench. In particular, voodoo fascinated him, and he believed that the spirit of an American Indian inhabited his body. He spent time with professed witches and occultists. Morrison embraced the ideal of expanding one's consciousness through drugs, mysticism, and music. His band's name, the Doors, comes from Aldous Huxley's book *The Doors of Perception*, which refers to unlocking doors (through drugs) and passing through to a higher state.

When Morrison died in his Paris apartment in 1971 of heart failure—although authorities performed no autopsy—rumors began to circulate that his death had something to do with his occult connection, such as a curse from a spurned lover. Other more mundane tales suggested that it was a drug overdose. Perhaps more interesting than either, however, is the conspiratorial theory that he faked his own death. At the time of his death, Morrison was wanted by the police in the United

OR SOMETHING ELSE!!!!!! Someone tried to curse me once!

States for public drunkenness, obscenity, and indecency. More than twenty paternity suits named him as the father of little "lizard princes" around the world. He'd grown fat and belligerent, a mockery of his former self—not unlike Elvis would before his death a few years later. And like Elvis, Morrison told people he had grown weary of public life. He even joked to his friends about sloughing off the burdens of celebrity by faking his death and disappearing into some out-of-the-way locale.

Morrison lived in Paris with his common-law wife, Pamela Courson. Writer Thomas Lyttle claims that Courson and the doctor

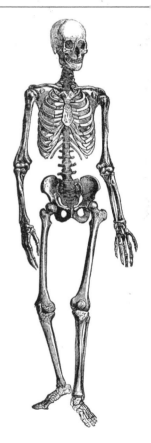

PAUL IS DEAD

If Elvis and Jim Morrison aren't really dead, where does that put former Beatle Paul McCartney? According to conspiracists, he really is dead, but "They" want you to think that he's not.

On November 9, 1966, Paul McCartney died in a car crash. Not wanting to lose out on the millions the biggest music group in history could still make, the Beatles' management and record company found a double from a recent McCartney lookalike contest. His name was either William Shears or William Sheppard. Presumably he was not just a lookalike but a soundalike. The Beatles themselves were horrified at the cover-up and left clues in their songs and album covers. For example, on the Abbey Road album cover, Paul is shown in a suit with bare feet, his eyes closed, like a corpse. He's out of step with the rest of the Beatles. The license plate on the car on the cover contains a phone number in England you could call to find out the "truth." "A Day in the Life," from the Sgt. Pepper album, contains the lyric, "He blew his mind out in a car, he didn't notice that the lights had changed," describing the accident. There are literally hundreds of other similarly intriguing photographic and lyrical clues.

Paul's death broke up the Beatles and, understandably, ended his relationship with fiancé Jane Asher. Of course, there was his subsequent marriage to Linda Eastman and their formation of the band Wings.

Inside the album, Paul is the ONLY ONE facing away from the camera!!!

And where's the Yoko Ono conspiracy? She must have been a CIA AGENT or something.

who signed the death certificate were the only people to see the body. According to other sources, there may have been a medical personnel and police involved. But in any case, the body was quickly sealed up in a locked coffin, and no one was allowed to view it. Information about his death wasn't even widely circulated until days after his burial.

Sightings of Jim Morrison around Paris occurred frequently in the two years following his death, but other evidence seems to suggest that Morrison, still alive, returned to the United States. Walt Fleischer, a Bank of America employee in San Francisco, claimed to have done business with a James Morrison who looked like the famous singer. A legend related by authors James Riordan and Jerry Prochnicky contended that he showed up at an obscure radio station in the Midwest in the middle of the night and gave a live interview where he explained the entire ploy and then mysteriously disappeared. No recordings of that interview exist.

Further, Morrison supposedly wrote *The Bank of America of Louisiana* in 1975, four years after his death. This book, published by a company that Morrison reportedly owned while alive, is the story of a dead rock star returning to life as a banker from Louisiana.

Jim Morrison's father was an admiral in the United States Navy and may have worked with the Office of Naval Intelligence. Lyttle contends that there is a James Douglas Morrison working with various intelligence agencies, both foreign and domestic. He also claims to have a courtroom transcript focused on the FBI's and CIA's cover-up of Jim Morrison's death. Other writers contend that because of Admiral Morrison's activities, Jim was assassinated by foreign intelligence services.

Some evidence—or at least wild speculation and dubious testimony—ties up all of the various theories into one. In this scenario, an intelligence agent uses voodoo-related occult rituals to steal Morrison's "mojo" (his *ti bon ange*; to use a more common term, his life force), killing him and disfiguring the body so badly that it had to be sealed in a coffin immediately. This man, now operating as "James Douglas Morrison," is able to use Morrison's bank accounts, his underground connections, and his vast reserves of spiritual energy to excel in his secret profession. Multiple "Morrisons" are created by the CIA and used as sleeper agents across the globe. *MORE CLONES!!!! CREATED by the Illuminati. Lots of them stored*

If only the real world were so interesting. (And is there really *in AREA 51!!!* enough "mojo" for all them?) Much of this comes directly from Mr. James Douglas Morrison of Louisiana, who at the very least has a wild imagination and a powerful fixation on dead rock stars.

Still, Ray Manzarek, keyboardist for the Doors, said, "If there was one guy that would have been capable of staging his death—getting a phony death certificate and paying off some doctor . . . and putting a hundred-and-fifty-pound sack of sand into a coffin and splitting to some point on this planet—Africa, who knows where—it is Jim Morrison who would have been able to pull it off." In 2008, he told the *Daily Mail*, "Jim was a restless soul, always looking for something else in his life, and even six years of success—and excess—with the Doors hadn't been enough. A year earlier, he had shown me a brochure for the Seychelles and said, 'Wouldn't this be the perfect place to escape to if everyone believed you were dead?' At the time, I never thought anything of it."

TWO KINGS

Some people, it would seem, cannot die. They are too big for that in our minds. They transcend such mortal concerns. For figures like John F. Kennedy or Martin Luther King Jr. we develop conspiracy theories because we need to find reason in their deaths. For men like Elvis Presley and Jim Morrison, we dream of them not being dead at all. They are too smart, too cool, or simply *too famous* to die. *The author's trying to COVER UP something here!! WATCH OUT!!!*

Faking one's own death appeals to us because it's a way to start a new life. Renewal gives us hope where otherwise there is only loss. And if our heroes go into hiding, remaining incognito, they might be living just down the street.

CONSPIRACY RUNDOWN

PLAUSIBILITY:

1/10. Oh come on. Elvis? Even most of the kooks laugh at that one.

HIGH STRANGENESS:

9/10. Elvis in spaceships and multiple Morrisons created through voodoo by the CIA. Definitely counts as high strangeness.

CONSPIRACY CHECKLIST:

- ☐ Illuminati
- ☐ The Freemasons
- ☑ CIA/intelligence community/the military
- ☑ Aliens
- ☑ The occult
- ☑ The Mafia

FOR MORE INFORMATION:

Elvis: The Biography by Jerry Hopkins

Break on Through by James Riordan and Jerry Prochnicky

Secret and Suppressed: Banned Ideas and Hidden History, edited by Jim Keith

ON THE WEB:

Official Elvis website: www.elvis.com

Elvis's will: www.ibiblio.org/elvis/elvwill.html

Official Doors website: www.thedoors.com

Paul Is Dead Hoax: www.paulisdeadhoax.com

CONSPIRACY INVESTIGATOR SEARCH TERMS:

Elvis lives, Elvis Is Alive Museum, Bubba Hotep, Lizard King, Kingtinued, Church of Elvis, ti bon ange, Morrison voodoo

13. TO THE MOON

IT'S MAY 25, 1961. A small group of coworkers sit around a table in the break room at NASA. Each wears dark rimmed glasses and a short-sleeved, white-collared shirt. Most have pens and pencils filling their shirt pockets. Numerous coffee cups surround an ashtray full of butts on the table. The radio plays in the background with the news of a speech the president just gave before Congress.

In a break from the laughter and talk of the engineers around the table, the radio plays a clip from Kennedy's speech from earlier that day.

But was it REALLY KENNEDY?!

"I believe that this nation should commit itself to achieving the goal, before this decade is out, of landing a man on the moon and returning him safely to the earth."

The room goes silent.

"What did he just say?" one man blurts out.

"The Moon?" another whispers.

"By the end of the decade? This decade?" The man's mouth hangs open.

"We just put Shepard into space. Isn't that good enough?" He slaps his hand to his forehead.

"And we just barely pulled that off. We don't know how to get to the Moon."

"What on Earth are we going to do now?"

What indeed. The tale of how NASA engineers, scientists, and astronauts reached the Moon is well known. It culminates with Neil Armstrong's famous words, "One small step for man, one giant leap for mankind."

Or there was something up there they didn't want us to know about!!!!!!!!

But what if it never happened? They just couldn't pull it off in the time allotted. They had to do something.

So they faked it.

They put it all together in a television studio and sold the American public—the entire world—a tremendous lie. It may be the biggest lie ever told.

EVIDENCE FOR A FAKE

You know the guy. He sits in front of the television and tells you how it really is. He's more than just a skeptic—he doesn't believe *anything* he's shown. He's convinced that every scientist since Newton is full of it because he's given it all some thought (over a few beers) and "it just don't add up."

If this armchair physicist and thousands like him don't understand something, it's not truth. And they don't believe in the moon landing.

Such conspiracists point out that blueprints and design drawings of the machines used in the moon landing are missing. This is evidence, they say, that the blueprints don't exist other than as stage props. The telemetry and high-quality video of the first moonwalk also seem to be missing. Because they would show it all to be a fake. The video footage we have is blurry and shaky, all the better to cover up the fakery.

On the other hand, the lunar conspiracy buffs say, the still photos are *too* good. The conditions on the moon and the restrictions of the space suits would make it impossible to take such great photos. Radiation from solar flares would distort the pictures and ruin the film. This same radiation should have killed the astronauts or at least given them cancer later on, since the walls of the lunar lander were only the thickness of aluminum foil.

Conspiracists rest a lot of their case on the various photographs brought back from the moon. Misplaced shadows, the absence of stars in the sky, the difference in the moon dust footprints of the astronauts and the lander, and other incongruities present a vast array of problems.

THAT'S TRUE!!

To survive on the Moon, the Nazis had to use alien technology!!

AND . . . ACTION!

So if it was a fake, how was it pulled off? Nearly the whole world watched it live on television. How do you fool 600 million viewers? First of all, you need some remote place to film in order to make it look like the moon. For instance, a television studio in a hidden location filled with cardboard moon mountains and papier-mâché terrain. Or you could film in the American Southwest, in New Mexico or Arizona, outside at night. Or how about in an underground cave in Nevada? Or maybe you could even use a Borehamwood soundstage in England, with director Stanley Kubrick, at the same location where he made 1968's *2001: A Space Odyssey*. Although it would appear that this last bit of speculation started as a joke, Kubrick's secret involvement is now bandied about seriously by those who believe the moon landings were faked. Other conspiracy theorists who are dedicated Kubrick fans point out that the director was far too precise and careful to allow so many mistakes into one of his films, so he couldn't have possibly been involved.

Next, you need some special effects wizardry. Again, we look to Kubrick—not because he had to be involved, but because he showed it was possible to create a film at that time that actually looked like men were in space and on the moon. Many of the same techniques used in *2001* were used in the fake moon landing. To make it all the more plausible, NASA shot a real Saturn rocket into space (with no one on board). When they were done filming the moon landing, NASA shipped the astronauts out to the Pacific for their "splashdown."

Lastly, you need a vast conspiracy of silence. As with all huge conspiracies, this may be the prickliest thorn of all. How to keep all those on the inside—the astronauts, the technicians, the engineers, the special effects people, and so on—from blabbing the horrible secret? According to author Bill Kaysing, you can do that with big payoffs, including corporate directorships in the private sector for many of the "stars" (the astronauts). Some people just can't be bought off, however, and need to be silenced in other ways. Astronaut Gus Grissom, for example, who died in an "accident" on the launch pad in 1967, may have been murdered because he was threatening to blow the whistle. NASA also wanted to send a message to anyone else who might get a similar idea. The government may have even used mind-control techniques à la *The Manchurian Candidate*.

Or film in AREA 51!!!

Or maybe the TRINITY SITE OF THE ATOMIC TEST!!!

Kubrick's DEAD now!!!

Another one!!!!!! Who's next???!

He WAS murdered!!!

A FUNNY THING HAPPENED ON THE WAY TO THE MOON

Perhaps the biggest question about a faked moon landing is, why do it at all? The most obvious answer is that NASA just couldn't pull off the real thing. They tried, but there was too little time and too few resources. When it became clear that Kennedy's deadline was looming and the program still couldn't get a man to the moon, they whipped up a fake so they wouldn't look like idiots to the American public and to the Soviets. It's possible that some of the later Apollo missions were legitimate, but most of the luna-tics who advance these theories don't believe that.

The most extreme believe that virtually the whole of NASA operated like an empty storefront for various U.S. intelligence agencies, which used the nearly $30 billion in its budget for black operations around the world. The fake moon landing provided a way to fool the citizenry into believing that all those tax dollars went to something worthwhile.

No!! It's because of the NAZI MOON BASE!!!! Built by Nazis who came to the U.S. after the WAR!

Or perhaps it's not because they can't get to the moon, but that they're afraid. Perhaps they learned of something on the moon, like ancient ruins or an alien base and they don't want to go there. *They've been WARNED OFF!!!* Researcher Richard C. Hoagland would like to know why, if we did go to the moon, we haven't been back? He speculates that NASA found something quite dangerous and knows that to go back would be to risk disaster or at least to let the public in on a dark secret.

Ken Johnston, the former manager of the Data and Photo Control Department at NASA's Lunar Receiving Laboratory during the Apollo missions, agrees. Johnston, in his book, *Dark Mission: The Secret History of NASA*, contends that America's recently renewed interest in moon exploration comes from the fact that other nations, like China and Russia, plan moon missions and the United States wants to get there before they do.

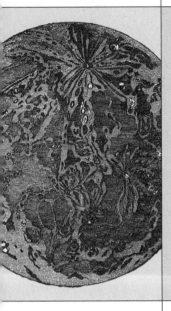

ALTERNATIVE 3

Although some conspiracy nuts claim that we never went to the moon, others disagree. Except these guys say that not only did we go, we never stopped going. A television program called *Alternative 3*, which aired in the UK in 1977, claims that the sudden disappearance of top scientists in the seventies, as well as the disappearance of thousands of other people, can be explained by the fact that a joint U.S./USSR space program has been kidnapping these people and forcing them to build a massive moon colony, with the ultimate goal of traveling to and colonizing Mars. The wealthy and elite of the world will populate these colonies while the rest of the world collapses into inevitable ecological disaster.

That's what the Nazis are doing on the Moon!!!

Even though the people behind *Alternative 3* admit it was a fictional "mockumentary," some conspiracy theorists, like Jim Keith, believe there is truth behind the story.

NASA'S RESPONSE

Sure! They covered up!!

AGAIN!!!!

NASA usually avoids even mentioning arguments of the naysayers. However, in 2001 when Fox aired a special suggesting the Apollo missions were faked, NASA and other top science writers went over every allegation and <u>refuted them in detail</u>. Even the television show *Mythbusters* in 2008 debunked the myths that suggest a faked moon landing. Not that this made any difference in the minds of the conspiracy theorists. The websites, the books, and the low-budget documentary films are still out there.

CONSPIRACY RUNDOWN

PLAUSIBILITY:
1/10. We should probably err on the side of the people who actually know what they're talking about.

HIGH STRANGENESS:
3/10. Aliens beat us to the moon!

CONSPIRACY CHECKLIST:
- ☐ Illuminati
- ☐ The Freemasons
- ☑ CIA/intelligence community/the military
- ☑ Aliens
- ☐ The occult
- ☐ The Mafia

FOR MORE INFORMATION:
We Never Went to the Moon: America's Thirty Billion Dollar Swindle by Bill Kaysing

ON THE WEB:
Questions and photo analysis: www.ufos-aliens.co.uk/cosmicapollo.html

Moon landing hoax documentary: www.moonmovie.com/index.htm

Science rebuttal: www.badastronomy.com/bad/tv/foxapollo.html

Kennedy's "Go to the moon" speech: http://history.nasa.gov/moondec.html

NASA's Apollo program: http://history.nasa.gov/apollo.html

CONSPIRACY INVESTIGATOR SEARCH TERMS:
Capricorn One, astro-nots, Apollogate, Moon landing hoax, Masonic NASA

14. THEY'RE HERE

ROSWELL. TODAY EVEN THE NAME conjures up images of conspiracists dressed in silver jumpsuits and tourist-trap diners decorated with flying saucers. But back in July 1947, the people living in Roswell, New Mexico, lived ordinary lives without much thought of little green men. That is, until the United States government told the world that an alien spacecraft had landed there.

Only a few weeks earlier, Kenneth Arnold's sightings of some UFOs coined the term, "flying saucer" (see Chapter 5). On July 8, the Roswell Army Air Field issued a press release stating that they had recovered a crashed flying disc. Later in that some day, the Air Force corrected its announcement, saying that it had recovered a weather balloon, not a flying saucer. And thus began sixty years (and counting) of argument. The UFO community insists that there really was a UFO and secret government forces are doing all they can to cover it up. Among ufologists, the term "weather balloon" means "it's really a spaceship, but we don't want you to know that."

They ALWAYS say it's a "weather balloon"!!

SAUCER DOWN!

Sometime between a week and three weeks before the government's gaffe, William Brazel found some debris while working on the Foster Ranch thirty miles from Roswell. Brazel finally reported his strange finding to authorities, and the military soon arrived to investigate. Major Jesse Marcel arrived with another man who may have been Army counterintelligence officer Sherdian Cavett. Cavett's presence is somewhat curious. The men loaded truckloads of material and sent it to the air base (Hanger 84). According to UFO lore, among the debris lay child-sized bodies of alien beings. The base commander, Colonel William Blanchard, then issued the now-famous press release.

Roswell Army Airfield is a significant place for aliens to be buzzing, actually. At the time, it's where the United States kept most of

I've been to Roswell!!! It's SCARY!!! All the alien vibrations in the air!!! And LIGHTS AT NIGHT!!!!!!!

YES!!! The GREYS!!! And this WASN'T THE FIRST TIME THEY'D BEEN HERE!!!!!!

its atom bombs and the planes—in the 509th Bomb Group—to carry them. Maybe the little guys were sizing up our defensive capabilities.

Not surprisingly, the press across the nation, and all of the world, went crazy with the story. Soon, however, word reached Blanchard's superiors who immediately released a second announcement stating that the debris was a high-altitude weather balloon.

Strangely, security around the weather balloon was very tight. The Air Force forbade photographs of the debris, though it was too late. Some had already been taken by folks around Roswell. Civilian witnesses, including Sheriff George Wilcox, had a hard time swallowing the new version of the story. Many had seen the debris. Some, including Major Marcel's son, remember seeing strange alien writing on a few pieces. Some of the witnesses, including Wilcox, claim that the military eventually intimidated them into agreeing with the weather balloon story.

Brazel himself showed up the day after the pair of announcements for a press interview—in the company of military officers. While he said that the debris had come from a weather balloon, he said later in the interview that he had found weather balloons before, and that this debris was nothing like that. *They got to him! But they won't get to ME!!!*

Major Marcel also made a statement to the press that backed up the weather balloon story, but now many of the details from the original press release, such as when the debris was found, changed. Marcel later admitted to UFO researcher Stanton Friedman that he was ordered to back up the weather balloon story, and that he did not believe it. He was convinced that the government was engaged in a massive cover up. (Government cover-ups are never small. Always massive.) ← *He's RIGHT! Even though he's covering up HIMSELF!!!*

Glenn Dennis, Roswell mortician, says that he received a phone call from the airbase requesting child-sized hermetically sealed caskets. Dennis also said that he then went to the base, and as he wandered around he saw some crazy things and was kicked out. He's also a co-founder of Roswell's hokey UFO Museum.

FREEDOM OF INFORMATION *It was TRUE!!!*

For fifty years, the Roswell story got <u>crazier and crazier</u>. Multiple UFOs crashing. Former Nazi scientists involved. Alien autopsies. Telepathic communiqués from orbiting saucers. Secret government meetings with aliens. By the mid-1990s, a CNN/Time poll showed that two-thirds of Americans not only believed in aliens visiting Earth, but thought they had crashed at Roswell and the government covered it up.

In 1995, the Air Force conducted an internal investigation and announced that the debris was a balloon, but a super secret balloon from something called Project Mogul. Such balloons were used to monitor Soviet atomic bomb tests. They were top secret and the cover-up was needed to preserve national security. In 1997, the Air Force suggested that reports of bodies in the debris must have come from a likewise top-secret program called Operation High Dive involving high-altitude parachutes and anthropomorphic dummies (as well as confusion or lies on the part of the witnesses).

The Roswell crash/government cover-up crowd didn't buy it for a minute.

The Gulf War was because Saddam Hussein had a secret UFO base in Iraq!

POST-ROSWELL UFOLOGY

Roswell, of course, was only the start (although, arguably, Kenneth Arnold's sighting in Washington State was the real start). UFOs, flying saucers, and aliens with gray skin and big bald heads have become a part of our culture. A majority of Americans believe in alien life beyond Earth. The number of officially reported UFO sightings in the United States in the past fifty years has been estimated at around 200,000, with many thousands of new reports each year. And most sightings go unreported. Around 6 percent of Americans claim to have seen a UFO, including former president Jimmy Carter. Nevertheless, the study of UFOs has gained little respect. Amid the scientific community, researchers into such phenomena are routinely dismissed. But even that may be changing. In 2008, Martin Plowman received a doctorate in ufology from Melbourne University in Australia (where they have had their own major UFO flaps).

After Roswell, various government groups, from the publicly known Project Blue Book to the more secretive (and possibly mythical)

LONNIE ZAMORA

Of the thousands of UFO reports investigated over the last fifty or so years, one of the most intriguing also takes place in New Mexico. Police officer Lonnie Zamora, a former aircraft mechanic and expert in conventional aircraft, worked in the town of Socorro. Considered trustworthy, level-headed, and upstanding on the force and in the community, Lonnie Zamora was an unimpeachably credible witness. On April 24, 1964, he heard a loud explosion. Investigating, he saw a cone of flame and heard a loud roaring sound. Officer Zamora then spotted a white, shiny oval on the ground with two child-sized humanoid figures nearby wearing white. He knew what he was looking at was no conventional craft and thought it might be an experimental vehicle from the nearby White Sands Proving Ground. Closer, he saw that the craft had a mysterious red insignia. The figures disappeared into the vehicle, which then took off into the sky, leaving behind impressions where the landing pads had been and footprints from the human-like figures. The sand in the area had been fused into glass and vegetation lay smoldering. Other witnesses corroborated by stating that they had seen an egg-shaped object in the sky at around the same time.

After a thorough investigation, this is the only UFO case in Project Blue Book's files declared unexplained involving physical evidence and a sighting of occupants in the alleged craft.

My UFO had RED WRITING TOO!!! And there was a big control panel with stuff like on Star Trek!!! But that's all I can say about it!!!!!

THEY'RE HERE | PAGE 135 OF 272

Majestic 12 and Interplanetary Phenomenon Unit, have investigated UFO sightings and evidence for many years. If these investigators found any hard evidence of alien visitors, they haven't told us. Interestingly, Dr. J. Allen Hynek, a self-styled UFO debunker who worked with Project Blue Book, is now a believer and a well-known advocate for UFO sightings. Supposedly, many military and intelligence officials privately believe that Earth may be visited by alien beings but keep those opinions to themselves. Officials from other countries, such as Sweden, the UK, France, Germany, and Brazil are more willing to admit that some UFOs may be of extraterrestrial origin.

Since Roswell, there have been at least eleven different supposed alien crashes around the world and thousands of UFO reports, some of them from credible sources. Some of the UFOs have left intriguing pieces of physical evidence, including scorch marks on the ground, photos or film of objects in the sky, radar blips, increased radiation levels, and so on.

One question no one seems to ask is, if they're so advanced why do these aliens keep crashing? Are they terrible drivers?

Today even many UFO believers now dismiss the Roswell incident as hokum. Worse, they claim, it diminishes real evidence and legitimate reports. Some people might call that splitting a very fine hair, but if you're a UFO believer, it's understandably an important one. "I'm a UFO guy," you might say, "but not one of the *crazy* UFO guys."

The UFO I saw was a bright light in the sky! And some really strange music playing in my head. That's all I can say about it!!!!

CONSPIRACY RUNDOWN

PLAUSIBILITY:
2/10. It's cool, in a science fiction-y sort of way, that the government actually admitted for about a minute that it found a flying saucer, but, unfortunately, it looks like it really was a weather balloon this time.

HIGH STRANGENESS:
4/10. Yeah, aliens are pretty odd. But if they were Nazi Mafia Freemason mind-control aliens with occult powers, then it would be high strangeness.

CONSPIRACY CHECKLIST:
- ☐ Illuminati
- ☐ The Freemasons
- ☑ CIA/intelligence community/the military
- ☑ Aliens
- ☐ The occult
- ☐ The Mafia

FOR MORE INFORMATION:
The Roswell Incident by Charles Berlitz and William L. Moore

The Truth About the UFO Crash at Roswell by Kevin D. Randle and Donald R. Schmitt

ON THE WEB::
Roswell cover-up: www.roswellufocrash.com

Roswell UFO Museum: www.roswellufomuseum.com

UFO Research Center: www.uforc.com

CONSPIRACY INVESTIGATOR SEARCH TERMS:
Jesse Marcel, CUFOS, MUFON, Roswell UFO Festival, Project Blue Book, J. Allen Hynek, Jacques Vallee, CSICOP

15. IMPLAUSIBLE DENIABILITY

AMONG CONSPIRACY THEORISTS, there's an idea that the government's secrets pass down from one president to the next. A new president learns top-secret information known only to the very upper echelons of the government. However, there exists some information so top secret that even the president does not know. According to the tinfoil hat crowd, the shadow government that *really* controls things knows things the president does not. Some say the president doesn't know certain things to give him "plausible deniability." This means he can say with a straight face that there are no Nazi bases on the moon and that the CIA does not use cyborg Bigfoot assassins because he doesn't know about them. The ufologists suggest that that's why even the president doesn't know what is really going on at Area 51. *OR ELSE the PRESIDENT is ONE of THEM!!!! A MASON! OR Illuminati!! MAYbE EVEN A GREY IN DISGUISE!!!!!!!????!*

GROOM LAKE

If "weather balloon" has become code for the government cover-up of a single UFO sighting, "Area 51" has come to symbolize a veil of secrecy over the entire UFO phenomenon.

Area 51 is a military facility ninety miles north of Las Vegas, Nevada. On the south shore of Groom Lake lies a military airfield used to develop and test experimental aircraft like the U-2 spy plane. Thus the base is sometimes known as Groom Lake. At other times, it is referred to as Dreamland, or Paradise Ranch, or just the Ranch. Officially, it is sometimes called Watertown Strip.

They could Admit it existed BECAUSE THEY WERE PLANNING A NEW SECRET BASE!! IN fact, they've AlREAdy got it set up!!

In 2003, the government finally admitted that Area 51 existed. Before that, they denied it, despite the massive amount of attention the place received from conspiracists. Many called it the worst kept secret in the world.

The main reason for the attention came in the 1980s when rumors began to circulate that the military was using the site to experiment with alien technologies recovered from the debris at the Roswell Crash (see Chapter 14). According to believers, they brought crashed spacecraft from various bases to Area 51 (probably in the late 1940s, but possibly as late as the 1950s). Some believers say that the Rosewell alien ship was sent to Wright-Patterson Air Force Base in Dayton, Ohio, before being transported to Area 51. In the secret hangers and laboratories on the site, for more than a half century top-clearance scientists and engineers have examined the alien wreckage.

Those interested in such things speculate that Area 51 is nothing less than the headquarters for the government's program for dealing with all things extraterrestrial. This plan is headed by a group called Majestic 12, or MJ 12. A group of twelve military officers, scientists, and intelligence agents oversees the work at Area 51, prepares for various contingencies (such as alien invasion), and even from time to time interacts with alien representatives. Some evidence, in the form of memoranda from the Eisenhower administration, suggests that MJ 12 has existed since 1947.

Is MJ 12 the group that's following me? It might be!

Supposedly, through the study of alien wreckage, the government has developed amazing new propulsion systems, energy weaponry, time travel and teleportation technology, and weather control.

In 1989, a man named Bob Lazar revealed that he was a government scientist working on an antigravity propulsion system developed from studying alien spacecraft in Area 51. He said that the *really* interesting stuff is going on in an even more secret base hidden beneath the mountains somewhere nearby called S/4—presumably, a top-secret base wasn't enough; he had to work at the top-secret part of the top-secret base. In various interviews, Lazar gave a detailed account of the goings on in Dreamland and some of the technology being developed there.

Lazar says that he saw no fewer than nine different recovered flying saucers there, built using knowledge that could not have come from this world and powered by something called Element 115, which could only be processed in space, like inside a supernova. The interiors of the craft were designed for beings smaller than humans, with almost liquid-smooth surfaces.

Really cool technology!! Like basically a WARP DRIVE for SPACE TRAVEL!! No wonder the government is covering up!!

Both skeptics, such as Glenn Campbell (no, not the country music star from the seventies), and UFO believers, such as Stanton Friedman, question Lazar and his story. Attempts to check his credentials and work history have suggested that he has no degree and has never worked in the scientific field. However, the reporter who first interviewed Lazar, George Knapp, claims to have uncovered evidence that the man did work and attend school where he said he did, but those records have been erased. The science Lazar discusses is regarded as iffy at best by those knowledgeable in the fields, yet former astronaut Edgar Mitchell spoke with him personally and at length and came away believing that Lazar had been involved with some secret government project.

ERASEd by the GREYS!!!!

Truth or delusion? Facts or hoax? The debate over Lazar's testimony rages. George Knapp, covering his butt, says that even if Lazar's personal story isn't true, some or all of the information could have been somehow implanted in his head to test the public's reaction to it.

It's also worth noting that in 2008, five former employees and military personnel stationed at Area 51 came forward and discussed with the *LA Times* what went on there. According to Colonel Hugh "Slip" Slater, Edward Lovick, Kenneth Collins, Thornton "T.D." Barnes, and Harry Martin, while they tested experimental aircraft and reverse engineered foreign technologies, there were no alien spaceships in Area 51. But with the cutting-edge, weird-looking stuff there, it's easy to see how such rumors could start.

ALIENS AND AUTOPSIES

In 1995, a film producer, Ray Santilli, claimed to have discovered footage of the autopsy of an alien being. Santilli's film supposedly showed one of the aliens from the Roswell crash being dissected by military experts. The film shows some kind of humanoid being with six fingers on a table with surgeons cutting into it. Although Santilli has some

Six is TWO TIMES THREE!!!!! THERE'S ANOTHER CONNECTION!

HIGH SECURITY

Don't just drive down to Nevada and expect to see some UFOs flying around. Despite the fact that the nearby stretch of State Route 375 has been officially dubbed the Extraterrestrial Highway, gawkers leaving that stretch of road to head toward Area 51 are not welcome. It's almost impossible to get closer than thirty miles from the facility. Wackenhut, a private firm, oversees security there and takes its job very seriously. Maybe they should be called "Whack-a-nut," considering their duties there. Many of Wackenhut's executives and employees are former intelligence operatives, and the firm itself may be involved in conspiracies all its own (see Chapter 26). The surrounding area is patrolled by men in jeeps and trucks, called "cammo dudes" because of their camouflage clothing. Some regions of the perimeter also use motion sensors to detect unwelcome truth seekers. Some say that unmarked black helicopters also monitor the entire area, and a few speculate that some of the extraterrestrial technology investigated in Area 51 better allows them to protect their secrets, such as an innovation that allows the guards to "smell" intruders at great distance. All these detailed reports come from the society of civilian UFO believers and truth seekers who regularly attempt to get into the base, or at least get close, to find out what's going on in there.

followers, most regard his film as a hoax. Forensics and biology experts point out that the supposed surgeons in the film disregard conventional autopsy procedures, and special effects artists say that everything in the film could have easily been created. In 2006, Santilli himself says that he "restored" the film and had to "recreate" portions of it.

The scientists in Area 51 supposedly have conducted many such experiments, because not only are crashed flying saucers brought there, but also their occupants, some of whom are still alive. According to a mechanical engineer named Bill Uhouse, who claims to have worked for the government on secret "flying disc" projects, an alien scientist named J-Rod lives and works at Area 51. Confusingly, there might be another J-Rod who lives and works at Los Alamos. Are all the aliens named J-Rod? It's hard to make much sense of Uhouse's story, but that's why they're called aliens.

I UNDERSTAND Uhouse!!! AUTHOR'S just COVERING UP!!!

PUTTING THE "FICTION" IN "SCIENCE FICTION"

If this all sounds like a science fiction movie to you, you're not alone. Movies, TV shows, and video games have featured Area 51 extensively. So much so that it's hard for many people to take it seriously. Of course, this could all be a part of some massive disinformation campaign to draw people away from the truth.

If forces within the U.S. government, with knowledge even the president does not have, possess information or evidence of UFOs, such evidence may very well be in Area 51. Even Bob Lazar claims to have had clearance levels higher than the president himself, and he was not high on the S/4 totem pole. Are there really things *that* secret?

Some of the true believers now say that Area 51 has closed up shop, at least as far as alien technology development goes. As soon as the government admitted the base existed, it clearly lost some of its cool mystique . . . that is, its ability to safely and secretly examine alien spaceships.

The new Area 51 supposedly lies somewhere in Utah.

MORMON CHURCH is INVOLVED IN AREA 51!!!???!

CONSPIRACY RUNDOWN

PLAUSIBILITY:
4/10. Area 51 exists, and the aircraft there lie at the cutting edge. You can go there and see them—but don't get too close or you'll be arrested. It *is* a top-secret military facility. Whether the planes are based on alien technology is much more up in the air.

HIGH STRANGENESS:
4/10. Aliens named J-Rod are always worth a few points.

CONSPIRACY CHECKLIST:
- ☐ Illuminati
- ☐ The Freemasons
- ☑ CIA/intelligence community/the military
- ☑ Aliens
- ☐ The occult
- ☐ The Mafia

FOR MORE INFORMATION:

The UFO Conspiracy: The First Forty Years by Jenny Randles

Open Skies, Closed Minds by Nick Pope

Beyond Roswell: The Alien Autopsy Film, Area 51, & the U.S. Government Coverup of UFOs by Michael Hesemann, Philip Mantle, and Bob Shell

ON THE WEB:
Area 51 (non-UFO related) information: www.dreamlandresort.com

UFO information: www.ufodigest.com

Bob Lazar's website: www.boblazar.com

How Area 51 Works: http://science.howstuffworks.com/area-51.htm

Santilli's alien autopsy footage: www.youtube.com/watch?v=0UP1OU9uQ2k

CONSPIRACY INVESTIGATOR SEARCH TERMS:
Area 51, Dreamland, Groom Lake, Bob Lazar, J-Rod, alien autopsy, Zeta Reticuli

16. THE SLOW INDOCTRINATION

IN 1982, WE ALL FELL IN LOVE with a cute, big-eyed alien in Steven Spielberg's *E.T.: The Extraterrestrial*. Just a couple of years earlier, we sat entranced watching the same director's film, *Close Encounters of the Third Kind,* where at least one man learned the truth behind UFO sightings. These movies introduced the public to terms like "extraterrestrial" and "close encounters." They presented the idea that aliens didn't have to be scary invaders, but instead could be our friends in peace. Spielberg may have been trying to shape public opinion when it comes to aliens, some conspiracists believe, because he knows that in fact they're already here and that soon they will need to officially announce that fact to the public. But this conspiracy theory isn't really about Steven Spielberg, or even about Hollywood. In this scenario, the movie makers and television media are tools of the government. Or perhaps those who really control the government—the Illuminati.

According to Bill Cooper, who claims to have had access to intelligence secrets while in the Navy, not only are aliens visiting this planet, but the government is working with them. The secret existence of these alien beings, who look just like the aliens depicted in *Close Encounters*, cannot remain a secret forever. But the powers that be feel that the world needs to be prepared for such an earth-shaking announcement or else there would be panic.

So we get *Close Encounters*. We get a television show called *Roswell*. We get *Third Rock from the Sun* and *Star Trek*. The number of movies and TV shows showing us aliens as potentially friendly, altruistic, and likeable is too numerous to list. They're not scary; they're funny and lovable, or wise and helpful (like Mr. Spock). Even *ALF* (1986–1990) is a part of the conspiracy. What other explanation for that show could there be?

So where do movies like *Alien* or TV shows like *The X-Files*—where the aliens are none-to-friendly and perhaps oh-so-hungry—fit in? Perhaps they're counterprogramming from those on the inside who know some sinister truth. Or perhaps they're just entertainment.

ON THE OTHER HAND

According to author Richard M. Dolan, the media is, in fact, intentionally *not* reporting on or talking about UFOs and downplaying their significance and seriousness when they do. Even in fiction, we see the UFO believer portrayed as a nut, unstable, strange, and unlikable. UFO sightings on the local news, if they're discussed at all, are laughed off at the end of a nightly broadcast as a "lighter moment."

Why aren't the major news outlets reporting on all the strange discoveries being made on the moon and Mars, a ufologist might ask. Why are they wasting our time with politics and natural disasters when there are stories of a much larger, cosmic significance at hand? Don't they listen to author and lecturer Richard Hoagland? Hoagland loves the face on Mars. If you've seen photos of it—a giant eerie-looking face that appears in NASA photos taken by the Viking 1 orbiter in 1976—it's probably because of Hoagland's attempts to get the word out. NASA says that the face is a trick of light and shadow and has produced other photos of the same region from the much more recent Mars Global Surveyor that make it clear it's just a hill. Hoagland insists that it is just one example of the many structures on Mars created by an ancient civilization—probably the same civilization that has come to the moon and Earth, and may still be coming. And as for NASA's explanations, Hoagland cries cover up.

Maybe not ancient! I think the Nazis might have gone as far as Mars. THIS COULD BE ANOTHER BASE!!! Run by MJ 12!!??

Not only are there structures on Mars, according to Hoagland, but they're on the moon as well (see Chapter 13). He displays official NASA photos from lunar missions that feature crop marks showing that things have been cut out of backgrounds of the photos. These missing objects, he contends, are huge alien structures.

The fact that the media won't cover this story, he says, proves it's legitimate. He believes that there has been a "complete blackout" in the United States of the data he has provided to the news. Interestingly, the Russian media gives Hoagland far more attention than their contemporaries in the United States.

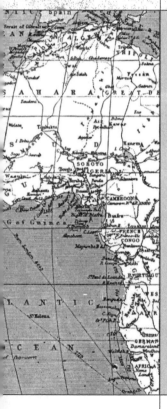

Hoagland also believes that movies are being used as a tool to prepare us for the truth. He writes on his website, "Present the truth as a sci-fi story and you have 'plausible deniability'. . . while also whetting the public's appetite and imagination for the idea that there could be 'something' out there, waiting to be found. Or, perhaps we already did find it . . . and have just been waiting for the right moment to reveal it publicly, without creating socioeconomic chaos."

DOG-GONE

The relatively isolated Dogon people of Mali in West Africa possess a rich culture including a very interesting mythology. Starting in the 1930s, two French researchers spent twenty-five years with the Dogon and became inducted into their tribe. After this initiation, the Dogon revealed that divine beings called the Nommo had come down from the stars in ancient times and taught their people many things. When asked specifically where these beings had come from, the Dogon indicated the star Sirius in the sky. The Dogon then revealed information that they could not have possibly known, the most significant being that Sirius is in fact a binary system. Without ever having laid eyes on a telescope, they also knew about Saturn's rings and the moons of Jupiter. Some people, including author Robert Temple, wonder if this is perhaps the purest evidence for alien contact with Earth. And even stranger, a case can be made that the Dogon language shows that their ancestors—the ones that had contact with the Nommo—may have influenced such great early societies as the Sumerians and the Egyptians, hinting that the very existence of civilization on Earth as we know it could have been jump-started by alien contact.

Or not. Even Temple himself wasn't willing to admit that he believed any of it. He mainly wanted to point out that it's an intriguing mystery.

Sirius is where Illuminati come from!!

DISCLOSURE SOON?

Most of the proponents of these theories believe that the government is going to make the announcement about aliens any day now. Ufologists like to point out that President Ronald Reagan declared the idea that aliens coming to Earth would be a way to unite all mankind. He broached the idea for the first time in a speech on December 5, 1985, and then *four more times* over the course of his presidency.

In November 2007, a number of noteworthy officials, including former Arizona governor Fife Symington, joined with the Coalition for Freedom of Information to insist that the U.S. government reopen Project Blue Book, the Air Force's eighteen-year probe of the UFO phenomena, and reveal what they know about aliens on Earth.

In May of 2008, a Vatican official announced that there is no conflict between Christianity and the existence of life on other planets. Such beings, should they come to Earth, should be welcomed as brothers.

As of autumn 2008, the latest news from NASA, thanks to its Phoenix mission, shows definite evidence of water on Mars, making the idea of life there, particularly ancient life, all the more believable.

Science fiction movies and television with humans and aliens interacting continue to come out with great frequency. (As do movies about superheroes, ghosts, vampires, and zombies. Do you think the government knows something that we don't there as well?)

Conspiracy theorists can use both the lack of media attention and an increase in media attention as evidence for their beliefs. That's resourceful. They look at what's presented as fact and call it lies, and they sometimes look at fiction and wonder if it's truth.

It's interesting that some people can't accept great works of imagination like *2001*, *Close Encounters*, or even *Star Wars* as just that: works of imagination. The irony that of all people conspiracy theorists don't accept acts of imagination seems utterly lost on them.

Handwritten margin notes:

RoNAld REAgAN met THREE TIMES with GREYs!!! That's bEEN PHOTOGRAPHED ANd publishEd oNliNE. ThE AliENs hAvE REPRESENtAtivEs iN thE OvAl OfficE!!!!!!!!

DoN't forget thE PoPE is PARt of thE IlluminAti/ MASoNS/GREYs!!!!

NOT ImAGiNATION!!!!!! IT'S REAL!!!!!??!

CONSPIRACY RUNDOWN

PLAUSIBILITY:
2/10 As Freud said, sometimes a movie alien is just a movie alien.

HIGH STRANGENESS:
3/10 The idea of the government using Hollywood as a propaganda tool to prepare us for alien contact is stranger than aliens themselves.

CONSPIRACY CHECKLIST:
- ☑ Illuminati
- ☐ The Freemasons
- ☑ CIA/intelligence community/the military
- ☑ Aliens
- ☐ The occult
- ☐ The Mafia

FOR MORE INFORMATION:

Dark Mission: The Secret History of NASA by Richard C. Hoagland and Mike Bara

Nothing in This Book is True, But It's Exactly How Things Are by Bob Frissell

Behold a Pale Horse by William Cooper

The Sirius Mystery by Robert K. G. Temple

ON THE WEB:
Richard Hoagland's site: www.enterprisemission.com

CONSPIRACY INVESTIGATOR SEARCH TERMS:
lunar ruins, face on Mars, UMMO, Richard Hoagland, mystery Babylon, Russian UFOs

17. ALIEN ABDUCTIONS

IT'S LATE AT NIGHT. You awake to a strange sound, but you find that you can't move to look to see what it is. You're frozen in your bed. Then comes the bright light. It spills into your bedroom through the windows and the door. You still can't move, despite the terror you feel. Suddenly, you are aware of a presence in the room with you. Then—if you're fortunate—you can move again. The light and the presence are gone. You're in your bed, but many hours have passed. And you can remember the alien hands, the strange craft, the sinister figures around you who initiate mysterious and invasive procedures. And while most of those figures are tiny and unlike anything you've ever seen, a few are recognizable. Human.

That's what HAPPENED TO ME!!! It's like the AUTHOR WAS THERE!!! OMG!! MAYBE HE WAS!!!!!!!!!??

The accounts from alien abductees follow a pattern. Sometimes the abductee isn't in bed but on the couch watching TV, outside, or in a car. The experience is usually horrific (but not always—sometimes it is enlightening and peaceful). Some abductees have strange marks on their bodies. Many find they can no longer sleep or conduct normal lives. Some become seriously ill, as though they'd been exposed to radiation. Most abductees recall their experience only through hypnosis. The most famous case is the account of Betty and Barney Hill.

NOT THE RUBBLES

Betty and Barney Hill were driving home to Portsmouth, New Hampshire, from upstate New York in September of 1961 when they saw a bright light in the sky. It followed their car, and eventually a disc-shaped craft landed in the road in front of them. Barney got out to investigate. When he saw what appeared to be humanoid figures inside the craft, he ran back to the car, and they continued their journey home. Although they experienced some odd sensations immediately afterward, it wasn't until later that Betty began to have dreams about what had happened to them. Barney dismissed the dreams, but eventually both found aid in the form of hypnosis, under which they revealed that the inhabitants of the craft took them aboard and gave them physical examinations.

The Hill case offers some intriguing features. It is the first occurrence of an alien encounter with creatures fitting the now-common description of what became known as the Greys: small beings with large, hairless heads and big, dark eyes. It's the first case of what is now the classic alien abduction scenario. And it's the first time that an alien revealed to a human where it came from: Zeta Reticuli, shown to Betty on a star map.

The case of Betty and Barney Hill is extremely detailed, as are the experiences of Whitley Strieber, who wrote about his own abduction in the book *Communion*. While Strieber remains neutral regarding the exact identities of "the Visitors" that come to him, his experiences seem to match the Hills' and many others'. Like so many others, Strieber has been abducted not once but many times.

What's really going on here?

MOTIVES FOR ABDUCTION

Some abductees claim that their abductors placed implants inside their bodies. In many cases, the implants can't be detected by modern science. But not always. Dr. Roger Leir, the world's (self-proclaimed) leading alien implant specialist, relates that he has surgically removed thirteen alien implants. These contain both biological and inorganic components, sometimes emit radio signals, and have magnetic properties as well. Whatever that means.

Alien implants may be tracking devices, allowing the aliens to find and abduct the same person again, the way humans tag animals for study. Many abduction experts believe that any abductee should be examined for implants and if any are found that they should be immediately removed.

STREIBER's stuff is cool!

I've got ALL his books!

I HAVE A SCAR ON my chest that WASN'T THERE BEFORE!!! And my head hurts sometimes!!

The aliens may be using some implants for mind control. This could be a part of some larger alien plan for humanity. Of course, this would place alien abductees at the forefront of that plan, whatever it is. Will the abductees be leaders when the aliens reveal their presence, helping usher in an alien agenda, or will they be a fifth column, acting as assassins and saboteurs when the alien invasion comes? Maybe we ought to lock these people up, just to be safe.

Others speculate that the implants may be something entirely . . . well, alien and thus something we are incapable of understanding. Researcher Derrel Sims, for example, points out that the implantation occurs in different places but almost always on chakra points used in pseudosciences like acupuncture.

Information from so-called experts suggests that the aliens require something from the abductees: information or fluids—even blood. Alien vampires?

Sometimes abductees say the aliens showed them a child. The child is a hybrid of both aliens and humans. The sight of these hybrids often creates an emotional bond between the abductee and the abductor, as though it were a shared offspring. If true, then the alien procedures must involve genetic manipulation and artificial insemination. Indeed, many female abductees discover they are pregnant after an abduction, though in a subsequent abduction the aliens remove the fetus.

One intriguing (if even more outlandish) theory identifies the aliens not as aliens at all but as humans from the far future. They come from a time when humanity's treatment of the Earth has left it almost uninhabitable. In order to survive in the polluted environment, humans genetically engineered themselves into different forms (smaller, bigger heads; grey, hairless skin; and so on). However, in so doing they have doomed the race and need genetic material from true humans to revitalize the gene pool. Thus, they come to the past in timeships, not spaceships, to find and extract DNA samples to create hybrids of past and future humans.

I asked a girl in a bar about that once, but SHE WOULDN'T TALK TO ME!!!

She must have been one of Them!

AND THEY KNOW ABOUT IT?

On Air Force One, President John F. Kennedy was once supposedly asked by one of the stewards, "What do you think about UFOs?" The president replied, "I'd like to tell the public about the alien situation, but my hands are tied." *That's why They killed him!!!!*

Ask any UFO researcher, conspiracy theorist, or even a majority of the average folks on the street, and they'll tell you that, yes, the government knows the truth about UFOs. The humans who stand alongside the alien abductors are almost always men and usually wear dark suits. Conspiracists say they must be government agents either working directly with the aliens or at least observing.

The source of the cover-up of alien presence on our planet, the shadow looming behind the government's involvement with UFOs, is a group called MJ 12.

Phillip Schneider, ex-Navy man, geologist, structural engineer, and UFO lecturer, claimed to have worked on an underground government structure in Dulce, New Mexico, in 1979 when his team accidentally uncovered an underground alien base. The Greys reacted with anger and shock, killing all the humans involved except for three, one of whom was Schneider. After that incident, Schneider worked tirelessly to spread the truth about not only the alien presence but the government's complicity. According to Schneider, the Greys arrived in 1954 and immediately made a deal with President Eisenhower. The agreement, called the 1954 Greada Treaty, said that the U.S. government would allow the abduction of humans for testing and implantation in return for extraterrestrial technology. The group created to oversee the Greada Treaty may be the NSC 5412/2 Special Group, a subcommittee of the U.S. National Security Council to oversee and coordinate government covert operations, formed in 1954 by President Eisenhower. Membership of the then-secret Special Group included Allen Dulles, head of the CIA, James Douglas, secretary of defense, Gordon Gray,

This is REALLY IMPORTANT!! Explains connection to Masons/Illuminati and Roswell! Greys have controlled the government since 1950s!!!!!!!!

national security advisor, and Livingston T. Merchant, undersecretary of state for political affairs.

Conspiracy theorists find it easy to link the Special Group and the background boogey-men of Schneider's tale into one group, called MJ 12, Majestic 12, Majic 12, or sometimes just Aquarius. This ultrasecret government organization may have been formed before 1954, however. Researchers like Greg Bishop put its creation in 1947, immediately following the Roswell crash and the flying saucer hysteria that gripped the nation.

To dedicated conspiracists, MJ 12 ranges from some secret government program to the actual shadow government itself. To these guys, MJ 12 *is* the Illuminati. Their contact with aliens has allowed them to take control of the government. The problem with this theory is that it would mean the Illuminati are new, not old. These Illuminati must be very different than Weishaupt's group described in Chapter 2, let alone the ancient Atlanteans. Most of the theorists who link MJ 12 with the Illuminati proceed down the well-trodden paths, assuming the Illuminati has always been around. It doesn't hang together well.

Some who approach MJ 12 more realistically and thoughtfully describe it as a group of military, scientific, and intelligence officials interested in studying the UFO phenomena. Previously secret documents that surfaced in 1984 describe the group and name the initial members, including Rear Admiral Roscoe H. Hillenkoetter, Secretary of the Navy James Forrestal, General Nathan Twining, and others. Some sources claim scientists such as Robert Oppenheimer, Albert Einstein, and Wernher von Braun were also involved. The government officially denies the existence of MJ 12 and calls the various "MJ 12 Papers" forgeries.

If Schneider, Bill Cooper, and others are right, however, at some point this secret group not only discovered that UFOs really are aliens visiting Earth but made some kind of alliance with them. The aliens' representative here on Earth was supposedly His Omnipotent Highness Krlll. Such a deal might be sinister—a trade of humans for technol-

THEY ARE THE SAME THING!!!!!

VON BRAUN WAS A FORMER NAZI!!! That's the connection to the Moon Base, too!!!!

ogy—or it might be far more benign. It all depends on one's view of aliens and the government. Perhaps the technology that MJ 12 has secured will allow us—or is already allowing us—to fight back against evil aliens. Schneider suggests, for example, that the Strategic Defense Initiative, the so-called Star Wars defense system of putting lasers on satellites, might come from the Greys. If so, perhaps it's being used to fight off the aliens, not protect us from missiles. (Since currently all tests of the Star Wars defense system have failed, this doesn't say much for the quality of Grey technology.) As strange as it may seem, some

THE STRANGE AND, FRANKLY, EMBARRASSING TALE OF ANTONIO VILLAS BOAS

The abduction of Betty and Barney Hill is technically not the first such story. Take, for example, the tale that Antonio Villas Boas, a native of Brazil, had to tell in 1957. It seems that Boas, a farmer, saw a strange light in the sky and then an egg-shaped craft, which landed in his field. He tried to escape, but his tractor's engine died mysteriously, and small beings in gray suits and helmets came out and grabbed him, dragging him into the ship. Once subdued, the aliens took his clothing and washed him with some strange, thick fluid. Then they placed him in a room with a woman. She was nude and beautiful, although her head was somewhat triangular, her eyes large and dark, and her mouth and nose very small (very similar to portrayals of alien Greys, although those portrayals did not exist in 1957). Despite the situation, Boas found himself excited. He speculated that perhaps the aliens had done something to him to entice his arousal. Boas had sex with the woman, twice. She never spoke, although she did make almost animal-like growls. When they were done, she pointed at her stomach, smiled, and then left.

I have a picture of a woman like that on my wall!!

The aliens then allowed Boas to dress and put him back in his field before taking off. Boas reluctantly shared his story with doctors who found that he had light radiation poisoning. He did not want to sell his story or let it be known, but it did get out, and Boas found only public ridicule and humiliation. He died in 1992.

people believe there is a war going on in space and all around us right now. That secret agents of our government ward off the actions of technologically advanced beings but can do so only in secret.

The more widely believed scenario is one in which both factions, the aliens and the government, are up to no good. They kidnap and murder innocent civilians without hesitation. For their trouble, the government gets the new toys and the aliens get . . . well, whatever it is that they're after. This includes as many as seventy-five secret underground bases built by the government. These bases exist throughout the southwestern United States and include Area 51 and the Denver International Airport. Huge underground tunnel systems connect all of these bases.

The secret forces in the government, armed with their advanced tech, control not only the United States but most of the rest of the world. According to Cooper, the entire Cold War was a sham to hide the fact that the shadow government actually controlled both East and West. Using alien technology, the secret rulers established a secret moon base long before the public Apollo missions. In 1962, astronauts of MJ 12 landed on Mars where today they have whole cities. Richard Hoagland's photographs of the face on Mars (see Chapter 16) may not be covering up alien bases but our own. All these iterations, and more, have their support among the UFO community.

However, there's another school of thought as well. MJ 12 really is a hoax, or was created as disinformation. That doesn't make UFOs or alien abductions any less real, of course; it just means that the government is as much in the dark as the rest of us. Comforting? Not really. This theory is not popular among most ufologists.

I'm SCARed to go NEAR the Southwest!!!

NOT ALIENS AT ALL

Bible scholars, or at least those tinfoil-hat wearers who purport to be, tell us that the Nephilim were the offspring of human women abducted by angelic beings (Genesis 6). Many Christian ufologists believe that aliens and biblical entities—some say angels, some say demons—are one in the same. Ezekiel saw wheels in the sky, and the Jews, leaving enslavement in Egypt, followed a flaming pyramid in the sky. Other religions have similar tales of gods riding in flying craft that sound a lot like UFOs. The Hindu gods traveled in "vahana," for example. Of course, writer Erich von Daniken would have you believe that it's not angels and gods we're mistaking for aliens but rather the other way around.

Regardless, there's apparently a strong connection between belief in the supernatural beings of the Bible and the supernatural experiences and sightings relating to UFOs. Theorists like Ron Patton describe beings that are really demons in aliens' clothing abducting, harassing, and otherwise frightening humans. The "aliens" lie to their abductees, filling their heads with "truths" about the nature of the world that do not correspond with the Bible. They encourage "New Age" beliefs, which distract people from the truth of Christianity. Patton even links occult figures like John Parsons and Aleister Crowley (see Chapter 18) to alien encounters. Researcher and author Sherry Shriner, however, claims that there are different kinds of aliens—some are demons while others are angels. The former are called the draco-reptilians who are allied with the Greys from Zeta Reticulum, and the latter are "Nordics" and look like humans. She'll even tell you what planet Lucifer lives on (it orbits Orion, if you're curious). *NO WAY!!??????! REAlly????*

SCIENCE

The abduction phenomenon is large enough, serious enough, and mysterious enough to attract the attention of serious researchers. There are kooks aplenty discussing the topic, to be sure, but there is also scientific study going on.

While many abductees already have some kind of predilection for pseudoscience or supernatural belief, many others do not. Few seem interested in publicity or attention—in fact, many cases go long unreported. It seems unlikely that it's simply imaginary or an elaborate hoax involving thousands of people who have no contact with one another.

Hypotheses put forward by scientists include hallucinations in a hypnogogic state of near sleep, temporary schizophrenia, and temporal lobe epilepsy.

Like cases of satanic ritual abuse (see Chapter 18), alien abduction memories often surface only with the help of hypnosis. In fact, therapist Gwen Dean has found no fewer than forty-four parallels between the two experiences, including focus on sexuality, abuse, and missing time. Most importantly, both seem to occur while the victim experiences an altered state of consciousness, and both involve contact with something supernatural. Both could result from psychological phenomena we're only now beginning to understand, such as a repressed trauma that manifests as a memory of something supernatural or impossible.

Various authors, starting with Carl Sagan, have pointed out that the alien abduction reports map closely to tales from the past, but in those stories, the role of aliens is played by faeries, angels, shamanic spirits, or other mythical creatures. Even if one cannot accept the literal truth of "abductions," perhaps science should investigate what has long been a part of the human experience.

Temporal lobe epilepsy is of particular interest in regard to the abduction phenomenon because symptoms can include temporary paralysis, unexplainable fear, a bright light, the sensation of other presences nearby, an altered state of consciousness wherein one seems to come into contact with a higher intelligence, and temporary amnesia. This could explain not only alien abduction experiences but other paranormal incidents, such as visions, encounters with ghosts and spirits, as well as mystical religious experiences. This, perhaps, is why most of the ufologists and paranormal believers hate it and argue strongly against

That's why I only sleep two hours a night!!!!

So They CAN'T HYPNOTIZE .ME!!

it. They don't want a simple scientific explanation to take away the mystery and mystique of aliens, visions, and ghosts.

One group of conspiracists argues that there are in fact no aliens involved in alien abductions—even though such kidnappings occur. Secret government agencies abduct the victims. The CIA has experimented with mind control before and perhaps continues to do so (see Chapter 24). Black ops scientists use hypnosis and drugs to alter memory and perception in their victims, so when the events finally surface, the abductees' minds confuse reality with aliens. Researcher Philip Coppens contends that Betty and Barney Hill, for example, were test subjects in a psychological experiment conducted by the CIA.

Because it's PART OF THE COVER-UP!!!!! That's why REAL investigators don't believe it!!

OR the Illuminati! OR maybe the Men in Black!! Who work for MJ 12??!!!

CONSPIRACY RUNDOWN

PLAUSIBILITY:

6/10 There are too many alien abduction reports, from too many reputable sources, for us to doubt that something is going on.

HIGH STRANGENESS:

5/10 Government-built alien bases underground. Alien mind-control implants located at chakra points.

CONSPIRACY CHECKLIST:
- ☑ Illuminati
- ☐ The Freemasons
- ☑ CIA/intelligence community/the military
- ☑ Aliens
- ☑ The occult
- ☐ The Mafia

FOR MORE INFORMATION:

The Interrupted Journey by John G. Fuller

The UFO Experience by J. Allen Hynek

Fire in the Sky: The Walton Experience by Travis Walton

Communion by Whitley Strieber

ON THE WEB:

Whitley Strieber's site: www.unknowncountry.com

The MJ 12 Papers: www.majesticdocuments.com

Dr. Roger Leir's site: www.alienscalpel.com

Alien abduction experience and research: www.abduct.com

Aliens as angels: www.alienresistance.org

Sherry Shriner's website: www.thewatcherfiles.com

CONSPIRACY INVESTIGATOR SEARCH TERMS:

Bill Cooper, temporal lobe epilepsy, Derrel Sims, NSC 5412/2 Special Group, Krlll

18. THE DEVIL MADE THEM DO IT

The Bohemian Grove is connected to the Illuminati. Bohemia is in Germany!!!!

Where the Illuminati started!!!!!

So the News Media is PART OF IT!!!! Just what I thought!! That's how everything is covered up!!!!!!

IN JULY 2000, FILMMAKER ALEX JONES infiltrated a secluded campground near Monte Rio, California, called Bohemian Grove. This was the meeting place of the Bohemian Club, an elite group of wealthy and influential politicians, corporate CEOs, and entertainment icons, a group some claim lies at the very heart of a worldwide satanic conspiracy.

That's right. If you didn't hate them enough for hoarding all the money, having all the power, and getting all the girls, the wealthy elite also worship the Devil. They got where they are because of devil power—evil magic, occult forces, demonic possession, everything that's bad in the world. If you've got images of Ronald Reagan in a black robe chanting to His Dark Majesty and George Bush Senior presiding over a virgin sacrifice, you're not far off. At least, that's what some people believe.

Regarding the Bohemian Grove, that it exists lies within public record. The group that has met there since 1872 is a secretive organization for the very wealthy, and by just about anyone's standards it is at least a little odd. There's a forty-five-foot-tall concrete shrine carved in the shape of an owl looming over an artificial lake, for example. Jones and his cameraman videotaped a ritual in the grove called the Cremation of Care, in which individuals in black hooded robes receive an effigy from a ferryman who has made his way across the lake. They place it on the altar and set it on fire while famous news anchorman Walter Cronkite gives voice to the owl and intones the ritual.

Every Republican president since Coolidge (and some Democrats) has been a member and watched or participated in this rite, along with leaders from Henry Kissinger to the former head of Procter & Gamble. So that is a little freaky. But is it satanic? The explanation most give is that it's simply an excuse for the wealthy and famous to gather and relax, and the ceremony is a ritual to show that they should burn their cares and woes and enjoy their time in the beautiful surroundings.

Good cover story, but many don't buy it.

The world's elite gathering in secret for strange ceremonies? That lies at the core of what many call proof that the world is indirectly ruled by Satanists. The theorists fall into two camps. The first, not surprisingly, are Christians with extreme beliefs. To them, Satan is the enemy and the "prince of this world" (John 14:30), so it's not a great leap to think he has a network of mortal agents working in the world for his evil ends. Since he can offer great power (at a great price), it figures that those in power (politically, economically, or in terms of fame and prestige) probably got it by selling their souls.

Others who subscribe to this idea don't focus on the religious aspect of it but link the Bohemian Club to the Illuminati. They believe that the world's elite are indeed dark and twisted cultists paying homage to the Devil, but that's really only icing on the conspiratorial cake.

And it's not just the Bohemian Club. Yale's secret society known as Skull and Bones, whose membership has included many presidents and influential men (including many in the intelligence community), practices occult rituals and indoctrinates future leaders into the satanic conspiracy. The list of so-called Bonesmen includes both George Bush Junior and his father, William Howard Taft, William F. Buckley, John Kerry, Chief Justice Morrison R. Waite, and many others.

Further, satanic cultists like Anton LeVey in California and the Process Church in England are thought to have had a lot of influence on various popular musicians and celebrities, such as the Rolling Stones and the Beatles, as well as on science fiction authors like Clarke Ashton Smith, August Derleth, and Fritz Leiber, and filmmakers like Kenneth Anger. Trailblazing rocket scientist Jack Parsons and retired Army intelligence officer Michael Aquino led secretive occult organizations as well.

With powerful leaders, celebrities, and scientists in its pocket, what does the worldwide satanic conspiracy hope to achieve? Nothing less than the complete domination of the world, and the installation of Satanism as the one true religion. This puts the Devil himself in charge,

SEE!!!!!!! That's what I said!!! Why Doesn't Anyone Believe Me???!!!!

THE WICKEDEST MAN IN THE WORLD

One thread that weaves its way through all the different parts of this conspiracy is a single name: Aleister Crowley. Born in 1875, Crowley was an extremely influential occult writer and leader. His book *The Book of the Law* serves as a centerpiece for many modern occult organizations and pagan religions. Said to possess magical powers and forbidden secrets, he wove together science, magic, drugs, and sex to create a philosophy that differed radically from the society around him. "Do as thou wilt, shall be the whole of the law," he wrote. Although he likely would not have called himself a Satanist, others believed that he was the very heart of a massive satanic organization. It is certainly true that Crowley led a Masonic-like order (yes, the Freemasons again) called the Ordo Templi Orientis. He also belonged to the infamous occult organization, the Golden Dawn (which also had Masonic ties) and was influential in the life of L. Ron Hubbard, founder of Scientology. Dubbed both "the Beast" and "The Wickedest Man in the World" in his lifetime, Crowley died in 1947.

Another connection!!!

Crowley DIDN'T REALLY DIE!!!!

He's living in Argentina. Part of a Nazi secret cell!!!!

The Templars were connected to Satanism!! Everyone knows that!!!!! .

with all our souls his to burn. But even with the help of politicians, celebrities, and the very wealthy, the secret cult of Satan knows that the world's not quite ready for that. So the conspirators must still operate in the shadows, their influential members helping to cover up the violent and illegal activities of the rest of the cult.

THE DEVIL'S WORK

You've heard of Charles Manson, the Night Stalker (serial killer Richard Ramirez), and Son of Sam? They're all linked, and not just because they've all spawned scary movies based on their exploits. They're all soldiers in the worldwide satanic conspiracy. Possessed by demons and serving the will of Lucifer, the murderers commit "ritual slayings" dedicated to the Devil. They take their marching orders directly from the conspiracy, or through subliminal messages hidden in music.

In fact, some contend that the whole idea of "serial killers" is simply a media/FBI fabrication to either explain or cover up the fact that thousands of people—mostly children—are abducted and killed by satanic cults each year. Likewise, they claim the number of teen runaways, child abductions by parents, and so on is exaggerated to explain the disappearances actually resulting from the bloody work of the cultists. They point out that many of the missing disappear on days sacred to followers of the occult, such as the equinoxes and solstices, Halloween (October 31, also called Samhain), or Candlemas (February 2), and on sites with known or suspected satanic cult activity.

I stay in my house on Halloween. IT'S SAFER!!!! And I keep four flashlights lit at the corners of the room. TO KEEP THEM OUT!!!!

Evidence of the conspiracy—well, evidence of secretive and freaky occult activity—turns up all the time. Authorities find locations covered in satanic symbols, used candles, and mutilated animals. These may be the leftovers of meetings and rituals conducted by those involved.

PLEASED TO MEET YOU . . . HOPE YOU'VE GUESSED MY NAME

The best evidence of a worldwide satanic conspiracy is in plain sight. One need look no further than the heavy metal section of the local music store. Almost since it began, people have associated rock music with the Devil because, they claim, it advocated promiscuity and drug use. However, in the late 1960s and particularly the 1970s, bands like Black Sabbath and Judas Priest used actual satanic imagery such as pentagrams, inverted crosses, and demons on their album covers and satanic themes and words, including the Black Mass, human sacrifice, cannibalism, murder, and suicide in their lyrics. *That's true!!!!*

I've listened to some of their music!! VERY DANGEROUS!!!!

According to Christian writer Jack Chick, most popular rock music is based indirectly or directly (and thus intentionally) on "ancient

Druidic rhythms," which have inherently occultic power. Others contend that the vibrations created by rock music beats dull the mind, making it more receptive to control. But it's the lyrics that worry still more people. Songs about murder and death are so commonplace in heavy metal music that there are subgenres known as death metal and black metal. The conspiracy lies in plain sight with lyrics like "God of rock 'n' roll, we'll steal your virgin soul." (Kiss, "God of Thunder").

Richard Ramirez claimed that the AC/DC album *Highway to Hell* influenced him to commit his murders. In 1990 Judas Priest was blamed for a suicide pact made by two teenaged boys. In 1985, Dr. Joe Stuessy, author of *The Heavy Metal User's Manual*, testified before Congress that messages recorded backward (called backmasking) can influence the subconscious mind listening to the recording forward. Various rock bands have been accused of placing backmasked satanic messages on their albums. Led Zeppelin's "Stairway to Heaven," for example, is believed to contain the message, "Oh here's to my sweet Satan. The one whose little path would make me sad, whose power is Satan. He'll give those with him 666, there was a little toolshed where he made us suffer, sad Satan," when played backward. You would think that "Buy more records" would be an even smarter, simpler, subliminal message, but perhaps the cult thinks differently than we do.

Today the signs of the satanic cult are pervasive: goths, vampires, and death-obsessed emo kids seem to be everywhere. Investigators into this conspiracy see its unmistakable thumbprint in New Age beliefs, holistic medicine, paganism, yoga, the television show *Bewitched* (no, really), trick-or-treating, and He-Man. And they're not so sure about Santa Claus, either. (Rearrange the letters in "Santa" and what do you get?) A few, like Jack Chick, would go a bit further and add Mormonism and even Catholicism to the mix, placing some secret meetings at the Vatican at the heart of the satanic conspiracy. If the latter is true, those priests in the movie *The Exorcist* evidently didn't get the memo—otherwise they would have realized that the little girl vomiting pea soup was actually on their side.

No, that's stupid!! Now the author's just trying to be funny!!!

HE'S NOT!!!

LURKING DEMONS EVERYWHERE

Satanic ritual abuse has been uncovered by using hypnosis on patients who had no conscious memories of the incidents. These testimonies of physical and sexual abuse contain further evidence of a worldwide conspiracy. In the book *Michele Remembers*, author Lawrence Pazder chronicles the terrifying ordeals of a young girl recounting formerly suppressed memories of a globe-spanning satanic cult involved in human sacrifice and cannibalism. In 1983, the owners and teachers of the McMartin Preschool in California were put on trial for the abuse of many children after evidence suggested that they were a part of an international satanic cult. Some children testified about animal sacrifice, flying witches, and secret underground tunnels. Oddly, as *Michele Remembers* sold more copies and the McMartin trial became the center of media attention, more such claims surfaced.

But the cult, widespread as it is, isn't content. In fact, it's apparently looking for new recruits. In the 1970s, Satanists created seemingly innocuous pastimes like Dungeons & Dragons to indoctrinate kids into the occult. Evidently they got tired of getting stuck with only the nerdy kids, because they later developed something with more mass appeal to grab them while they were young: Harry Potter. You probably didn't realize it, but the beloved kids' book series isn't just single-handedly revitalizing the Young Adult section in your bookstore and turning more kids onto reading than ever before. It's turning them into zombies for an occult army that uses wands and spells rather than guns or bombs—or at least into people who will better accept the idea of occult powers and practices as normal.

And just in case you thought we were going to get through a conspiracy theory without bringing up aliens, author John Ankerberg believes the alien Greys are actually demonic entities. Perhaps the demons disguise themselves in this way to deceive and confuse (as demons do), or their appearance is simply mistaken or misinterpreted by modern minds as being alien (suggesting that perhaps in earlier

SOME PEOPLE I KNEW PLAYED DUNGEONS & DRAGONS. THEY WOULDN'T LET ME PLAY!!! BECAUSE I KNEW TOO MUCH!!!!

times they might be mistaken for spirits or faerie folk; see Chapter 17). Either way, the strange lights in the sky, the mysterious abduction experiences, and the aliens themselves are a manifestation of the conspiracy's success.

The conspiracy can be found the world over (although no one seems to talk much about Satanism outside the United States, Mexico, England, Scandinavia, and maybe Australia) made up of the most sinister forces imaginable. They seek not just world domination but the very souls of those they wish to subjugate. Is this truly the world's most terrifying conspiracy theory? Maybe. But it's also one of the most tenuous.

Secret cabals aside, most law enforcement agencies refute the idea that thousands of people are being abducted by evil cults for sacrifice. The link between most heavy metal music and *actual* believers in the occult is tenuous at best. And backmasking has yet to be established as an actual way to influence the subconscious—the case against Judas Priest, for example, was thrown out of court. Satanic ritual abuse and the recovery of such memories through regression hypnosis is denounced by the majority of the psychiatric community as well as law enforcement, who claim it owes more to the power of suggestion than of Satan.

There are, of course, a number of different groups that call themselves Satanists: the Church of Satan, the Temple of Set, and others. They seem to have little to do with the worldwide conspiracy discussed here, although it's unlikely that they would admit to such a thing on their websites. Still, the Church of Satan doesn't even seem to believe that there is such a thing as "Satan" and uses the term only metaphorically. Many people confuse Wicca and other pagan religions with Satanism, making the sinister, shadowy cult seem even larger.

Believers contend, however, that anyone who does not see this diabolic cult for what it is simply ignores the obvious.

That's because they're covering up for the GOVERNMENT!!!! They think we won't notice!

Many of the people who believe in the worldwide satanic conspiracy also believe that at least some of its members have demon-granted powers to perform feats of supernatural ability. The cultists cloud the minds of innocent victims (particularly the young), they hide in plain sight, and they possess great cunning and strength. The Devil grants them the wealth, position, and authority that they could not have otherwise achieved on their own merits.

Perhaps this fascination with the secret circles the rich and famous move in is a deeply held resentment against the kids who didn't pick you for kickball in gym and went on to be class president and quarterback of the football team. Isn't it a lot easier to accept that they got where they are because they made a deal with the Devil?

The Illuminati can do that!! There are lots of stories about Templar Knights raising people from the DEAD!!!!! And now the Masons-Templars-Illuminati-Satanists are doing it AND NO ONE'S WATCHING BUT ME!!!!!!!!! •

CONSPIRACY RUNDOWN

PLAUSIBILITY:

3/10. The Bohemian Club and Skull and Bones are real, and Black Sabbath is a real rock band, but it's hard to think of Walter Cronkite, George W. Bush, and Ozzy Osborne all being in the same conspiracy.

HIGH STRANGENESS:

5/10. Despite the fact that many who worry about the worldwide satanic conspiracy believe its members have supernatural powers, most of the activities of the conspiracy are decidedly mundane.

CONSPIRACY CHECKLIST:
- ☑ Illuminati
- ☑ The Freemasons
- ☑ CIA/intelligence community/the military
- ☑ Aliens
- ☑ The occult

FOR MORE INFORMATION:

Satanic Panic: The Creation of a Contemporary Legend by Jeffrey S. Victor

The Ultimate Evil: The Truth About the Cult Murders: Son of Sam & Beyond by Maury Terry

Painted Black by Carl A. Raschke

The Bohemian Grove and Other Ruling Class Retreats by G. William Domhoff

ON THE WEB:

Backmask Online: www.backmaskonline.com

Jeff Milner's Site: http://jeffmilner.com/backmasking.htm

The Church of Satan Official Website: www.churchofsatan.com

The Official Site of the Temple of Set: www.xeper.org

CONSPIRACY INVESTIGATOR SEARCH TERMS:

Bohemian Grove, Kenneth Anger, Michael Aquino, Anton LeVey, The Process Church, sign of the Devil, Black Mass, Jack Chick

19. THE NEW WORLD ORDER

BEFORE TACKLING THE NEW WORLD ORDER, one should probably understand the Old World Order. This is the 1950s, as portrayed in black-and-white television programs like *Ozzie and Harriet* and in old issues of *Life* magazine. Under the Old World Order, America fought the Communists at every turn but always came out on top. We were the good guys, and they were the bad guys. Men were men, and women knew their place. Everyone was white, spoke English, and went to church on Sunday. Goods were plentiful, technology was understandable (anything could be fixed with the tools you had in your garage), big corporations could do no wrong, kids were always safe, and there was never anything to be afraid of. Andy Griffith was the sheriff, and the Cleavers were our neighbors.

And then everything went to Hell.

In the New World Order, America has no sovereignty, for the world is ruled by a single entity, the United Nations, which has established power in the guise of world trade and the abolition of war. Patriots who love America are rounded up and put in prisons by foreign troops operating on U.S. soil. On May 12, 1989, in his commencement address at Texas A&M University, the first President Bush said, "Ultimately, our objective is to welcome the Soviet Union back into the World Order. Perhaps the world order of the future will truly be a family of nations." In 1991, he also stated: "If we do not follow the dictates of our inner moral compass and stand up for human life, then this lawlessness will threaten the peace and democracy of the emerging 'New World Order' we now see, this long dreamed-of vision we've all worked toward for so long."

And it's all happening right under our noses!!

PALEOCONSERVATISM

Author H. G. Wells wrote of the benevolent New World Order in 1940, describing an inevitable world social democracy. Many now see Wells's vision coming to fruition. The Commission on Global

Wells also wrote about a MARTIAN INVASION!! Not a coincidence!!!!

Governance, NAFTA, the World Trade Organization, the World Bank, the International Monetary Fund . . . these are the tools of the New World Order. Oh, it sounds great at first. Global trade, expanding new markets, greater cooperation, and so on. But what it leads to is a one-world government. And that's a bad thing, according to those behind this theory.

Some of the major voices describing the New World Order conspiracy theory are not tinfoil-hat wearing nuts living in their mother's basement. At least, they don't wear their hats in public. These are actual movers and shakers in the political arena, often called paleo-conservatives for their old-school, right-wing, anti-Communist, antiauthoritarian views. (Not all paleoconservatives are conspiracy theorists, of course.)

Here's what author, politician, and paleoconservative commentator Pat Buchanan has to say on the subject: "You may be sure that in this 'new international system,' the American citizen will count for precious little. Already, we are told that, henceforth, U.S. Marines may be put at the command of the United Nations' [Secretary General] Boutros Boutros-Ghali, to fight and die for the new world order." Buchanan also points his finger at the Council on Foreign Relations, a nonpartisan foreign policy think tank in the United States that Buchanan and others believe is nothing more than a front for international banking interests ultimately seeking to subvert U.S. sovereignty and the creation of a socialist world state. CFR co-chairman Robert Pastor called for a North American Union, similar to the European Union, in 2005 and referred to the U.S., Mexican, and Canadian governments as "zealous defenders of an outdated conception of sovereignty."

This organization is controlled by the Illuminati!!

OTHER BELIEVERS

At the other end of the social spectrum, although not the political one, lie the militia groups and so-called survivalist colonies found throughout the United States but often thought of as being tied to Idaho and other nearby states. People like Timothy McVeigh, who blew up an office complex in 1985 killing 168 people and injuring more than 800, believed in the New World Order. So does Randy Weaver, who held off federal agents in a violent twelve-day siege in 1992 at Ruby Ridge, Idaho. These are people who take their beliefs seriously. They're not just writing about them in online message boards, they're acting upon them. They're convinced that the government—under the direction of the New World Order—is going to come to take their guns. And they're ready to fight back. These same people often mix strongly racist views in with their conspiracy theory. Groups such as the Aryan Nation and Christian Identity believe that Jews ultimately pull the strings of the New World Order, and list interracial integration and marriage among the NWO's tools to create a one-world socialist state.

In fact, the militia groups and their members—like McVeigh—figure into other people's conspiracy theories. McVeigh in particular has been called a dupe, a tool, or a member of various pro-Islamic, neo-Nazi, and secret government theories. McVeigh and his ilk criticized the government continually for its so-called Nazi-like tactics, when in fact they themselves had connections with, or at least sympathy for, admitted antigovernment neo-Nazi groups.

NEW WORLD ORDER IN THE UNITED STATES

The New World Order's members know that they must control the one superpower left in the world, the United States. After all, Henry Kissinger, former secretary of state, said, "Our nation is uniquely endowed to play a creative and decisive role in the new world order which is taking form around us."

The Federal Emergency Management Act of 1978, according to some theorists, is the New World Order's first major stride in gaining

handwritten margin notes:

I don't have any guns. SHOULD I GET ONE???!!! To defend against ALIEN INVADERS!!!

McVeigh was in touch with Argentina Nazis about the Arctic base!! He was PLANNING TO BLOW UP THE WORLD TRADE CENTER!!! But the GOVERNMENT beat him to it!!!!!!!

BIG BROTHER

In 1944, George Orwell wrote *1984*, a dystopian novel of the future (at the time) in which Big Brother ruled with an iron fist through media manipulation and surveillance of the population. Since then, Big Brother has come to be synonymous with the idea of the government watching and monitoring the lives of its citizenry. Big Brother is an important part of the New World Order as well, for in order to dominate the world completely, they—or rather They—must eliminate all personal freedoms, and the first to go is privacy. As each year passes, technology increases the ability of the few to monitor the many. Employers can watch what employees do on their computers and can even track their movements using new sophisticated technologies. The United States government has used its war on terror as an excuse to monitor its people. In 2007, it was revealed that the NSA increased the number of phone calls it listened in on, without warrants. The number of letters opened by the FBI in recent years has increased tenfold. Governments likely to one day be subsumed into the New World Order already keep vast databases of personal information on its citizenry. They track not only things like names, addresses, and so on, but travel, medical history, and even your DNA. You can't even rent a movie or check a book out of the library without that information being stored somewhere. Perhaps worst of all, not all of the information gathered is accurate. The number of people, for example, in California's database of criminal information exceeds California's entire population. All of this, theorists speculate, is because of the New World Order and its ultimate plans. Like a terrible beast that feeds on information, the NWO must know everything in order to control anything.

control of the United States. Like a Trojan horse, it has been wheeled into the American landscape where the New World Order secret police can leap out and take over whenever they wish. Researcher Harry V. Martin of FreeAmerica refers to FEMA as nothing less than the "secret government" itself and claims that it is the most powerful single entity in the country, made up entirely of nonelected officials with

FEMA has secret communications set up with Area 51 about INTERNMENT CAMPS!!! FOR PEOPLE LIKE ME!!!!

HURRICANE KATRINA WAS ENGINEERED by ALIEN technology to destroy A SECRET LABORATORY in New ORLEANS. LEE HARVEY OSWALD SPENT time in New ORLEANS! That's what they WERE trying to cover up with the hurricane!!!!!

no public oversight. Through a number of executive orders, FEMA has been granted the power to seize the media, as well as all means of transportation, hospitals, and schools. They can relocate populations, conscript civilians into work brigades, and control the flow of all natural resources and money in the country.

On the other hand, emergencies such as Hurricane Katrina in 2005 may suggest that FEMA isn't so much frighteningly powerful as it is frighteningly incompetent. Not fazed, conspiracists say that it's possible FEMA was so unprepared for Katrina because dealing with natural disasters isn't what it's actually designed to do. That's what author Jim Keith contends. He writes that only 10 percent of FEMA's personnel are involved in anything having to do with disaster relief. The rest? They're compiling records of possible dissidents in the United States who could cause trouble if the country became politically destabilized.

Or maybe the New World Order itself is entirely incompetent. Maybe that's why they haven't seized power yet.

According to Martin, the New World Order intends to use FEMA to take control of the U.S. military and suspend the Constitution under the auspices of quelling a large-scale domestic disturbance. This unrest could come from an extraneous (perhaps engineered) event, or it could come from patriots who oppose the New World Order. Thus the conspiracy's real plan will come to fruition only when enough people speak out against the conspiracy. Insidious. They don't seem so bumbling now.

The next big step for the New World Order, according to this school of thought, was the creation of the Department of Homeland Security. Like FEMA, Homeland Security was created to alleviate public fear when in fact it intends to steal the very rights, freedoms, and ultimately the sovereignty it allegedly protects. Through Homeland Security, the New World Order can detain whomever it wants, can monitor all communication and gain access to all information, and can suspend the rights of citizens. It is George Orwell's Big Brother.

PEOPLE who ARE SEARCHing for THE TRUTH!!!!

But wait, you say. I thought we were talking about a world government, but FEMA and Homeland Security are just in the United States. Well, if pressed, those behind this theory would tell you that FEMA and Homeland Security are just the U.S. branches of the NWO that's going to eventually rule the world. Americans, they believe, need special attention in getting us primed for this takeover. And you know, maybe they're right about that. Getting Americans to do something is like herding cats.

Remember the metric system?

AND THEY'VE GOT SATAN ON THEIR SIDE (AND ALIENS, AND FREEMASONS . . .)

According to many conspiracy theorists, the New World Order is prophesied in the Bible—it is the one-world government of the Antichrist himself. Some of these, like Jack Chick, lump in the Catholic Church as a part of the New World Order. The Vatican serves as a prophet for the Antichrist. The Catholics, these believers contend, help legitimize the NWO, particularly in Third World nations where the Church is still very strong.

Writer Ron Graff points out that just as the New World Order strives for a one-world government, so too does it look to control a one-world religion through the National and World Council of Churches. The New World Order is in fact a front for Satan and his attempt to destroy Christianity.

Often the same conspiracy theorists—like, say, David Icke—not only contend that the New World Order is backed by Satanic occultists, but also by the Freemasons and by secretive extraterrestrials either living in underground New World Order bases, or passing among us as shape shifters. Or both. Imagine Satanists, Freemasons, and aliens all working together with the United Nations and FEMA to take over the world. *THAT'S WHAT'S REALLY GOING ON!!!!!! PEOPLE NEED to WATCH out!!! It's closer than you think!!!!!*

NEW WORLD TECH

The New World Order wields a vast arsenal of secret technology to accomplish its ends. "Pro-scientism" appears to be a major tenet of the NWO's dogma, and its opponents seem to be terrified by that. In fact, much of what's written about the New World Order is laced with an undercurrent of technophobia. Computer logins, barcodes, credit cards, and so on are employed by the conspiracy to track us and gather information that can be used against us. Afraid of this kind of Big Brother monitoring, some people choose to live off the grid, using only cash (and not ATMs), keeping no permanent residence, and avoiding activities that force them to submit any kind of personal data. Of course, in today's modern society, this is almost impossible, and even those claiming to do so are still likely well within the grid they fear. But what really seems to keep them up at night are more imaginative technological advances like subliminal advertising, implanted computer chips that track us, and more.

One of the most discussed technologies is something called HAARP. In 1993, the U.S. government began the High-frequency Active Auroral Research Project in Alaska to study atmospheric processes affecting communication and surveillance systems. The site boasts a high-frequency transmitter that can temporarily alter the ionosphere in order to study it. But conspiracy theorists like Nick Begich and Jeane Manning believe it capable of much more than that. High-frequency radio wave transmissions can disrupt and perhaps even modify human mental processes. HAARP, they argue, is really a giant mind-control device. But there's more. It can be used to jam all communication systems in the world. It can control the weather. It can knock out enemy satellites or spacecraft. It can harm wildlife and human health. It can disrupt the entire atmosphere. It slices, it dices, it's a weapon worthy of any supervillain you can name. As Begich and Manning say, this is a HAARP that angels do not play.

The anti-HAARP folks really do put tinfoil on their heads or on the insides of their homes to block its rays. Really. And this same

I NEVER USE ATMS. They keep track of my money!!!

I have tin foil shades around my room! They're GOOD PROTECTION!!!!

crowd seems awfully worried about chemtrails. When you look up in the clear sky and see the trails made by jets as they fly—those are chemtrails. Most people call them contrails, and know that they are composed of water vapor and ice crystals. But the folks on the kookier end of the Internet and talk radio claim that they are in fact the spray of chemical or biological agents to pacify and control the population or perhaps even eliminate some percentage of the citizenry with disease and contamination. Or perhaps they're intended to modify and control the weather. At least one politician believes in chemtrails, too. Dennis Kucinich, congressman from Ohio, introduced legislation in 2001 that would prohibit weapons in space and specifically mentions chemtrails. Everyone from the Air Force to the EPA, FAA, NASA, and NOAA deny chemtrails exist. Of course, every conspiracy theorist knows what that means: cover-up.

New World Order foes also fear psychiatry. The NWO uses psycho-analysis, hypnosis, psychiatric medication, and institutionalization to control the populace and dull the minds of the people they wish to sub-jugate. This part of the conspiracy's plot is important now, as they need to keep us docile and stupid while they get their plans into motion. We won't even know what will hit us until the UN tanks are rolling up our streets and the dissenters are rounded up.

In order to deal with the vast number of people (likely the ones not doped up on drugs and therapy) who will require detention in the United States, the New World Order is already building secret deten-tion camps throughout the country. According to author Jim Keith, a program called Operation Rex 84, ordered by President Ronald Reagan, authorized the creation of at least twenty-three emergency detention centers to be used to hold dissidents in times of national emergency. More have been built since then in places like Madison, Wisconsin; Tulsa, Oklahoma; and Fairbanks, Alaska. These facilities are considered top secret and many are well hidden. If this seems like science fiction, Keith urges us to remember that the United States

chemtrails could be mind-altering drugs!!!

REAGAN WAS A DUPE of the ALIENS!!! THE MASONS ARE PLANNING HUGE DETENTION CENTERS!!!!!!!

It's coming!!

government detained 100,000 citizens of Japanese descent during World War II.

GOALS OF THE CONSPIRACY

Of course, the New World Order wants complete control of the world and all the people in it. That goes without saying. Everyone wants that, from the Illuminati to the Freemasons to the Satanists to the Reptilian aliens from Orion.

But the New World Order feared by the political far right seeks to create a planned global economy entirely controlled by the technocracy of the wealthy elite. In the NWO, the population of the world will become little more than slaves.

But the elites know that to properly control the people of the world and, more importantly, to manage its resources most efficiently, the global population must drop. Drastically. According to researcher Ken Adachi, the New World Order seeks to eliminate approximately five and a half billion people through orchestrated conflict and bioengineered disease. Some of the spread of disease comes from the use of vaccines and inoculations, so everyone should avoid those like the . . . well, like the plague. If you believe Adachi. Of course, before you cancel your flu shot, realize that Adachi also believes that the New World Order has been building a vast network of underground cities on Earth and bases on the Moon and Mars where the wealthy elite will live with the extraterrestrials to wait out the ecological catastrophe soon to occur here when the Earth collides with the planet Nibiru.

What else need be said?

That's RIGHT!!!! We need to fight for freedom from Masonic Templar Alien Enslavers!!!

CONSPIRACY RUNDOWN

PLAUSIBILITY:
3/10. The books and websites will show you photos of the secret concentration camps, and you can read the various executive orders giving FEMA too much power. But it's all just too big to really believe that it's a coordinated effort.

HIGH STRANGENESS:
6/10. I'm going to say that chemtrails, mind-control machines, and plots to control the weather are very strange.

CONSPIRACY CHECKLIST:
- ☑ Illuminati
- ☑ The Freemasons
- ☑ CIA/intelligence community/the military
- ☑ Aliens
- ☑ The occult
- ☐ The Mafia

FOR MORE INFORMATION:

The Late, Great Planet Earth by Hal Lindsey

Angels Don't Play This HAARP by Nick Begich and Jeane Manning

The New World Order by Pat Robertson

Black Helicopters Over America: Strikeforce for the New World Order by Jim Keith

New World Order: The Ancient Plan of Secret Societies by William T. Still

ON THE WEB:

New World Order Truth: www.nwotruth.com

Ken Adachi's site: http://educate-yourself.org

FreeAmerica's site: www.sonic.net/sentinel

CONSPIRACY INVESTIGATOR SEARCH TERMS:

NAFTA, police state, world state, chemtrails, HAARP, global governance, Rex 84, Ruby Ridge, Timothy McVeigh, Aryan Nation

20. THE OTHER NEW WORLD ORDER

BILLIONAIRES SAY THE DARNDEST THINGS. David Rockefeller, grandson of oil magnate John D. Rockefeller and influential banker and statesman in his own right, wrote the following in his autobiography in 2002: "For more than a century ideological extremists at either end of the political spectrum have seized upon well-publicized incidents . . . to attack the Rockefeller family for the inordinate influence they claim we wield over American political and economic institutions. Some even believe we are part of a secret cabal working against the best interests of the United States, characterizing my family and me as 'internationalists' and of conspiring with others around the world to build a more integrated global political and economic structure—one world, if you will. If that's the charge, I stand guilty, and I am proud of it." *HE ADMITS it!!!!!*

Not surprisingly, a lot of conspiracy theorists didn't react well to this statement. The idea that bankers, tycoons, and wealthy aristocratic families operate in a secret cabal to rule the world has been around a long time. This secret cabal seeks to form a New World Order in which these elites rule secretly, not by taking over the government (as described in Chapter 19), but by being more powerful and influential than any government.

Call this cabal the Illuminati. Or you can call them the Committee of 300, as former MI6 agent John Coleman does in his book by that title. Coleman claims that the cabal patterns itself after the British East India Company's Council of 300, founded by the British aristocracy in 1727. They call themselves the Bilderberg Group, the Council on Foreign Relations, the Trilateral Commission, and similar names. These secret groups of elite, extraordinary wealthy and influential people, many of them related in ancient bloodlines, work together, manipulating politics and economics, to control everything. Literally everything. New members are recruited through programs like the Rhodes Scholarship, for example, which was set up by diamond magnate Cecil Rhodes to promote a secret society of the wealthy and intelligent to rule over the

They're all part of the same thing!! The SECRET GROUP that's running things!!!!

Like Bill Clinton!!!!!!!!! He was a Rhodes Scholar!!

rest of the world's inferior population, according to authors like Carroll Quigley and Frank Aydelotte.

These authors believe that the activists who speak out against the United Nations and globalization have the right idea, but they're looking in the wrong direction. The Illuminati aren't interested in using the government. They aren't controlling FEMA. They don't pass laws or abolish constitutions. The true New World Order lurks in the shadows and is likely far more insidious. It's not going to use governments or establish a world government to enact its control. It isn't going to roll into your town with tanks or drop bombs. That's so twentieth century. It's going to use wealthy families and corporations.

THE FAMILIES

Since the eighteenth century, wealthy, aristocratic families such as the Rothschilds and the Vanderbilts have controlled much of international commerce. Later, the Rockefellers, the Carnegies, and other families would join them. For some conspiracists, these are modern-day dynastic monarchs who rule not by divine right but by the right conferred by wealth.

They not only manipulate events, but they do so in such a way so as to throw attention away from themselves. For example, according to author Eustace Mullins, the Rockefellers helped create the John Birch Society. The John Birch Society in turn helped create the Red Scare, which fueled the Republican Party. The society also served a vital role in creating the so-called Christian Right, according to Barbara Aho, putting all Christians—and thus a huge number of votes—into the camp of the Republicans. Convenient that the party in the United States most concerned about the Communist menace and upholding Christian morals is also the one friendliest to the corporation, the banker, and the industrialist. The *international* corporation, banker, and industrialist. This is, of course, ironic, because the John Birch

They're all connected!!

The Carnegies have been training secret scientists for years in their "Foundation" to do experiments in Area 51 and other places!!

Society, well known for its anti-Communist stance, supposedly holds the idea of globalism and a one-world government with the highest contempt. The Illuminati use the strengths of their enemies against them. In fact, they *create* their so-called enemies to distract the world from their real goals. The New World Order conspiracy described in Chapter 19 is, in fact, a ruse put forward by the real New World Order conspiracy. Confused yet? It always gets crazy when conspiracy theorists get accused of being a part of a conspiracy themselves.

And it gets still more complex. Gary Allen's work, *None Dare Call It Conspiracy*, suggests that the growing (in 1971) Communist threat, dangerous and terrible as it may be, might itself be a front for the very industrialists we're talking about. Industrialists likely bankrolled the Bolshevik Revolution in 1917. That would mean that both Commu-

The Illuminati were in control of the U.S.S.R.! AND THEY STILL CONTROL RUSSIA!!

RESISTING THE SIREN SONG

While conspiracy theorists focus on aliens, ancient cults, and long-dead knightly orders, and governments chase terrorists or confront each other, the very real and very easy-to-believe-in bankers and industrialists slowly take over everything. In fact, that may be their very plan. Gobbledygook about Freemasonry, reptilians, satanic rituals, and even Zionist conspiracies might simply be disinformation of the strangest kind to make naysayers of very real organizations like the Bilderberg Group, the Trilateral Commission, and the Council on Foreign Relations seem silly by association.

Some conspiracy theorists, like James Perloff, do manage to avoid charged words like "Illuminati" and so forth in order to try to investigate and expose the actions and motives of these elitist and extremely secretive organizations. Because as soon as you take that first turn into weirdville, you lose all respect you could have ever had. If any. Clearly, however, the temptation to take that one extra step into high strangeness is too much for most authors and researchers. *They're wrong!!!*

nists and the anti-Communists were created by the same secret cabal of billionaire supercapitalists. All to help them get what they want—complete control without anyone noticing. *They already have complete control!!!*

Author Stewart A. Swerdlow says that there are in fact thirteen bloodlines of the Illuminati, including the Rothschilds, the Rockefellers, and more (including, among others, the Sinclair/St. Clair family popularized by *The Da Vinci Code* and discussed in Chapter 3). He even manages to drag in the Kennedys. (You can't spell conspiracy without Kennedy.) Swerdlow also says these families report to the reptilians who inhabit the Inner Earth.

The idea of important bloodlines and power transferred solely through familial ties does not actually fit in with the dogma of the Illuminati at all; the original Illuminati believed in keeping power in the hands of the enlightened and disdained dynastic monarchy. As well, many (but not all) conspiracy theorists pointing fingers at the Jewish Rothschild family really intend to point their fingers at the Jews.

THE WHATA-BURGERS?

The Bilderberg Group is an invitation-only conference of influential individuals held each year. The first conference, held at the Hotel de Bilderberg in the Netherlands in 1954, gave the group its name. Members of the group, known as Bilderbergers, wield influence in politics, business, and media. They range from foreign policy and military experts to prime ministers and presidents to royalty and international financiers. Most hail from Europe or North America. Donald Rumsfeld, Paul Wolfowitz, Prince Philip and Prince Charles, Madeleine Albright, Gerald Ford, Henry Kissinger, David Rockefeller, Pierre Trudeau, Bill and Hillary Clinton, Tony Blair, Otto von Habsburg, Helmut Schmidt, Peter Jennings, and William F. Buckley Jr. have all been members. There are hundreds of members, and not all attend each year. According to author Mick Farren, most profess a conservative and staunchly

They control Britain, the U.S., and Germany! Are they also secret Nazis?!!

anti-Communist outlook. Author Phyllis Schlafly postulated that this group controls the modern Republican Party in the United States and uses it to shape policy friendly to the ultrarich and megacorporations. Their ideology revealed at Bilderberg conferences remains extremely pro-capitalist, suggesting that the best interests of the common people are served when banking and big business thrive and grow. Members preach capitalism like a religious dogma. New members invited into the group often have high political aspirations. The existing membership determines how well they fit into the organization's worldview—and thus, whether they should be supported or opposed.

Bilderbergers control BOTH Democrats and Republicans!!! Part of their plan for domination!!!

No reporters are allowed in Bilderberg conferences, unless they attend as members, which is not at all uncommon. Like all other members, they must keep what happens at the meetings in strict confidence. Conspiracy theorists speculate that all manner of dastardly deeds are plotted in these closed-door sessions. However, when Denis Healey, former U.K. Labour chancellor and current Bilderberger, was confronted with the accusations of conspiracy and world domination, he told a reporter that it was "crap." *He would!! He's one of them!!!*

THE REST OF THE ROUND TABLE

The Bilderberg Group is just one portion of a larger secret society known as the Round Table, which includes the Committee of 300, the Olympians, the Illuminati . . . if you're that rich, you can afford a lot of names for your conspiracy. When Cecil Rhodes died in 1902, he left his vast fortune in the hands of the Rothschilds to create the Round Table. Initially it influenced British politics, but eventually it manipulated events all over the world by creating organizations like the Bilderberg Group, the Trilateral Commission, the Club of Rome, and the Council on Foreign Relations.

The Trilateral Commission is the brainchild of David Rockefeller and first met in 1973. It consists of around 300 businesspeople, bankers, and political figures from Europe, the Asia-Pacific region, and North America. Ostensibly, it exists to promote trade and good relations between these three regions. Its ranks have included Jimmy Carter, George Bush Sr., Lloyd Bentsen, Zbigniew Brzezinski, Dick Cheney, Bill Clinton, John Glenn, Henry Kissinger, and many others. In 1975 the Trilateral Commission released a report called the Crisis of Democracy, stating that the United States had an "excess of democracy." Regarding growing democracies and the expansion of the middle class, commission members have said that "order depends on somehow compelling newly mobilized strata to return to a measure of passivity and defeatism. . . ." Even the name of this group strikes a chord of fear among those coifed in tinfoil. Trilateral suggests three sides, like a pyramid. You know, with an eye on top of it.

Tri-lateral Commission! In other words, THREE!!! very important!!

When Rockefeller created the Trilateral Commission, he was also chairman of the Council on Foreign Relations. The CFR (see Chapter 19) works to influence U.S. foreign policy. Its membership includes intelligence officials, CEOs of multinational corporations, politicians, and some media personalities, and its roll call includes familiar names like Bush, Cheney, and Kissinger as well as John McCain, Colin Powell, and many others. *Barack Obama is CONTROLLED BY THEM!!!*

Conspiracy theorists like Jim Marrs and David Icke suggest that even individual members of these groups may not fully comprehend the entirety of the secret society to which they belong. Only an inner circle, described in Rhodes's will as a small subset of the memberships of these organizations, know the entire plan. And since Icke's involved, we can be certain that the Inner Circle is made up of shape-shifting reptilian aliens from another dimension.

There were SECRET MEETINGS to arrange his election!! ORGANIZED by GREY AND OTHER ALIENS!!??!!!!

CAN YOU HAVE TWO WORLD ORDERS?

There's nothing worse than a sloppy conspiracy theory. This is particularly true of, but not entirely limited to, websites that try to bring everything together: the Bilderbergers, the United Nations, the Free-masons, Weishaupt's Illuminati, aliens, MJ 12, the Antichrist, the Satanists, the Rothschilds . . . whew. A grand unified conspiracy theory is a noble goal, but it doesn't really make a lot of sense, even consider-ing it's, well, a conspiracy theory.

The main difference is that one New World Order is feared by the Far Right and involves Big Brother and the United Nations—it might very well be a Communist plot. The other New World Order is feared by the crazy Left and involves the ultrarich, capitalism gone amok. Some aspects of one theory (say, the Bilderberg Group) fit just as easily into the other, but in their hearts these are not conspiracy theories that play together well.

That's not for lack of trying on the part of harried conspiracy theorists who struggle to put George Bush, Bill Clinton, the ancient Atlanteans, and FEMA, into the same conspiracy.

COVER-UP!!!!
HE'S COVERING UP
AGAIN!!!

IT ALL FITS
TOGETHER!!!!!!
LISTEN TO ME!!!!

CONSPIRACY RUNDOWN

PLAUSIBILITY:

5/10. It's easier to believe in a conspiracy about people just wanting to get richer than it is to believe in a one world government that's going to lock us all up in concentration camps out West.

HIGH STRANGENESS:

3/10. As long as we can resist the temptation to focus on the reptilians living at the center of the Earth, or something, we'll be okay.

CONSPIRACY CHECKLIST:
- ☑ Illuminati
- ☐ The Freemasons
- ☑ CIA/intelligence community/the military
- ☑ Aliens
- ☑ The occult
- ☐ The Mafia

FOR MORE INFORMATION:

A Choice, Not an Echo by Phyllis Schlafly

The Conspirator's Hierarchy: The Committee of 300 by John Coleman

None Dare Call It Conspiracy by Gary Allen

The Shadows of Power: The Council on Foreign Relations and the American Decline by James Perloff

The True Story of the Bilderberg Group by Daniel Estulin

ON THE WEB:

The Vast Right Wing Conspiracy: www.watch.pair.com/rockefeller.html

The John Birch Society site: www.jbs.org

The Trilateral Commission site: www.trilateral.org

The Council on Foreign Relations site: www.cfr.org

CONSPIRACY INVESTIGATOR SEARCH TERMS:

Bilderberg Group, Trilateral Commission, Council on Foreign Relations, Rothschilds, Rockefellers, Rhodes, Illuminati bloodlines, Committee of 300, Gnomes of Zurich

21. THE WAR ON DRUGS

JUST SAY NO. First Lady Nancy Reagan told us that was what we were to say to drugs in the eighties. But even as the president and his wife were saying no, some conspiracists believe the CIA was saying yes, yes, yes! While one part of the government fought an overt, costly war on drugs, another part fought a covert war with drug money, selling drugs to U.S. citizens. In a way, the War on Drugs may be another American Civil War.

The United States incarcerates almost 1 million citizens each year on drug-related charges. In fact, the United States holds a higher proportion of its population in jail than any other nation in the world. It spends billions each year and devotes thousands of agents and military troops to combating drug users, dealers, smugglers, and producers. Whether this is helping to decrease the number of drug users or even effectively curtail the drug trade is open to question.

Many authors and conspiracy researchers believe that a massive conspiracy has developed in the government involving the trafficking of drugs, primarily to fund covert CIA operations. This conspiracy involves not just the CIA but the Justice Department and federal judges, who have ignored the evidence, and various elected officials who have kept the knowledge secret and covered up the program's existence.

Much more than the CIA. This is PART of the FREEMASONS' mind-control conspiracy!!

SETTING UP THE BUSINESS

This conspiracy's roots extend to just after World War II. An increased interest in Southeast Asia and a need to feed the growing beast that was the newly formed Central Intelligence Agency spawned the idea of using drug money to support secret ops. But what did the government know about the smuggling and the trafficking of illegal goods? Back then, perhaps not much. But they knew who did: the mob. With the government acting as supplier and the Mafia as dealer, illegal drugs made their way into American culture (and the rest of the world as well). This quickly turned into such a profitable business for all involved that when President John F. Kennedy looked as though he would decrease American involvement in the region, conspiracists argue that he was assassinated as a result. *OMG!!! That might have been part of it!!!*

With their opponents in the executive branch largely out of the way, the conspiracy went into overdrive during the Vietnam War. Veterans report seeing operations in which the CIA took heroin produced in Vietnamese and Cambodian opium fields and smuggled it into the United States in order to fund covert operations during the war. The first customers were the troops themselves, in need of escape from the horrors of war. Not only did they quickly become good customers, but the government ensured they would be avid consumers when they returned home.

Crime syndicate boss Meyer Lansky worked with the CIA, according to author Michael Collins Piper. His syndicate moved the drugs from Southeast Asia to the United States. CIA operatives like Ted Shackley and Thomas Clines helped create heroin labs through the region. Thus, they actually fostered the drug trade and increased drug production. Coincidentally—or maybe not—Shackley and Clines had previously headed Operation Mongoose, the agency's program to oust Cuban dictator Fidel Castro, a program that may have had some hand in the assassination of President Kennedy (see Chapter 6).

The Watergate operation was partly to hide drug smuggling out of the White House??! THAT WAS WHY THEY KILLED ELVIS!!!!

CREATING THE DRUG CULTURE

But what if the government's real drug-related crimes were even more insidious than that? According to many authors, including Doug Moench, Andy Smith, and George Piccard, the CIA *created* the drug culture in the United States. It began with the OSS during World War II, when interrogators wanted to develop a truth serum. They experimented with a potent extract of marijuana that could be secretly injected into normal cigarettes and tested it upon unknowing subjects, including suspected Communists in the U.S. military.

Did the Government give me drugs???

Meanwhile, Nazi scientists used captives in concentration camps to test drugs for similar purposes, and even took matters a step beyond: mind control. The Nazis used primarily mescaline. Even in combination with hypnosis, however, they couldn't make it work. After years of experimentation, the United States had a breakthrough. Allen Dulles, who would one day head the CIA, learned of a discovery made at Sandoz Laboratories in Switzerland by Dr. Albert Hofmann. Hofmann, who may have been working indirectly for the Nazis, discovered lysergic acid diethylamide, or LSD. By this time, the CIA had its own mind-control project in the works (see Chapter 24), and they believed LSD would work well for them.

The project required extensive testing. So the CIA began spreading LSD onto college campuses by offering grants for drug-related studies using academic fronts such as the Society for the Investigation of Human Ecology at Cornell University. Meanwhile, Operation Midnight-Climax (winner of the I-can't-believe-it's-really-named-that contest) created brothels that served as CIA fronts in which prostitutes could secretly drug the drinks of their patrons and record their actions on hidden cameras. The point of all this? To see what would happen to normal people using different dosages of the drug in different situations.

What's hardest to believe about all this is that it contradicts the stereotype of the FBI or CIA agent. We think of him—especially in the fifties and sixties—as a straightlaced fellow with a dark suit and a crew cut, ignorant of anything but baseball, hot dogs, apple pie, and Chevrolets. But if the conspiracists are to be believed, some of these guys were pimps and pushers. Some CIA agents supposedly saw this as an opportunity and sold LSD and other drugs on the side into the black market. Maybe we should think of a government agent as a shifty guy in a trenchcoat whispering, "Hey man, you need a hit?"

As the CIA tests increased in frequency, the Army got involved. In 1958, at Edgewood Arsenal, ninety-five men—all of them black—were

They might have put drugs in MY WATER!!!! It's been tasting funny!!

WATCH OUT!!!

Don't drink the Kool-Aid!!!!!!!!!!!!

secretly given LSD and then observed, given polygraph tests, or placed in isolation. In the 1960s, the military tested LSD on at least 1,500 unwitting people. The military tested other drugs in this way as well, including PCP, powerful hallucinogens, and hundreds of others.

It became clear, however, that even LSD wasn't a useful mind-control agent and was only partially useful as a truth drug. However, it and a powerful hallucinogen called BZ (3-quinuclidinyl benzilate) did offer another benefit: they could be powerful incapacitating agents. The Army created BZ bombs and even bullets, testing them at least five times during the Vietnam War between 1968 and 1970. Researcher Andy Smith contends that the Army still keeps fifty tons of BZ, enough to send the entire planet into a three-day trip from which it might never return. There's an apocalyptic scenario you don't hear about too often.

The CIA began ordering LSD doses from the chemical company Sandoz in the tens of millions. When Sandoz refused to fill the order in 1953, another company figured out how to produce the drug, and the CIA upped its order to billions of doses. Were they planning to drug all the Communists in the world? Possibly. It's not so hard to believe that they wanted all the Reds to see a few other colors. Far out, man.

LSD also had its uses right here in the United States. By the 1960s, a counterculture arose that rejected typical 1950s-era values and embraced antigovernment sentiments and sympathy for the Communists. One way to fight them was simply to drug them. According to authors Martin Lee and Bruce Shlain, the CIA and the FBI did just that, setting up LSD labs in San Francisco. Drug culture gurus like Allen Ginsberg and Timothy Leary worked—intentionally or not—for the CIA. "Turn on, tune in, and drop out" was the mantra of the day. Activists become advocates of peace and love. Rebels became flower children. Rather than protest against the government, the counter-culture became an apathetic mass, turning from LSD to abundantly available heroin, also supplied by the government.

The Military-Industrialists wanted to use the drugs to protect the Greys from discovery. BY PEOPLE LIKE ME WHO KNOW THE TRUTH!!!!!!

That's why I have to watch out for drugs!! No more vitamins!!????!

That's right!! The Secret Government was USING THEM!!

HIP-HOP CIA

According to researchers Jon Hillson and Eli Green, the drugging of America continued well past the 1960s. In the 1980s, even as Nancy Reagan told us to Just Say No, the CIA supported the Contra rebels in Nicaragua by selling Colombian cocaine in South Central Los Angeles. Worse, the government may have also sold the young black gang members their weapons. This was not only a way to raise secret funds for covert operations, but at the same time it suppressed members of the impoverished and disaffected black community, drugging them and encouraging them to use violence against one another.

Decades of high drug use among all young people have created a culture whose members are ill informed and apathetic. Conspiracists argue that these qualities prevent change and support those in power. Meanwhile, the government has used the War on Drugs as an excuse to exercise more authority, imposing stiffer penalties for drug-related crimes, expanding search and seizure powers, and placing more limitations on personal privacy. The War on Drugs also keeps street prices high.

It's not just American intelligence agencies, either. James Casbolt, former MI6 agent, says it's British intelligence (MI5 and MI6) that reigns supreme in the global drug trade.

Embarrassing, hypocritical, unethical, and illegal . . . if it's all true. While some critics have referred to the CIA as something akin to the Three Stooges, it may turn out they're more like Cheech and Chong.

And their Secret Agenda!! They want us drugged and helpless!! BUT NOT ME!!!

CONSPIRACY RUNDOWN

PLAUSIBILITY:

8/10. Like so many conspiracy theories, this one has its hard-to-swallow portions, but the wealth of evidence pointing to CIA drug trafficking is disheartening.

HIGH STRANGENESS:

2/10. Trippy, sure. But high strangeness? Not really.

CONSPIRACY CHECKLIST:

- ☐ Illuminati
- ☐ The Freemasons
- ☑ CIA/intelligence community/the military
- ☐ Aliens
- ☐ The occult
- ☑ The Mafia

FOR MORE INFORMATION:

Mind Control, World Control by Jim Keith

The Politics of Heroin: CIA Complicity in the Global Drug Trade by Alfred W. McCoy

Drugging America: A Trojan Horse by Rodney Stich

ON THE WEB:

Overview of the CIA drug trade: www.ciadrugs.com

We The People CIA-Drugs: www.wethepeople.la/ciadrugs.htm

CONSPIRACY INVESTIGATOR SEARCH TERMS:

CIA drugs, Society for the Investigation of Human Ecology, Meyer Lansky, Operation Midnight-Climax

22. THE TWO TOWERS

WE ALL REMEMBER what happened on September 11, 2001. It's a date that's been etched into our memories. Two planes smashed into the World Trade Center and another struck the Pentagon in Washington, D.C. Nearly 3,000 people died in the worst act of terrorism in American history. It was the costliest attack of any kind, both in money and in lives, on American soil.

I WAS IN MY ROOM, checking out stuff online!! SO I KNEW THERE WAS SOMETHING WEIRD RIGHT AWAY!!!!!!!

In many ways, 9/11 has become the current generation's JFK assassination. We can all remember where we were on that day.

But if you think there's more to the 9/11 story than what we've been told you're not alone. A poll in 2007 indicated that about 5 percent of Americans believed that the U.S. government was involved with the September 11 attacks in some fashion.

Many believe September 11 was a false flag operation—that is, one in which a government conducts a covert operation designed to appear as if it was perpetrated by someone else. Conspiracy nuts argue the attacks were allowed to happen by the government. The more extreme fringe claims the attacks were, in fact, engineered by the government.

WE'RE NOT NUTS!!! THE SECRET GOVERNMENT PLANNED THE WHOLE thing!!!!

WHY?

Let's get the most obvious question out of the way first. Why would the government do such a thing, or even allow such a thing to happen, to its own people? The answer is fear mongering. After 9/11, according to the theorists, the Bush administration relied heavily on fear to motivate the country. In the aftermath of the tragedy, President Bush launched his so-called War on Terror, and in so doing gathered unprecedented powers for the executive branch. He pushed through the Patriot Act and created the Department of Homeland Security, which many claim are dangerous threats to civil liberties in the United States. Bush used the September 11 attacks as an excuse to wage a war in Afghanistan. He used it as a reason to invade the country of Iraq because Saddam Hussein supposedly supported the attacks (a claim that was later proven false). In 2000 a conservative think tank, the Project for a New American Century, released a report that claimed it was necessary to increase spending for the military, but pointed out that doing so would be difficult unless there was some "catastrophic and catalyzing event—like a new Pearl Harbor." Members of this think tank include Vice President Dick Cheney, Secretary of Defense Donald Rumsfeld, Deputy Secretary of Defense Paul Wolfowitz, and Jeb Bush, George Bush's brother (and then governor of Florida). *Cheney is a MEMBER OF THE TRILATERAL COMMISSION!!! Makes lots of SENSE NOW!!*

Of course, all of this starts with the assumption that the president is in charge of the country—something many conspiracists reject. Filmmaker and researcher Alex Jones says the attacks on September 11 were ordered by the Illuminati to launch the War on Terror, which served their needs (violence and fear of violence is good for business, and fear makes it easier to control the masses). Bush had to dance when his Illuminati masters pulled his strings. *YES!!!!!!!!! That's EXACTLY what happened!!!!*

Researchers point to a quote from David Rockefeller in 1994: "All we need is the right major crisis and the nations will accept the New World Order." Were the attacks on 9/11 an attempt to create that crisis? Many would have us believe that the Illuminati, or the New World Order, orchestrated the attacks.

Some, like writer Peter Allen and filmmaker Michael Moore, point out the links between terrorist Bin Laden and the Bush family. Bin Laden is part of the Saudi royal family, and the Bushes have long had a close relationship with the ruling house of Saud, both on a business and a personal level. The second President Bush, before he came to office, engaged in a joint business venture with Bin Laden's half brother Salem. *Saudi Royal family CONTROLS OIL, which is converted by the GREYS into hyperenergy bursts to POWER THEIR SHIPS with faster-than-lightspeed drive!!!!*

Although this fact might surprise many, it's hardly a conspiracy. It's just odd, and embarrassing to Bush, at least in front of his more right-wing supporters. Unless of course you want to make it a conspiracy. . . . Author and nutcase David Icke suggests that the connection between the Bushes and Saudi royal family was engineered by the

• That's the REAL reason oil is so important!!!! GREYS WERE behind the
• WHOLE THING!!!!!!

Illuminati. To put it another way, the connection proves that both are members of the Illuminati and thus, according to Icke, are reptilian shapeshifters. Or they're possessed by a force from an alien dimension so that they can better serve the reptilians. Or something like that.

While on the topic of billionaires, let us not forget the economic repercussions of the 9/11 attacks. Analysis of the stock market shows that someone appeared to know ahead of time which companies would be hurt by the attacks and which companies would be helped, based on the selling and buying patterns in the days before September 11. Similarly, the World Trade Center was privatized just before it was destroyed; its new owner took out a huge insurance policy that specifically included terrorist attacks. And during the attacks themselves, millions of dollars in suspicious transactions were conducted through the offices in the World Trade Center (WTC) that could then never be traced. We can't overlook that the offices in WTC 7, another building destroyed that day, contained records of hundreds of fraud investigations being carried out by the Securities and Exchange Commission.

Perhaps the president and other top officials didn't know anything about the attack, and they were fooled as much as the rest of the public by a smaller, compartmentalized conspiracy within the government. As with the Kennedy assassination, obvious suspects include high-ranking personages in the military-industrial complex. These people would benefit from an America afraid of terrorism and foreign aggressors. Military spending skyrocketed after the attacks, for example, with both the Afghanistan and Iraq conflicts resulting in trillions of dollars in military and rebuilding contracts for companies such as Halliburton, in which Vice President Cheney has a vested interest.

Mafia figure Tony Gambino stated in 2007 that he knows for a fact that President Bush knew about the 9/11 attacks and played a part in organizing them and carrying them out. According to Gambino, who also says he knows who killed JFK, the administration orchestrated the attacks in order to stage the invasion of Iraq as well as to get at all the (gold) buried in vaults below the World Trade Center. Gambino contends that the Mafia knows many of the government's dirty secrets, since they've worked together for decades. He also says the Vatican was in on the whole operation as well and got a share of the profits.

Gold used to finance the moon base???!!

Or maybe the government was just horribly incompetent. Before the attacks, U.S. intelligence sent the White House a memo telling the president an attack by Bin Laden was imminent and might use planes as weapons. Bush and his staff appear to have ignored it. Sibel Edmonds, who worked as an FBI translator, said, "My translations of the 9/11 intercepts included [terrorist] money laundering, detailed and date-specific information . . . if they were to do real investigations, we would see several significant high-level criminal prosecutions in this country . . . and believe me, they will do everything to cover this up." Edmonds is currently under a gag order that keeps her from testifying.

ATTACK AND DEFENSE

Many of the 9/11 hijackers were under close scrutiny by the CIA, the FBI, the military, and even Israeli intelligence. Under such surveillance, how could they have pulled off the attacks? Some reports even suggest that FBI investigations prior to September 11 that might have uncovered the plot were obstructed, further evidence of government complicity.

NORAD, the United States' air defense system, released a time-line of events, specifically in regard to its response to the attacks, that contradicted what the Federal Aviation Administration said. NORAD then contradicted itself as well. It seems that someone is lying (or is just inept). But who, and more importantly, why?

At least five different military drills and war games occurred on September 11, including some that simulated terrorists hijacking air-liners. This meant that NORAD registered as many as twenty-two hijacked airliners that morning. Many of these war games diverted mil-itary aircraft away from the eastern seaboard and sent them to Alaska and Canada. Researchers like Robert M. Bowman wonder why there were so many and whether it was to intentionally sow confusion. After the exercises, only a few fighter planes were left at the ready to protect the East Coast.

What might surprise many readers is that Osama Bin Laden himself initially denied that he or Al-Qaeda had anything to do with the attacks. While it's easy to believe that he would lie, it's odd that he wouldn't take credit for such a "victory." Many believe that the November 2001 video he released in which he takes credit for the attacks was faked or at least mistranslated by the State Department. It's at least interesting to note that the genesis of Al-Qaeda lies with the CIA back during the 1980s when the United States supported Afghani rebels against Soviet invaders. Bin Laden may have met with a CIA agent as recently as July 2001 in Dubai. Conspiracy theorists suggest that he may have been a CIA asset right up to the time of the attacks.

If the attacks were not perpetrated by Bin Laden, then who was behind them? Some say that the real villains were Saudi Arabian—a connection overlooked because of the Bush family's ties with the Saudi royal family. It is certainly true that most of the hijackers were from Saudi Arabia, which provides most of Al-Qaeda's funding. Bin Laden himself is a distant member of the Saudi royal family. Many credit a man named Prince Turki as the driving force behind the initial Al-Qaeda organization and the recruitment of Bin Laden. Today Prince Turki is the Saudi ambassador to the United States.

Of course, it could also have been Pakistan. According to an article in the *Guardian* written by journalist Michael Meacher, Pakistan's intelligence service, the ISI, wired $100,000 to the leader of the hijackers just before the attacks. A Pakistani man, Khalid Sheikh Mohammed, was a known terrorist recruiter and may have helped organize the 9/11 attacks. The ISI has funded and assisted both Al-Qaeda and the Taliban in Afghanistan. It is a powerful, well-organized, and well-funded force in the region. And it owes its origins to the CIA as well.

Who was controlling NORAD????!!! Possibly Men in Black, if they were working with the GREYS!!!

OBVIOUSLY Bin Laden was working with the CIA!!!!!!

EVERYBODY KNOWS THAT!!!!!!!!

REACTION TO THE CONSPIRACY THEORIES

On November 10, 2001, Bush specifically denounced "outrageous conspiracy theories" dealing with the attacks. He couldn't have fanned the flames of the conspiracy theorists more if he had then given a Masonic hand signal and ended his statement with "Hail Satan." That's the way this works. In 2006 he indicated that terrorism itself comes from misinformation and that lies and conspiracy theories create terrorists. At the same time, the State Department launched a campaign to debunk the theories and studies to answer outstanding questions and address the physical analysis of the attacks. That trick never works.

Some conspiracy theorists also claim that counterintelligence techniques have poisoned the well by releasing more outlandish conspiracy theories, such as the so-called No Planers, who believe that the World Trade Center wasn't hit by airplanes at all, those who doctor photographs or video of the event to try to prove a conspiracy, or for that matter, the people who attempt to blame it all on aliens. ←

Whether it was done to them or whether they did it to themselves, the 9/11 Truth organization has fallen in with the Flat Earthers and the tinfoil hat brigade as far as most average Americans are concerned. That's a tough hole to crawl out of. The fact that this is a chapter in this book and not some text on serious ongoing investigations alone says much.

THERE WERE PLANES. But the PART About ALiENS IS TRUE!!!!!!!!!

THE WORLD TRADE CENTER

Built in the early 1970s, the two towers of the World Trade Center (WTC) were the tallest buildings in the world at the time of their construction. Billionaire David Rockefeller (advocate of a New World Order—see Chapter 20) initiated the project. Although the two towers were the ~~most dramatic part of the complex, there were actually seven~~ buildings.

And member of the TriLATERAL Commission- BilderbERg GROUP!!!

Some conspiracy theorists doubt even that the buildings were struck by planes at all. These guys, called no-planers or pod people, think that what struck the twin towers were missiles, remote control drones, or even

UFOs! No-planers get little love from their conspiracy theorist brethren. Outcasts even among fringe thinkers . . . that's got to be a tough life.

Most 9/11 conspiracy theorists call themselves "9/11 Truth." These people have no problem accepting that airplanes hit the World Trade Center. But that's about all of the official story they do accept.

Conspiracy theorists like Mike Berger don't believe the impact of an airplane would cause a huge steel-framed building to disintegrate. According to him, the buildings must have also been rigged with explosives.

Witnesses on the scene, from bystanders outside and television reporters on the scene to workers and firefighters inside who got out before the collapse, say that they heard secondary explosions inside the buildings, much lower than where the planes hit or where the fires raged. The lobby of Tower 2, before the collapse, showed damage as if from an explosion. Video footage of the falling towers shows small explosions below the level of the collapse. Even seismic data from surrounding recording stations provides evidence indicative of explosions low to the ground or underground.

The official story contends that jet fuel from the planes, burning at high temperatures, weakened the internal structure and caused the buildings to collapse. The 9/11 Truth guys point out that many other similarly constructed buildings withstood fires just as hot for far longer without collapsing. In fact, only three steel-framed buildings have collapsed due to internal fires ever—all on September 11, 2001. And 7 WTC doesn't even have the jet fuel excuse. Researchers also point out that watching the video footage from the attacks, one can see most of the jet fuel being consumed outside the buildings in the explosions as the planes struck.

Speaking of Building 7, the fact that it too collapsed in the same fashion is particularly odd since nothing crashed into it. By many accounts, the building exploded, or at the very least explosions came from within it. This building housed, among other things, important files concerning investigations into fraud cases on Wall Street.

I saw explosions on television!!! They're there if you know what to look for!!!!

Housed OTHER FILES TOO!!!

Maybe some important stuff on OIL AND THE GREYS!!!!!

But if the true weapons were bombs and not planes, where did the bombs come from? How did they get there? According to some who worked in the buildings, a number of strange security measures and drills got people out of the complex on numerous occasions shortly before September 11. The bombs could have been brought in then with few people knowing about it. Foreign terrorists could never have organized such a project, but the government could.

Of course, examining the wreckage could provide conclusive proof as to what brought the buildings down. However, officials quickly disposed of the ruins—and in particular the tell-tale steel supports—before this could happen.

THE PENTAGON

Meanwhile, the attack on the Pentagon raises questions of its own. Where is the airplane debris in the initial photos of that attack? Why does the damage seem so different than at the twin towers—or virtually any known airliner crash? The hole the attack made in the building (seen in footage and photos before the wall collapsed) is much smaller than the Boeing 757 that supposedly made it. Some conspiracy theorists believe a missile struck the building. The damage seen at the Pentagon seems more consistent with a missile attack, say a cruise missile, than with an airliner crash. *The government launched a missile at the Pentagon*

If the terrorists attacked with a missile, why cover it up? Unless of course the public was only supposed to *think* it was a plane. Conspiracy theorists suggest the United States military fired the missile.

to cover up something!!!

Even if you can't buy the "No plane . . . missile" theory, there's still a lot about the Pentagon attack that doesn't add up. How could the attackers possibly use the same tactic that they had used against the WTC against the Pentagon an hour and twenty minutes later? It defies credibility that the entire capital, let alone the Pentagon, was not on high alert for wayward airplanes. Why wasn't the plane shot down

Maybe BIGGER THAN ANYTHING BEFORE!???! Pentagon is AN OCCULT SYMBOL!!!!!!

or intercepted? Why didn't any help come from Andrews Air Force Base just ten miles away, particularly when one of the duties of those stationed there is the defense of the nation's capital from air attacks? These questions make conspiracy theorists suspect that the Pentagon attack was allowed to happen, perhaps was even directed from within that very building. The fact that the plane (or missile) struck the Pentagon on a relatively empty and unimportant side, far away from such figures as Donald Rumsfeld, is also strangely convenient.

Supposedly, there was to be yet another airplane strike on 9/11, this time flying into the White House. However, on United Flight 93, the passengers fought back against the hijackers and forced the plane to crash in Shanksville, Pennsylvania. Some conspiracy theorists, such as author David Ray Griffin, contend that the story of the passengers fighting back is false. The airliner, according to Griffin, was shot down by U.S. fighter planes. It certainly is true that Vice President Cheney gave the order to shoot down any planes that were being used as weapons. The debris field from the crash is spread out miles from the impact point, indicating an explosion or two before the crash. So why the cover story? To avoid the bad publicity of having to shoot down one of our own planes?

Passengers on the hijacked airplane made cell phone calls to authorities and to loved ones before they took on the hijackers. This, according to many experts, should have been impossible. At 30,000 feet, the signal would have been intermittent if it existed at all. Even an AT&T spokesperson called it a fluke. Could this be evidence that the story of brave passengers fighting against evil terrorists is a cover-up?

The crash site in Shanksville also raises questions. Those immediately on the scene report nothing more than a small hole in the ground. No debris, no bodies, not even flames. The hole appeared too small for a commercial airliner. A coroner on the scene said that there were no bodies at all. The official report contends that the airplane disintegrated upon impact. Conspiracy theorists cry foul.

YES!!! I tried calling on my cell phone from a plane, and THEY MADE ME PUT IT AWAY!!!!!! PART of the COVER-UP!!

But if Flight 93 didn't crash in Pennsylvania, what happened to it? According to one news report, on the morning of September 11 Flight 93 landed at an airport in Cleveland, Ohio. The passengers were escorted off. This report was later described as a mistake. But then what (if anything) crashed in Shanksville? And where are the (presumably still alive) passengers of Flight 93? Answers do not seem to be forthcoming.

They're being held in a secret location in Wyoming!!!
Along with other hostages captured by aliens!!!!!

THE 9/11 COMMISSION

The similarities between the conspiracy theories surrounding 9/11 and the JFK assassination are many. In both instances, a terrible event happened in broad daylight, and still eyewitness testimony contradicts the official story, which itself was the result of hastily formed conclusions. In both cases, evidence disappeared before it could be properly examined. In both cases, the government assembled an official committee to study the situation, and the study verified with the hasty, original official story in every way, apparently ignoring contradictory evidence.

In the case of the September 11 attacks, the government assembled the 9/11 Commission, a bipartisan group, in response to the growing number of conspiracy believers and to answer the questions of the families of those who died in the attacks. Ironically, the commission did little to address the concerns raised by either group.

Typical!!! Just like the WARREN Commission!!!!

The members did not look into the possibility that a missile, not an airplane, struck the Pentagon. They did not properly investigate what happened at Building 7 of the World Trade Center. They overlooked a great deal of evidence pointing to Al-Qaeda's noninvolvement. The 9/11 Truth Movement points out the significant conflicts of interest of those involved. Max Cleland resigned from the commission, calling it a sham.

Critics of the commission also contend that it was not given enough resources to complete its job. The 9/11 Commission itself stated that it did not intend to assign blame, but that's exactly what the families of those who died and the conspiracy theorists wanted it to do.

Because the commission was COVERING UP!!!!

CONSPIRACY RUNDOWN

PLAUSIBILITY:

7/10. While some of the 9/11 Truth Movement's contentions are pretty outlandish, there do seem to be some disturbing unanswered questions regarding the whole affair.

HIGH STRANGENESS:

2/10. This stuff is all too real.

CONSPIRACY CHECKLIST:

- ☑ Illuminati
- ☐ The Freemasons
- ☑ CIA/intelligence community/the military
- ☐ Aliens
- ☐ The occult
- ☑ The Mafia

FOR MORE INFORMATION::

The 9/11 Conspiracy by James H. Fetzer

The New Pearl Harbor by David Ray Griffin

ON THE WEB:

9/11 Truth: www.911truth.org

Scholars for 9/11 Truth: http://911scholars.org

Loose Change: www.loosechange911.com

9/11 Commission site: www.9-11commission.gov

CONSPIRACY INVESTIGATOR SEARCH TERMS:

Project for a New American Century, War on Terror, Osama Bin Laden, WTC 7, anthrax, Hani Hanjour, NORAD, Sibel Edmonds, Phoenix memo, pod people, ISI

23. WE'VE GOT YOUR NUMBER

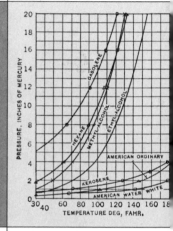

THERE IS A COSMIC SECRET that only some people know—an inner circle of those in the know. The Illuminated, you might call them.

This secret is a glitch in reality, a flaw, or maybe just a signpost put there by some unknowable higher power. Perhaps it's something trying to communicate with us. The message comes in the form of a number. The number 23.

It occurs again and again throughout . . . well, everything, but most noticeably whenever something strange is going on. Those in the know use the number as a sign to others in the know. Twenty-three is the secret high sign of the Illuminati, and whenever you see it, you might just get a glimpse of the Truth.

TWENTY-THREE, THE NUMBER OF COINCIDENCE

There's no conspiracy in this chapter. Not really. This chapter deals with knowledge shared by most conspiracy theorists, researchers, wackos, and nuts.

The conspiracy crowd, a group of people already predisposed toward numerology, have placed a special significance upon the number 23 for years. For some, it's the number of the Illuminati. Or the number of conspiracies. Twenty-three means that something's going on behind the scenes, in the background, just offstage, or in the shadows. It might be something dangerous, or something wonderful, but it's hidden from most people.

That's pretty much the essence of conspiracy theory right there.

What a tinfoil hat wearer will tell you is that 23 crops up in relation to significant events or paranormal occurrences. It's a secret signal used by the Illuminati. It's a number of mystical and cosmic importance.

Author Richard Dawkins coined the term "meme" to describe any idea or concept that transmits itself from person to person, almost

The NUMBER of CHAOS!! It's PART of the FABRIC OF SPACE TIME!!!!!! It's All AROUND us!!

It is!!! PAY ATTENTION HERE!!!

like a virus. In this sense, the so-called 23 Enigma is a meme that's been around for almost fifty years. Most attribute the establishment of the significance of 23 to writer William S. Burroughs, who told a story about a man named Captain Clark in Tangier. Clark bragged to Burroughs that his twenty-three-year sailing career had been entirely without accident. That same day, Clark's boat sank killing him and all aboard. That evening, just as Burroughs thought about the irony, he heard about an airplane that crashed in Florida. The pilot was another Captain Clark and it was Flight 23.

Thus it began. Twenty-three shows up in odd ways once you start looking for it. A statistician will tell you that it's called confirmation bias. If you look for it, you will find it. In other words, if you're on the lookout for 23s, you won't notice all the other numbers; you'll only notice the 23s.

You can take it a step further, as well. When someone claims to see patterns within random data, it's known as apophenia. Give a 23-obsessed apopheniac any number, and he'll come up with 23. For example, April 19 is the date of the Oklahoma City bombing in 1995: 4/19 is 4 + 19 is 23. Area 51 is 23 + 23 + 2 + 3. *OMG!! I NEVER NOTICED that!!! That's all A PART OF IT!!!!!!*

If it sounds like numerology, it should. Twenty-three aficionados use numerology and similar "sciences" to establish the significance of 23. For example, in many occult traditions, the number 5 is very significant. There are five points on a pentagram or pentacle, (or five points on a Pentagon, if you want to be political). Five elements make up the world—water, earth, fire, air, and ether (or metal, if you're east Asian)—and astrologically, there are five planets visible to the naked eye. But 5 is just 2 + 3.

And don't forget, W is the twenty-third letter of the alphabet, with two points down and three points up. Believers love to point out the significance of www (World Wide Web) to the world, and of course the second president George Bush's middle (and thus identifying) initial.

LAW of FIVES!!! You CAN RELATE EVERYthing to 5!!! You just have to LOOK HARDER!!!

Even real math fuels the 23 Engima. Two and three are the first two prime numbers. Twenty-three is also a prime number and the smallest odd prime number that is not also twin prime. A twin prime is a prime number that differs from another prime number by two, the smallest difference possible between two primes… except, of course, for 2 and 3.

And the first six digits of pi, 3.14159, all add up to 23.

MORE EXAMPLES OF THE SIGNIFICANCE OF 23

"Twenty-three skidoo" became popular American slang in the 1920s. It usually means something along the lines of "getting out while the getting's good" or just getting out while there's a chance. No one seems to know the exact origin of the phrase, although some believe that just the number 23 was used as slang around the turn of the century, mean-

DISCORDIANISM

The *Principia Discordia* is a holy book written by someone named Malaclypse the Younger around 1958, detailing the worship of Eris, the goddess of discord. Discordianism, however, is essentially a parody religion and Malaclypse the Younger is actually a man named Greg Hill. In his introduction to the *Principia Discordia* (5th edition) Hill's partner in crime, Kerry Thornley, writes, "If organized religion is the opium of the masses, then disorganized religion is the marijuana of the lunatic fringe." It is an absurdist faith based around the idea that chaos and disharmony are the paths to truth. Or a path to truth. Or just a funny joke. *NOT A JOKE!!!*

Conspiracy theories, the Illuminati, and the number 23 figure prominently in Discordianism, but that's just all part of the joke. It is similar to the even more irreverent and silly Church of the SubGenius—so similar, in fact, that they're virtually the same thing in the eyes of all but the purists. The point of it all, perhaps, is the realization that we all take the world far too seriously, and anything and everything needs a little fun poked at it from time to time.

ing to get away or clear out. ("Skidoo" or "skiddoo" might come from "skedaddle.")

Human cells have 46 chromosomes, arranged in two pairs of 23. Twenty-three chromosomes come from each parent. It's commonly said that it takes twenty-three seconds for blood to circulate through the human body. *Julius Caesar was stabbed 23 times!!!!!!!!*

The Twenty-Third Psalm in the Bible is the most quoted and best known of the Psalms. "Yea, though I walk through the valley of the shadow of death…"

Twenty-three expressed as 2 divided by 3 equals .666, the number of the Beast.

Dagobert II, one of the Merovingian kings (see Chapter 3), was murdered on December 23.

Remember the Dogon from Chapter 16 who believe that visitors came in ancient times from the Sirius star system? Sirius A has a luminosity of 23.5. The dog days of summer, when the Dog Star Sirius first rises from behind the sun in the constellation of Orion, begin on July 23. At least in some places. July 23 to August 23 is known as "rotting-month" in Sweden and Finland because of the high risk of food spoilage during the high temperatures.

On that theme, in the Kabbalah's Tree of Life, the Twenty-Third path is associated with the Hanged Man tarot card. And in the *I-Ching*, which is a Chinese divinatory system, Hexagram 23 means "All breaks apart." Twenty-three, it seems, can be a real danger.

In telegrapher's code, 23 means "break the line."

Twenty-three axioms open Euclid's *Geometry*. DNA bonding irregularities happen at every twenty-third angstrom.

And it gets sillier. The bomber in the movie *Airport* sat in seat 23. And in the follow-up, *Airport 77*, the flight number is 23. More UFO sightings are reported on July 23 than any other day of the year. One of the Blue Meenies in the Beatles film *Yellow Submarine* wears a shirt with the number 23 on it. There are twenty-three buildings on the

Original moon landing was at 23.63 degrees east!

Next one was at 23.42 degrees west!!

Microsoft campus in Redmond, Washington. And the number features prominently on many episodes of the *X-Files*.

The thing to take away from all this is not the importance of the number 23 but how important conspiracists *think* it is. Look for 23 in recent movies (not to mention *The Number 23* with Jim Carrey), for example, as the apartment number of a character. Is this just a coincidence? Maybe. Is it the director winking at us? Maybe. Some people know that others look for 23s, so they put them out there to be found.

And now that you know, you're a part of the conspiracy too. *We* are the Illuminati.

Maybe the author's GIVING SOMETHING AWAY!!!
Maybe he is PART of Them?????!!!

CONSPIRACY RUNDOWN

PLAUSIBILITY:
1/10. It's all a coincidence. Or is it? No, it really is.

HIGH STRANGENESS:
3/10. It's not strange at all that conspiracy nuts developed
something like this.

CONSPIRACY CHECKLIST:
- ☑ Illuminati
- ☐ The Freemasons
- ☐ CIA/intelligence community/the military
- ☐ Aliens
- ☑ The occult
- ☐ The Mafia

FOR MORE INFORMATION:

The *Principia Discordia* by Malaclypse the Younger

The *Cosmic Trigger* by Robert Anton Wilson

ON THE WEB:

The 23 Enigma: www.afgen.com/numbr23b.html

Discordianism: www.discordian.com

The Church of the SubGenius: www.subgenius.com

CONSPIRACY INVESTIGATOR SEARCH TERMS:

23 Enigma, 23 skidoo, Illuminatus!, *Principia Discordia*, Church of
the SubGenius

24. ULTRA SECRET

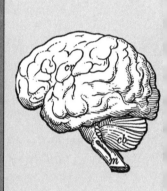

IF YOU'RE A CONSPIRACY THEORIST worthy of your secret decoder ring, you've got an opinion about the Central Intelligence Agency. And chances are that opinion is either:

1. The CIA is a sinister, almost supernaturally powerful organization that is behind every significant event in world history since the late 1940s. They can't be stopped.
2. The CIA is a nefarious group of bunglers that try to manipulate world events but end up picking the wrong side in every conflict and make things worse every time they stick their noses in.

BECAUSE THEY'RE NOT!!! They're smarter than you think!!! They're following me!!!!!!!!!

(You will notice that there is no third option, stating that the CIA is an efficient force for good in the world, or even a fourth, wherein the CIA is a government intelligence agency doing its best. That is not how conspiracy theorists think.)

Regardless of which describes your own feelings best, the story of the MKULTRA program has something for you.

MIND KONTROL ULTRA

During World War II, the OSS began experimenting with different methods to improve interrogation techniques. This research continued after the war, led by the OSS's successor, the CIA. By the 1950s, however, the idea evolved from getting a prisoner to talk to getting subjects to do whatever they were told. In other words, mind control. They called this experimental program MKULTRA. This may sound like something from a science fiction movie, but it's not. It's an established fact and one that the CIA has admitted was real.

At the end of World War II and for a short time thereafter, the United States helped smuggle Nazi scientists out of Germany and into the United States. This program, known as Operation Paperclip, led to many different research projects. The CIA even pursued some of the

It also led to the SECRET NAZI BASES!!! There's one in New Mexico and one in Idaho!!! I know someone who has a friend who knows someone who's behavioral modification techniques used by these nefarious researchers. *SEEN IT!!!!!!!* using experiments begun in the dark confines of concentration camps. Perhaps driven by rumors of Communist mind-control development, programs with names like Project Chatter and Project Artichoke took up brainwashing research where the Nazis had left off. It was, in fact, an escalating mind-control cold war.

In 1953, the most infamous and far-reaching program, MKULTRA, began on orders from the then CIA director Allen Dulles. The scientists involved with MKULTRA weren't just interested in interrogation of prisoners but in real mind control—the mass behavioral modification of foreign leaders, enemy troops, and even civilians.

Under the direction of psychiatrist and chemist Sidney Gottlieb, MKULTRA used drugs, electroshock therapy, radiation, subsonic transmissions, low-frequency radio waves, sensory deprivation, and various psychological techniques to affect behavior modification. And, according to author Kenn Thomas, they even placed mechanical implants *I was in the hospital once,* directly in the brains of test subjects. They were interested in lowering *and they used RADIO* victims' will, erasing memories, calming aggression, heightening aggres- *WAVES on me!!! They* sion, manipulating actions, and even creating so-called sleeper agents *said they didn't, but I* who lived normal lives until "activated" and compelled into service. *know they did!!!!!*

While working on MKULTRA projects, Gottlieb became known as the "Black Sorcerer" and the "Dirty Trickster." He served as the mastermind behind some of the outlandish schemes to eliminate or discredit Fidel Castro, including spraying the leader's belongings with LSD or putting chemicals in his shoes that would make his beard fall out (see Chapter 10 for more information).

To the CIA and the military's experimental drug programs (described in Chapter 21), MKULTRA mixed in hypnosis and sensory deprivation to create a synthesis of suggestibility for its targets. Its experimental targets were often unaware of what was going on. CIA scientists frequently used military personnel, prisoners, and mental patients as subjects as well as unwitting university volunteers. They sometimes conducted their tests in other countries, particularly in areas where there was little chance of intervention.

The CIA scientists discovered some people possessed a far greater vulnerability to their mind-control and brainwashing techniques than others. These subjects, according to John Gittinger, an MKULTRA veteran, can receive hypnotic instructions over the television or radio. Memories can be erased, suppressed, altered, or replaced.

MKULTRA officially ended in 1963, but immediately afterward the MKSEARCH program began and carried on the same studies with the same goals. MKSEARCH also investigated various types of non-conventional weapons, including biological and chemical, as well as odder things like using radar waves to assault the minds of the enemy.

MKSEARCH ended in 1973, but most conspiracy researchers believe that behavior modification experiments continue to this day.

DO AS I SAY, NOT AS I DO

If the CIA did develop the means to control people's minds, what has it done with this dangerous power? You won't be surprised to hear that the conspiracy crowd has plenty of answers to that question.

As mentioned in Chapter 8, witnesses describe notebook-scribbling assassin Sirhan Sirhan as being in a trance when he shot Robert Kennedy. Some theorize that he had been hypnotized, perhaps drugged, and possibly was the subject of behavioral modification. The infamous girl in the polka dot dress served as his "handler," perhaps the one administering hypnotic suggestions, giving him drugs or—who knows?—using a remote control device for the implant in his brain.

The granddaddy of all MK assassins, Lee Harvey Oswald, was perhaps given an electrode implant while in the military, or perhaps while in Russia (depending on whom he was working for). Authors Kenn Thomas and Lincoln Lawrence contend that Oswald and his killer, Jack Ruby, were mind-controlled assassins created by the government.

Like OSWALD!!!! OR Sirhan Sirhan!!???

Yes!!! That's what I thought!!! They WERE using him!!!!!!

Reportedly, MKULTRA tests and LSD experiments were conducted at the Atsugi Naval Air Base in Japan where Oswald was stationed in 1957.

Infamous murder-instigator Charles Manson appeared to use some of the same techniques to control his "family." Conspiracy maven Mae Brussell contends that Manson worked for an intelligence agency and his actions were all part of an elaborate experiment. Charles "Tex" Watson, one of the Manson Family, wrote in his prison memoir that the LSD Manson gave to the Family while convincing them of his insane, apocalyptic vision ("Helter Skelter") came from the CIA. Manson himself was in Vacaville prison at the time Project MKULTRA was experimenting on inmates there.

Patty Hearst, the granddaughter of publishing tycoon William Randolph Hearst, was kidnapped in 1974 by a radical group calling itself the Symbionese Liberation Army. In very short order, Hearst had become a brainwashed accomplice to the SLA's crimes, taking the name Tania. Was the Symbionese Liberation Army using MKULTRA techniques? SLA leader Donald DeFreeze, like Manson, had been in Vacaville prison when the CIA was conducting its research there. Were they both taught the techniques and instructed to go forth and create more mind-controlled zombies?

Candy Jones worked in the 1940s and 1950s as a New York fashion model. However, after she began exhibiting wild mood swings and other problems, a psychiatrist hypnotized her and discovered that she had been trained in an MKULTRA mind-control program. Apparently, Jones—using the name Arlene—operated as a clandestine courier in Asia while she toured with the USO. With each mission completed, she would remember none of what happened. Even memories of painful torture were suppressed. This was not just a case of imaginative scenarios recovered by hypnosis. Jones eventually discovered a passport with the name Arlene Grant, showing her with a dark wig and makeup.

Even Timothy McVeigh, perpetrator of the Oklahoma City bombing, claimed to have a microchip implanted in him by the military.

They tried to kill Ford!!! WHO WAS ON THE WARREN COMMISSION!!!!! PART of a bigger thing??????!!

And nobody investigated!!!!

TYPICAL!!!

The CIA contends that it only experimented with the various forms of mind control in order to recognize its use by the enemies of the state. Purely defensive, of course. While the CIA scientists were certainly looking for the ability to directly control the actions of a subject, no conclusive evidence exists that they ever succeeded in creating reliable mind-control techniques.

But there's every reason for a conspiracy theorist to believe that the Manchurian candidate is a reality. The world has a long history, it turns out, of mind-controlled assassins. The very word "assassin" comes from a sect of Shia Muslims around A.D. 1090 called the Hashshashin, who gain the name from their use of the drug hashish. These holy killers, under the influence of drugs, were convinced that if they murdered for Allah, they would be granted special access to heaven.

Interestingly, the Knights Templar could have come into contact with the original Hashshashin. (It's a stretch, but no larger a stretch than most conspiracy theorists make all the time.) They could have adopted some of their techniques or just simply learned the value of blood-thirsty killers under your complete control. Once you have the Templars involved, it sets off a chain reaction of historical conspiracy links.

So who's really behind all of this? According to author Doug Moench, the Freemasons are one of the primary driving forces behind the CIA. And if Masonry's inner circle were really the Illuminati of old, the ability to send mind-controlled infiltrators into other governments and disrupt or even subvert them from within . . . well, that would be right up their alley. And that's exactly what the most extreme fringe of conspiracy theory believes.

No!!! It happened!!!!! This explains SO MUCH!!!!!

YES!!!!!

DRINKING THE KOOL-AID

On November 18, 1978, in a small compound in the South American jungles of Guyana called Jonestown, 913 members of the so-called People's Temple died in a mass suicide/murder. Some conspiracy theorists, such as Fiona Steel, believe that Jonestown was in fact an MKULTRA test site. After the official end of the MKULTRA program, the CIA continued to use cults as testing grounds for their processes. The program didn't actually end at all. And the infamous Jim Jones, leader of the People's Temple, may have in fact been an intelligence agent.

Jones was a "faith healer" charlatan and an insane cult leader, but was he yet another in a long string of lone nuts? Did he have connections to more powerful organizations? According to those who knew him, while he lived for a time in Brazil, Jones was involved in military intelligence. On the one hand, he claimed to be a Marxist seeking to create a socialist utopia, but on the other hand he raised money for Richard Nixon's presidential campaign, and one of his advisors worked for the CIA's anti-Communist militant group, Unita, located in Angola.

AnothER NIXON coNNEctioN!!! Nixon hAd A hANd iN EVERything!!!!!

REMOTE VIEWING

MKULTRA wasn't the strangest clandestine government program. That honor would have to go to the Stargate Project. Stargate was the government's attempt to use psychics to spy on the enemy through a technique called remote viewing, as described in documents declassified in the 1990s. Like MKULTRA, it shows that the government is willing to explore all avenues of research, and also like MKULTRA, it came about because the United States was terrified that its enemies might make a breakthrough in some odd but dangerous field before it could.

In the Stargate Project, as many as fourteen different laboratories had agents using clairvoyance or out-of-body techniques to gather information at a distance. These psychics also practiced precognition, allowing them to predict enemy movements and actions before they happened. These techniques may have even been used during the Iranian hostage crisis of 1979–1981.

The actual usefulness and accuracy of the information provided by Stargate remains in question, and the government says that the project is now defunct.

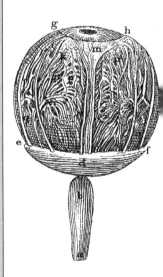

I'VE tried this but it's hard!!!!! MAybE that's what those drugs WERE USED foR!!!

Even while the People's Temple was still located in the United States, Jones used uniformed armed guards to keep his followers in line. Those in the cult lost all of their money and if they disobeyed in any way faced beatings and abuse. When this leaked to the press, Jones moved his cult to Guyana—with the help of the United States Embassy. Once out of the country, all pretense of being a religious cult seemed to fall away. Jonestown, as his "utopia" came to be called, was really little more than a slave labor camp. Investigators later discovered vast amounts of drugs on the site and learned from meticulous records that all of the people there were forced to take them every day. These drugs were the same that project MKULTRA had been studying in its experiments: sodium pentothal, chloral hydrate, Demerol, thallium, and others. The tortures the people in Jonestown experienced were like some of the more extreme measures MKULTRA had developed to brainwash subjects, using research gained from Nazi concentration camps.

Because the Nazis were still teaching them how to torture!!!

Just as disturbing, evidence shows that by the end, almost all of the people in Jonestown were black, and those running the camp were white. Many have speculated that at least some of what occurred in Jonestown was racially motivated: a concentration camp for blacks rather than Jews. The findings of Senator Frank Church in 1975 hearings into the program suggested that African Americans were among the "test populations" of Project MKULTRA. Most of those in Jonestown were also women, and there were many children in the compound as well. These too are now believed to be groups that MKULTRA scientists were particularly interested in experimenting upon.

Before the massacre, when the families of those in Jonestown complained to the government about mistreatment and forced drug use, Congressman Leo Ryan went to Guyana, despite resistance from the State Department. At Ryan's side were a number of reporters (including, strangely enough, Tim Reiterman, who had covered the Patty Hearst story for the *San Francisco Examiner*) as well as Richard Dwyer, a U.S. Embassy official later revealed to be a CIA agent.

At the airstrip in Guyana, Ryan and four of the reporters were shot and killed. Witnesses described the killers as "glassy eyed," "mechanically walking zombies," and "devoid of any emotion." Then the killing started at Jonestown itself.

Although the media reported at the time that the 913 people killed at Jonestown had all committed suicide by drinking Kool-Aid laced with cyanide, later evidence suggests that most, in fact, were murdered, either through injection, strangulation, or other violent means. Many tried to flee and were hunted down in the jungle, their bodies brought back to Jonestown. Jones supposedly shot himself, but the gun he reportedly killed himself with lay far away from his body.

Not a suicide!!! Who killed him? MKULTRA, obviously!!!!

Did Jones actually die at all? The man was known to frequently use body doubles (a common spook tactic). There seemed to have been some question as to the true identity of the corpse recovered there.

Author Michael Meiers contends that Jonestown was an experiment conceived and run by Dr. Laurence Laird Layton of the Army's Chemical Warfare Division as much as by Jones. Layton had reportedly been one of Jones's advisors from the beginning—an odd choice if Jones *was* creating a socialist cult.

It's also worth mentioning that Congressman Ryan was an outspoken critic of the CIA and had legislation pending to make the agency far more transparent. After Ryan's death, the legislation failed.

The Mafia- and CIA-linked P2 (Masonic) lodge, first mentioned in Chapter 1, also operated in that very area in South America, right around the same time as the People's Temple. Researcher Robert Serling maintains that the Solar Temple, a cult not unlike the People's Temple, was used by both the CIA and P2 as an intelligence-gathering front. (The Order of the Solar Temple also claimed to be the modern incarnation of the Knights Templar, just for good measure.) Like the People's Temple, the Solar Temple ended in mass "suicide" in 1994 in a compound in Switzerland. Further investigation showed that few of those people actually killed themselves. Just like Jonestown. A bit chilling, really.

Masons again!!! I thought so!!

∴ THEY'RE EVERYWHERE!!!!

Some theorists, like John Judge, speculate that many camps like Jonestown were still in operation in the 1980s and even later in remote areas of the world such as the Philippines and even still in Guyana. Some fascist camps in Chile under dictator Augusto Pinochet are similar to Jonestown. They also appear all-too reminiscent of the camps in Nazi Germany, where the dictatorship ruled with the support of Joseph Mengele and Martin Bormann. Full circle indeed.

A VISION FOR THE WORLD

An evangelical, right-wing charitable organization called World Vision has worked as a CIA front for decades, according to writer Fiona Steel. World Vision might have been the conduit through which Jim Jones communicated with his CIA superiors while in Guyana (they visited many times). After the massacre, World Vision worked to repopulate Jonestown with mercenaries from Laos that had worked for the CIA during the Vietnam War. But that's not all. World Vision provides us with links to two other well-known possible MKULTRA operatives.

Mark David Chapman, the assassin of John Lennon, and John Hinkley, who shot at Ronald Reagan, at first blush have nothing in common other than being lone nuts obsessed with pop culture icons. But Hinkley's father served as an official in World Vision, and Chapman also worked for the organization. Hinkley's father was a close friend of then vice president George Bush Sr., who had been director of the CIA. Witnesses who saw the men after committing their crimes describe them as glassy-eyed and in a trance. Perhaps hypnotized. Both had copies of *Catcher in the Rye* with them—a detail that would be insignificant except for its sheer improbability. Many conspiracists speculate that the book is some kind of hypnotic trigger used in MKULTRA conditioning. (In the movie *Conspiracy Theory*, Mel Gibson's character, a former MKULTRA subject, is obsessed with the book. Interestingly, author J.D. Salinger worked in military intelligence during World War II.)

Who else was behind World Vision?? Sounds like the Templars!!! It's all connected!!!! PEOPLE DON'T UNDERSTAND!!!!

An OSS-CIA-MKULTRA agent!!???

If what some conspiracy researchers say about World Vision is true, then the organization was and perhaps still is deeply involved in MKULTRA experimentation (and implementation) all over the world.

THE TINFOIL HABERDASHERY

This book has alluded many times to tinfoil hats. Now we finally learn what conspiracy-minded people are putting tinfoil on their heads *for.* They're afraid of the CIA mind-control rays. HAARP (see Chapter 19) might be sending low-frequency radio waves. But secret superimposed signals could be coming from many other sources, like cell phones, TV satellite transmissions, LED clocks, kitchen appliances, or even those new fluorescent energy-saving light bulbs. And even if you're not ready to be afraid of your toaster, there's always ultrasonics to worry about.

I'VE got foil COVERS on All my APPliANCES to stop THem!!!

Ultrasonic technology supposedly allows someone to change the brainwave pattern of a target using nearly undetectable transmissions. The government (or others) could use this for crowd control or subconscious suggestions incorporated into advertising on television or radio. It could even be used over the phone.

As interesting (or terrifying) as that is, the cutting edge mind-control method for all discerning conspirators appears to be microwaves.

For example, the Sierra Nevada Corporation announced in 2008 that it had developed the MEDUSA: Mob Excess Deterrent Using Silent Audio. Meant to be a crowd-control device, this weapon uses microwave audio transmissions to place sounds or even messages in the minds of its targets. Detractors claim that such a weapon would kill anyone who attempted to use it.

No!! Stolen from hostile AlieNS with the GREys' help!!!!

Where did all this amazing technology come from? Some say that government scientists reverse engineered it from the devices gained after the UFO crash at Roswell. Others claim that while it is alien in nature, it was given to mankind willingly. Still others postulate that mind-control technology is in the hands of extraterrestrials visiting Earth.

JFK WAS COVERING UP!! Hoover too!!!!! And they're dead!!!!!
• WATCH OUT!!!

MK-FALLOUT

Thank goodness MKULTRA and mind control are all well behind us. Stuff from the fifties, the sixties, maybe even the seventies—that's all past. Right?

Former CIA agent Victor Marchetti says that black programs like MKULTRA still exist today, with different names. And they're deeper undercover. But if the CIA has been trying to create mind-controlled assassins for fifty years, where are they today? Presumably, these people are still around. Perhaps the homeless people you see shuffling down the street mumbling to themselves are in fact MKULTRA subjects, now cast aside. In 1979, a congressional aide said that there were "120 white brainwashed assassins out from Jonestown awaiting their trigger word to pick up their hit." And that's just from Jonestown.

Remember the Unabomber? While the infamous Ted Kaczynski attended Harvard in the late 1950s, he participated in psychological studies that were a part of the MKULTRA program. Look where that got us. How many more Kaczynskis did the CIA inadvertently create?

Writer David McGowan contends that many modern serial killers may have been produced, intentionally or unintentionally, by MKULTRA or similar programs. In theory, such murderous terrors would be intentionally created to produce an atmosphere of fear in order to gain public acceptance of a stronger police state. Such tactics were supposedly used by the CIA in Southeast Asia during the Vietnam War to sow fear among the populace. Serial killers like Henry Lee Lucas—the only death row inmate to be spared death by then Texas governor George Bush—may simply be mind-controlled assassins gone "off the reservation." McGowan's research also suggests the chilling theory that mind-control techniques today may be used to supply the rich and powerful with sex slaves, some of them even children.

Other theorists ponder whether projects like MKULTRA could be going on in Iraq and other parts of the world even today. This could be an explanation of some of the strange goings on in places like Abu

Did they make clones of Kaczynski???!!!!!

Ghraib prison where inmates were subjected to bizarre and humiliating treatment and torture, evocative of Jonestown.

But all that aside, we can look at how the various events and people linked to the mysterious MKULTRA program have shaped our world today. The deaths of the Kennedys put the country more firmly in the hands of the military-industrial complex. The crazed and violent activities of the Manson Family and the SLA changed the way that people looked at the youth movements of the late sixties and early seventies. Despite the fact that Manson was no hippie, and his politics tended far right rather than far left, he and his Family convinced middle America that "drugged out hippies" were up to no good. Likewise, the SLA made the nation terrified of left-wing, radical black organizations. The People's Temple and other dangerous fringe cults used brainwashing to control their members and teach us that such things happen when you stray too far from the norm or dare to be a nonconformist. Slaughterhouses like Jonestown are the inevitable result of socialism. Lone nuts and serial killers make us worry about dangerous individuals while turning toward the protective embrace of the state.

Despite the fact that Project MKULTRA found its way into the public spotlight in 1975, when it was brought to the attention of Congress by the Church Committee, charged with looking into intelligence activities, CIA director Richard Helms destroyed the vast majority of files and records about the program before they could be made public. The government now acts as though MKULTRA was a silly dalliance into pseudoscience and that nothing ever came of it, of course. If people who did a lot of drugs in the sixties claim to hear voices in their heads, it's simply because they're crazy, not because of any actual, successful government project.

Which, conspiracy believers will tell you, is the perfect cover story.

Iraq War fought because Saddam Hussein was ALLIED WITH ALIENS????!!! That would explain the real weapons of mass destruction!!!

OMG!!!!! THIS IS SO IMPORTANT!!!

Helms has been in the pay of the Masons for years!!!

CONSPIRACY RUNDOWN

PLAUSIBILITY:

7/10. MKULTRA is real. It's only the details that are in dispute.

HIGH STRANGENESS:

8/10. *The Manchurian Candidate* for real? Mind-control rays? Sleeper agents? Zombie assassins? All very strange.

CONSPIRACY CHECKLIST:

- ☑ Illuminati
- ☑ The Freemasons
- ☑ CIA/intelligence community/the military
- ☑ Aliens
- ☑ The occult
- ☑ The Mafia

FOR MORE INFORMATION:

Programmed to Kill: The Politics of Serial Murder by David McGowan

Mind Control, World Control by Jim Keith

Mind Control, Oswald, and JFK by Kenn Thomas

ON THE WEB:

Primer on mind control: www.educate-yourself.org/mc

Make your own tinfoil hat: www.zapatopi.net/afdb/

Study on the effectiveness of tinfoil hats: http://people.csail.mit.edu/rahimi/helmet/

Remote viewing research: www.farsight.org

CONSPIRACY INVESTIGATOR SEARCH TERMS:

MKULTRA, tinfoil hat, Sierra Nevada Corporation, ultrasonic mind control, Jonestown, Solar Temple, Charles Manson, Patty Hearst, Sidney Gottlieb, José Manuel Rodriguez Delgado, neuroelectronics

25. MEN IN BLACK

YESTERDAY YOU SAW something strange. A bright light in the sky that moved in an inexplicable manner, changing direction and speed more than once. Then it got closer to you and you realized it wasn't an airplane. It was shaped like a long oval and had multiple lights on it. Then, in a flash, it disappeared.

This morning, you sit thinking about the event as you drink your coffee. You check the paper and the TV to see if anyone else saw anything odd. There's a knock on the door. Three men are on your doorstep. In front of your house is a big black Cadillac—a ten- or even twenty-year-old model, which is strange because it looks brand new. The men are all dressed in black suits and wear black hats. There's something else about them, but you can't quite put your finger on it. They look foreign, but for the life of you, you can't place what nationality they might be.

"We have a few questions," one of them says, his voice a low monotone. "We're from the government." The men question you about what you saw. Though you don't invite them in, they're inside your house. The men all talk in the same strange, toneless manner. They might even have an odd accent, but you're not sure. And it's hard to tell them apart. One picks an apple from the bowl on your table as if he's never seen one before. Finally, as you describe your experience of the day before, one of them interrupts you with a vague threat, warning that you should never speak of this to anyone, ever. And then they leave.

Many people report having had an experience much like this. Who are these men? Are they really from the government? Why are they so odd? Are they aliens? They're called the Men in Black, and they are almost always associated with UFO sightings. They never look like Will Smith or Tommy Lee Jones.

COMMONALITIES OF THE STRANGE

The first UFO-related Men in Black (MIBs) come from a story told by Albert K. Bender, editor of a UFO publication called the *Space Review*

I SAW MEN IN BLACK ONCE!!! I followed them, but they got AWAY!!! I don't know who they WERE AfTER!!

and head of an organization he called the International Flying Saucer Bureau (IFSB). In 1953, he claims that three very strange men dressed in black suits visited him and warned him not to spread any information about UFOs. Albert and his pals felt they had cornered the market on the truth behind UFOs—that they were spaceships from another planet.

Well, it was 1953. Maybe it sounded groundbreaking then.

In any case, the visit shook Albert so much that he stopped publication of the *Space Review*, dissolved the IFSB, and warned other UFO buffs to be very cautious. The last issue of the *Space Review* said that "the investigation of the flying saucer mystery and the solution is approaching its final stages." Whatever that means.

Ever since then, MIBs have entered the common lore of UFOs. Just as everyone seems to know that UFOs are often saucer- or cigar-shaped, or that they often knock out electrical appliances when they come near, everyone seems also to know that strange men might come knocking at your door after you have a UFO sighting.

The men usually wear black suits that are somewhat out of style, although the clothing appears new. They often wear fedora-like hats and dark sunglasses, even at night. They drive in big black sedans, usually Cadillacs or Lincolns. Like their suits, the cars are older models but look like they just rolled off the production line.

Men in Black are often described as "foreign." Some people say they appear Asian, sometimes Indian, or even described as "gypsies," but everyone agrees the MIBs are "not from around here." Apparently because of these allegations, in 1948 Air Force chief of staff General Carl Spaatz told a press conference that "there is no truth to the rumor that the flying saucers are from Spain, or that they are piloted by Spaniards."

Sometimes witnesses stress the MIB's long fingers or oddly shaped eyes. Their use of language is strange, sometimes very formal and then suddenly very casual, though their slang is wildly out of date. They can be secretive and distant but also awkward and inappropriate.

THE ONES I SAW WERE IN A TOWN CAR! And I couldn't see the license plates!!!! When I looked at the car I got a headache!!!!

Occasionally MIBs attempt to pass themselves off as Air Force or intelligence officers. They've also claimed to be census takers, journalists, or even Bible salesmen. Other times they make no pretense at all.

In most cases, they ask people about their UFO sighting or other odd experiences. (A few people have reported MIB encounters without ever having seen anything strange beforehand, showing that even the Men in Black get the wrong address sometimes.) Most of the time, they seem eager to learn anything they can about the experience, almost as if they're hunting for UFOs. Many other encounters end with the MIBs warning the subjects not to tell anyone else what they experienced. In all cases, the MIBs appear to know a great deal about whom they are speaking to. But who are they? There are many theories.

They're SCARY!!!!

I tried to take a picture of the ones I saw, but the picture on my camera phone didn't come out!!!!!!

THEORY 1: GOVERNMENT MEN

The Men in Black might be exactly who they (or at least some of them) claim to be: agents of the FBI, CIA, or NSA, looking into the UFO phenomenon. Or they might be in the military, investigating threats to national security. They could even be from some other, even more classified intelligence agency created to look into alien threats or other paranormal phenomena. Author Stephen Wagner believes they may be from the Office of Scientific Investigation and Research, a top-secret government program that has been around since the 1940s.

Lending credence to this theory is the fact that Men in Black (in modern times) seem to be an almost exclusively American phenomenon. On the other hand, they might not have any special connection to UFOs. Perhaps they work for a clandestine organization that has no intention of revealing itself. The odd behavior reported by those who have encountered MIBs makes it hard to believe that these are real agents or officers of the government.

Of course, that kind of thing can be exaggerated. Albert Bender's story, for instance, got stranger as time went on. Some of those on the

They're NOT!!!

They're from SOMEWHERE

• ELSE!!!! →

MOTHMAN

For a few months in the late 1960s, Point Pleasant, West Virginia, certainly did not live up to its name. When investigator John Keel arrived, there were numerous encounters with MIBs as well as UFO sightings, poltergeists, strange voices on late-night phone calls as well as from radios and TVs, and the frequent appearance of something now called the Mothman. Named by the press after a campy Batman villain, the real Mothman was nothing to take lightly. An eight-foot-tall figure of shadowy darkness with glowing red eyes, more like a massive bird than a moth, this strange creature/apparition was seen at night as well as in broad daylight by a number of disparate and often quite reliable witnesses. Those who saw it frequently experienced brief paralysis, terrible headaches, and even physical damage to their eyes. Many believe that creatures like this are seen as harbingers of some great catastrophe. And maybe they're right. On December 15, 1967, the Silver Bridge near Point Pleasant collapsed, killing forty-six people. After that time, sightings of the Mothman, MIBs, and other phenomena stopped.

THE MOTHMAN WAS A PROPHET!!!

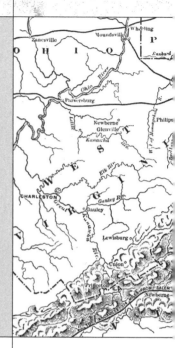

more paranoid end of the pool suggest that the more outlandish MIB stories are fabricated, spread to discourage serious belief in them.

THEORY 2: EXTRATERRESTRIALS

Maybe the Men in Black are so interested in UFOs because they *are* aliens. This would explain their odd, almost inhuman behavior, their unfamiliarity with seemingly common objects, and their strange appearance. The MIBs, then, are attempting to cover up their own existence, and that of their fellows. They are the Away Team, in *Star Trek* parlance.

Some have speculated that perhaps MIBs are from a different race of aliens, hostile to the alien Greys that are piloting the flying saucers (or cigar-shaped craft, or triangular vehicles, or whatever). Or maybe they are artificial creations of the aliens, like robots or androids, made to look (almost) like humans.

In one reported encounter, an MIB was offered some Jell-O and tried to drink it as if it were liquid. In another, the MIB reacted to a ballpoint pen as if it were some kind of mysterious treasure. Some MIBs have been known to giggle unnervingly. Imperfect mimicry indeed. If you can fly across the galaxy at faster-than-light speeds, you'd think you could do a better job of seeming human.

Not funny!!!!!

THIS IS NOT A JOKE!!!!!!!

The alien hypothesis would explain why some people have said MIBs don't always talk with their mouths. It might even explain how they know things a normal person couldn't know, including details of a subject's personal life, or even what will happen in the future. These kinds of psychic powers are more easily attributed to extraterrestrials than to, say, FBI agents with poor social skills.

THEORY 3: ULTRATERRESTRIALS

Investigator John Keel has had many encounters with MIBs and believes that they are something quite inexplicable. Literally. Using the term "ultraterrestrial," he thinks that they come from some indescribable "elsewhere." They are, almost by definition, something we cannot under-stand. Thus all the very odd behavior. And Keel knows odd behavior.

In 1966, he visited Point Pleasant, West Virginia, where he inves-tigated many different strange occurrences, MIB encounters being just one among many. Others included UFOs, animal mutilations, strange phone calls, time discrepancies, poltergeist phenomena, and mysterious flying creatures with glowing eyes. Not only did the people of Point Pleasant get phone calls from MIBs, receive (badly) written notes from them, and have encounters with them, they even learned one's name: Indrid Cold. Which, you have to admit, is a pretty creepy name.

This is probably just a disguise for his ALIEN NAME!!

Ultimately, Keel concluded that all these things, including the MIBs, were the result of some kind of crossing over between what we think of as reality and some other reality. The MIBs are an alien "other" trying to communicate. Thus the term "ultraterrestrial," a creature not just from some other planet but from *somewhere else*. Could he be right? If so, then Point Pleasant was some kind of temporary window into a completely different realm.

This theory capitalizes on the indescribable eeriness of the Men in Black. We react to MIBs with fear and paranoia because on some instinctual level we realize that they are not a normal part of our universe. These strange encounters are produced by our own minds attempting to interpret input we were never meant to experience. UFOs, MIBs, and other strange phenomena are all symptoms of the same thing—some kind of confluence with a plane, level, or frequency of reality that is not our own. We can no more understand them or explain their actions than an insect could explain ours.

Keel's hypothesis synchs up with the fact that if one stretches the definition, MIB encounters have been around far longer than the modern UFO situation. At various times in history—particularly the Middle Ages—mysterious strangers in black garb showed up at various times, saying and doing odd things. These were typically interpreted at the time as being encounters with demonic entities, or the Devil himself. Around the time of the Black Death in Europe, witnesses told of strange men dressed in black spreading the disease. So how long have the MIBs been with us, and what are they up to? Perhaps it is impossible to know.

That PROVES IT!!!! They were connected to the TEMPLARS!!

BLACK HELICOPTERS

Although witnesses associate MIBs with large black automobiles, it seems that in today's modern society the harried Man in Black on the go needs a way to get around faster. Reports of unmarked black helicopters have been around for the past forty years. These strange craft sometimes appear to be military vehicles, while others look like civilian helicopters. In all cases, they have no identifying markings. Sightings of these helicopters coincide with cattle mutilations and strange disappearances of animals and people. At least one report of a black helicopter has it turning into a classic flying saucer and back again, like a Transformer.

Some tinfoil hat wearers say that black helicopters are the vehicles of choice for the New World Order (see Chapter 19). They are the air wing of the Illuminati, piloted by foreign troops who seek to take away American freedoms.

It's possible that the mysterious men in the black helicopters are entirely different from the MIBs of UFO lore. It's as dangerous, sometimes, to mix conspiracies as it is to mix medications. Still, some think the Illuminati are in league with the aliens, and the Men in Black—some extraterrestrial and some all-too-human agents of sinister organizations—work for both in their scheme to take over the world.

THE ULTIMATE EXPRESSION OF PARANOIA

Doug Moench subtly suggests that perhaps the MIBs simply represent our own fears rather than anything real. In the 1950s, for example, when people imagined dangerous Commies around every corner and foreign powers infiltrating our society, the MIBs appeared to be mysterious outsiders asking too many questions and fueling our paranoia. In the nineties, however, people began to report women in black. (No, seriously.) These woman posed as social workers and sought to take away people's children, just as child abduction fears and rumors spread across every soccer field and school playground.

Today, Men in Black have appeared in movies, comic books, and on television. They're often seen as a joke. Kids—particularly hackers—use the term to describe any government employee, or even just any authority figure. Like the number 23, Men in Black figure into many different theories. They are a sort of conspiratorial mortar that holds various bits of various theories together.

I'm going to watch out for them! They won't catch ME!!!

I think I heard a Black Helicopter last week!!! It didn't sound like a regular helicopter. Maybe IT'S TIME FOR THE INVASION!!!!!!

CONSPIRACY RUNDOWN

PLAUSIBILITY:

3/10. When push comes to shove, the stories may likely be hoaxes and exaggerations more than truth.

HIGH STRANGENESS:

10/10. It hardly gets stranger than this.

CONSPIRACY CHECKLIST:

- ☑ Illuminati
- ☐ The Freemasons
- ☑ CIA/intelligence community/the military
- ☑ Aliens
- ☑ The occult
- ☐ The Mafia

FOR MORE INFORMATION:

Casebook on the Men in Black by Jim Keith

Black Helicopters Over America by Jim Keith

The Mothman Prophecies by John Keel

The Truth Behind the Men in Black by Jenny Randles

ON THE WEB:

A Review of MIB (Men in Black): A History: www.ufoevidence.org/documents/doc1692.htm

CONSPIRACY INVESTIGATOR SEARCH TERMS:

Point Pleasant, Maury Island incident, Albert Bender, Gray Barker, black helicopters

26. THE OCTOPUS

SOMETIMES CONSPIRACY THEORIES are vast connected webs of plots, organizations, and secrets, and sometimes they are smaller. Very rarely are they both.

This is the story of a writer named Danny Casolaro, who may or may not have discovered a massive conspiracy that ties together most of the theories that you have read about in this book. He called it the Octopus.

INSLAW

Casolaro was born in 1947 in Virginia. Charming, funny, and well liked, he worked as a freelance writer and novelist. In 1990, he began looking into a small information technology company in Washington, D.C., named Inslaw. Inslaw had helped develop a computer program called PROMIS (Prosecutor's Management Information System). PROMIS, a database system, manages information for courts and law enforcement agencies. In the 1980s, Inslaw founder William A. Hamilton claims that the Justice Department appropriated (or just stole) PROMIS and distributed it illegally. Casolaro worked with Hamilton investigating these events in the hopes of writing a book about it. In his investigation, Casolaro uncovered far more than just the theft of some software.

DANGER MAN

Casolaro's main informant was eccentric former child prodigy Michael Riconosciuto, whom he dubbed "Danger Man" due to Riconosciuto's involvement in so many dangerous pursuits. For starters, Riconosciuto modified PROMIS to give the CIA backdoor access to the information stored in the database no matter who was using it, or where. Riconosciuto claimed that one way or another (usually illegally), the software found its way into at least eighty-eight different foreign countries, including (and

That's how the CIA maintains their spy network!!!

perhaps especially) U.S. enemies like Libya, Iran, and Iraq, as well as allies such as Canada, Great Britain, Japan, and Israel. This allowed the CIA to use the backdoor and gather all the information stored in the database. Supposedly this information was used in such operations as the Gulf War. Ironically, author Kenn Thomas believes that Osama Bin Laden may be evading capture by using the same backdoor created for the CIA, peeking into the databases of various intelligence agencies—including the CIA—to stay one step ahead of them.

Riconosciuto did his work on the Cabazon Indian Reservation in California at the behest of the Wackenhut Corporation. Because of technicalities in the reservation's sovereignty, Wackenhut could do things there that they could not do elsewhere in the United States. These things ranged from illegally obtained software to weapons design. Powerful fuel air explosives were created there using technology that, according to writer Doug Moench, may be linked to antigravity and teleportation and may have some roots in the work of Nazi scientists and Operation Paperclip (see Chapter 4). The mad scientists of the Wackenhut Corporation were supposedly even working with data from the Human Genome Project in order to create biological weapons based on specific DNA codes. In other words, diseases that killed based on race. *WEAPONS of MASS destruction!! IRAq connection AGAIN!!!*

Riconosciuto didn't work alone. A man named Earl Brian also worked on the Cabazon Reservation. Brian was not only the architect of PROMIS's theft, but he had worked with Operation Phoenix in Vietnam (a CIA program of using terror tactics, assassination, and psychological warfare on the civilian population). He also worked with George Bush Sr. to arrange the so-called October Surprise in 1980, an agreement with Iran not to release their fifty-two American hostages until after the election, a move that ensured victory for Ronald Reagan over incumbent Jimmy Carter. In fact, Brian may not have stolen PROMIS; in fact, Attorney General Edwin Meese may have illegally given it to him as a reward for his work on the October Surprise.

WACKENHUT is a KEY PART of the MILITARY-INDUSTRIAL COMPLEX!!!!

Who KNOWS how POWERFUL they ARE??

WHITEWATER AND VINCE FOSTER

In 1992, President Bill Clinton assigned Webster Hubbell of the Justice Department to investigate the Inslaw affair. However, Hubbell had been involved with a company called Park-On-Meter (POM), which supposedly received a loan from the Arkansas Development Finance Authority, an organization headed by Hubbell, at then governor Clinton's request. According to Riconosciuoto, POM secretly, and possibly illegally, produced chemical and biological weapons as did Wackenhut. The Whitewater scandal, centered around a possibly illegal business venture involving Bill and Hillary Clinton, forced Hubbell to resign before ever really getting into the Inslaw case. However, after the Whitewater scandal broke, White House counsel and former Clinton financial advisor Vince Foster was found shot dead in a park. Foster had spent some of his last days with Hubbell and spent some of his last hours of work focusing on the POM improprieties. Foster's diary and some Whitewater documents were removed from his office immediately following his death. According to some conspiracy researchers, this all makes these Clinton-based scandals a minor tip of a tentacle of the Octopus. *It's so clear now!*

IT'S ALL ONE BIG CONSPIRACY!!!!! But it's dangerous to know too much! Be careful!!! They're all around!!

While at Cabazon, Brian supposedly used money gained from the sale of PROMIS to fund the weapons programs there and to supply munitions and biological weapons to the Nicaraguan Contra rebels. Was there any shady dealing in the 1980s that Earl Brian didn't have his fingers in? Did he steal Michael Jackson's other glove, too?

MOBSTERS AND ALIENS

Oh, and we're not done with Wackenhut. Casolaro identified Wackenhut itself as a major part of the Octopus. Long rumored to be a civilian front for the CIA, and certainly a career opportunity for ex-CIA operatives (as many Wackenhut employees are), the corporation is rumored by conspiracy nuts to be involved in shady projects, black ops, and conspiracies.

For example, Wackenhut interfaced with Mafia drug dealers (specifically the Gambino family) on the reservation, taking a cut of the family's proceeds and using them to further their arms smuggling operations. Further, Wackenhut apparently provides security for Area 51 (see Chapter 15) and according to Casolaro's own notes is linked with a number of supposed underground bases used by the government along with its alien allies. These include Dulce, New Mexico, and Pine Gap in Australia. Thus we have entered into the world of MJ 12 (see Chapter 15), where the shadow government works secretly in cahoots with the alien Greys. Riconosciuto's view, however, goes a step beyond that. He paints a picture of two different covert forces warring against one another in the shadows: "Aquarius," which is linked to the CIA (and Wackenhut) and the CIA's secret leaders, versus MJ 12 and "Com-12," which is linked to the Office of Naval Intelligence. Aquarius represents the surviving hidden cabal of Nazis who still seek to promote the Aryan race, although quixotically they've allied themselves with aliens (who are neither blonde haired nor blue eyed). Com-12 members work on the good side of the Force and have supernatural communication abilities. So in Riconosciuto's mind, there are two octopi, and they're at war.

Mob ALWAYS works with the government!! JUST LIKE IN THE KENNEDY ASSASSINATION!!

Riconosciuto has his own links to aliens. Like Bob Lazar (see Chapter 15), he worked for Lear Aircraft, specifically Bill Lear, who in addition to having created the Lear jet also supposedly experimented with antigravity technology. Riconosciuto also worked with John Lear, a proponent of the idea that the government secretly works alongside extraterrestrials. Also, as mentioned in Chapter 5, John Lear has connections with Fred Crisman, a friend of his father's who was involved in the infamous Maury Island incident, one of the first modern UFO encounters and certainly one of the most interesting. But Crisman also ties Riconosciuto into the JFK assassination, because Crisman may be one of the infamous three hobos (see Chapter 6) photographed just beyond the grassy knoll. Even lawman Jim Garrison believed that Crisman was involved, and he subpoenaed the mystery man to testify in

LEAR got ideas for this from the Roswell CRASH!!!!!

the trial of Clay Shaw. Besides the presidential assassination, it is likely that Crisman was involved with the CIA, Operation Paperclip, and all manner of other spook matters. *HE'S ANOTHER KEY who ties it All together!!!!!*

CLARK GABLE

In addition to Riconosciuto, another of Casolaro's informants was Robert Booth Nichols, whom the investigator called "Clark Gable" because of his likeness to the actor. Nichols warned that Riconosciuto was untrustworthy (Riconosciuto said the same about Nichols), and he also cautioned Casolaro that what he was investigating was dangerous stuff. Nichols worked at Cabazon developing weapons and other high-tech systems. He invented the modern submachine gun and was an admitted CIA agent. Nichols was a close friend of Earl Brian and may also have been involved in the October Surprise. He had connections with organizations all over the world, from postwar Japanese intelligence to the Chinese tongs. He laundered money for former Philippine president Ferdinand Marcos and controlled a significant portion of the heroin trade. His friend Steven Segal even got him a small role in the move *Under Siege*. He was a man with many fingers in many pies.

According to researcher and activist Sherman Skolnick, Nichols not only had ties to both intelligence and organized crime, he may have been involved in the World Trade Center bombing in 1993. Nichols provided Casolaro information about Hughes Aircraft, which Casolaro believed was a part of the Octopus. Of course, Nichols may simply have been a con artist. In 2004 he was under investigation for defrauding investors in a multimillion-dollar international scheme.

OMG!!! What about 9/11????? This is SUCH AN IMPORTANT CONNECTION!!!!

CASOLARO'S THEORY, TENTACLES AND ALL

Danny Casolaro wrote in his notes that "[exposing] the Octopus will help unravel the most compelling puzzles of the Twentieth Century."

He took the term "octopus" seriously, as he identified eight men (tentacles) who comprised a sort of shadow government involved in the Bay of Pigs invasion, the JFK assassination, Area 51, Iran-Contra, and virtually every other conspiracy hot topic of our time. They were not elected officials but instead men who could influence whole governments. They were not criminals but wielded criminal organizations—like the Mafia, the Japanese yakuza, the Chinese triads, and even terrorist groups—like weapons. They were all intelligence agents or former intelligence agents and included Operation Phoenix masterminds John Singlaub and William Colby as well as Watergate operatives E. Howard Hunt and Bernard Barker. *Both dead!!*

We'll never know the full extent of what Casolaro had uncovered. He never got to write his book, because he died in 1991.

A housekeeper found him floating in his Martinsburg, West Virginia, hotel room bathtub with slashed wrists. His death was ruled a suicide, despite the fact that his wounds showed signs of not being self-inflicted and the fact that there were bloody towels under the sink well away from where he died. *Another suspicious death!!!!*

Just a few hours before, he had been seen meeting with a man of Arab or East Indian appearance (and if you're wondering if he was wearing all black, you've likely just read Chapter 25). Those who saw him describe his mood as upbeat—excited even—regarding his research and his book. He had told his brother on multiple occasions, "If anything happens to me—and it looks like an accident—don't believe it." The housekeeper reported that he had received a number of mysterious, threatening phone calls earlier that day, and that many of his papers were missing. *I wonder if the housekeeper was in on it.*

One remaining piece of paper in his room drew links between "CIA," "Shadow Government," "Alien," and "Zapata." "Zapata" was the name of George Bush Sr.'s oil company based in Houston. Perhaps not coincidentally, the Bay of Pigs invasion of Cuba in 1961 was given the top-secret code name "Zapata" as well, using two disguised naval vessels bearing the name "Houston" and "Barbara" (as in Bush?). Was Casolaro on Bush's trail—did he think our former president was a part of the Octopus? Many believe that despite his denials, Bush Sr. was a long-time operative in the CIA and may very well have been present at JFK's assassination. (He was appointed the director of the agency in 1976.) Then again, Zapata is also Spanish for "shoe," so maybe the note meant Danny needed a new pair of sneakers.

IT ENDS IN TEARS

Was Danny Casolaro a victim of the Octopus? If he was, he didn't die alone. A number of the informants and sources that Casolaro talked with also died under mysterious circumstances, many of them "suicides."

Riconosciuto was arrested and sent to jail on drug charges—he claims he was framed by the people he was talking to Casolaro about. In February 2001, he contacted Attorney General John Ashcroft and Secretary of State Colin Powell offering them information in exchange for his freedom about Arab terrorists who wanted to hijack planes and destroy American sites. His offer was ignored.

Some of Riconosciuto's lawyers and contacts ended up on the wrong side of a gun barrel. Another reporter investigating the same things as Casolaro, Jonathan Moyle, was found hanged in his hotel room.

In all, nearly forty witnesses in the Inslaw case were murdered, as well as many others more tenuously connected to Casolaro, Iran-Contra, and the October Surprise.

Is it all true? Did Danny Casolaro happen to stumble onto a vast conspiracy? There's room for doubt, but most of the conspiracy theory crowd hails Casolaro as its posthumous hero-king. There are even "Danny Casolaro died for your sins" T-shirts.

I KNEW IT!!!

POWELL WAS PART of THE COVER-UP too!!! HE WAS A MEMBER of THE Council on FOREIGN RELATIONS, which is controlled by THE MASONS!!

YES!!!!!!!

CONSPIRACY RUNDOWN

PLAUSIBILITY:

5/10. Who knows? This may be one of the few attempts to really find proof of a secret government with careful research, or it might be as kooky and unbelievable as the rest. Without Danny's full manuscript or notes, how will we ever know?

HIGH STRANGENESS:

6/10. We've got underground alien bases again, as well as near-mystical, secret spook armies fighting on opposite sides like Jedi and Sith, so we'll call that strange.

CONSPIRACY CHECKLIST:
- ☑ Illuminati
- ☐ The Freemasons
- ☑ CIA/intelligence community/the military
- ☑ Aliens
- ☑ The occult
- ☑ The Mafia

FOR MORE INFORMATION:

The Octopus: Secret Government and the Death of Danny Casolaro by Kenn Thomas and Jim Keith

ON THE WEB:

Inslaw official site: www.inslawinc.com

Wackenhut official site: www.g4s.com/usw

CONSPIRACY INVESTIGATOR SEARCH TERMS:

Danny Casolaro, Inslaw, Wackenhut, Iran-Contra, Zapata, Hughes Aircraft, Lear Aircraft, Fred Crisman, E. Howard Hunt, Pine Gap

27. THE CONSPIRACY CONSPIRACY

IT'S NOT EASY being a conspiracy theorist. Conspiracies are everywhere, and their number one enemy is those who would seek to expose them: conspiracy theorists. The conspiracy theorist's main weapon is information, and thus its greatest weapon is disinformation. That's why conspiracy theorists always respond to challenges with statements like, "that's just what they *want* you to think!"

That means, then, that in the minds of many, this very book you're reading is a part of a conspiracy—the worst conspiracy of them all, in fact. The conspiracy to make conspiracy theorists look bad. The conspiracy to make everyone believe that there is no such thing as conspiracies. The conspiracy conspiracy.

Conspiracy theorists believe that, as a culture, we've been brainwashed to be too accepting of the mainstream media. We believe the official story but never the lone voice in the wilderness, regardless of where the truth actually lies.

The very word *conspiracy* has become a loaded term. Conspiracy simply means "a secret agreement between two or more people to perform an unlawful act." And that's certainly very real. It happens all the time, in fact. One in four criminal convictions includes a conspiracy charge. But "conspiracy" has become synonymous with "bogeymen." Hearing the word instantly makes us think that the person using it is a crackpot. This is why conspiracy theorists have recently adopted the term "parapolitics" to describe what it is they research and write about. We've yet to see that term catch on, however.

Sometimes, according to conspiracy believers under siege, the conspiracy has even muddied the waters with outlandish, blatantly ridiculous conspiracy theories to make the real theorists look foolish alongside them. The problem is separating the good nuts from the bad. The "government was behind 9/11" crowd, for the most part, doesn't want to be lumped in with the Area 51 fanatics. Serious investigators into ufology, like Stanton Friedman, don't want to be associated with

The answers are obvious!!!! YOU'VE JUST GOT TO SEE THEM!!!

The author keeps calling me a NUT. But HE KNOWS I'M RIGHT!!!!!!

people like David Icke, who think the president is really a shape-shifting alien. So one man's truth seeker is another man's nut job.

CONSPIRACY THEORY IS HARD

The conspiracy—whether it's the military-industrial complex, the New World Order, the Illuminati, or reptilian shape-changer overlords—has created a society in which we want simple answers. We'd rather learn more about some celebrity's time in rehab than the truth about 9/11, conspiracy theorists say. We don't like the truth conspiracy theorists have to offer. Conspiracists say that's for at least three different reasons.

First, the truth is complicated. It's just hard to manage the facts and understand the motives and plots of the conspiracy. The mechanisms perpetrators use to get away with their secret crimes are intricate and involve aspects of government procedure, legal processes, and economic principles of which most of us know nothing.

Second, conspiracy theories paint a picture of a bleaker world than we want to live in. It's easier to think that a lone nut killed a beloved president or famous personality than to think that it was a conspiracy involving a large portion of our government and law enforcement. As cynical as we can be, we really don't want to believe that our authority figures are up to no good. It's bad enough that someone killed Martin Luther King Jr., but it's far worse to think that it might have been a conspiracy of many people, some working under the auspices of our government. To accept a conspiracy theory is to accept that we've been lied to, and that we've bought into it until now. It means that we've been dupes. The world is awful *and* we're stupid. No one wants to believe that.

Third, believing in a conspiracy requires the believer to begin to question everything. If the CIA was behind the Jonestown massacre, what else has it done? It's one thing to question a single belief, but not many people like to have their entire worldview challenged. Rev. Ivan

THE GOVERNMENT TRIES TO MAKE US DUPES!!! BUT I SEE THROUGH IT!!!!! EVEN if THEY GET ME I KNOW THE TRUTH!!!!

Stang, in his introduction to the *Big Book of Conspiracies*, puts it this way: "They simply cannot *allow themselves* to believe that men whose portraits still hang in city halls and corporate headquarters were in fact amoral monsters and eager collaborators with Nazis. It implies that the smiling, rosy-cheeked, glad-handing politician they just voted for might be involved in something *worse!*" We are, for the most part, comfortable with our lives, and we don't want to have to spend the next year investigating everything that's happened to find the truth. It's easier to be lied to—it's less work.

MIND CONTROL IN ITS MANY FORMS

Conspiracy theorists like Cisco Wheeler and Al Bielek believe that a mind-control program of a massive scale is going on. As with the CIA's MKULTRA program (see Chapter 24), our minds have been conditioned via carefully designed traumas, like Vietnam or 9/11, as well as electronic transmissions and implants. Wheeler and Bielek argue that as many as 10 million people in the United States have been deliberately and artificially programmed via these methods.

Some more down-to-earth theorists (if there is such a thing) believe we are motivated by far simpler techniques. The first and foremost is fear. By making us afraid, "They" convince us to forgo our freedoms in order to be safe. We give up our right to privacy so They can listen to phone conversations and root out anyone who might pose a threat to us. We give up our right to criticize the government. We give up the right to free speech.

Is it time, then, to get ourselves measured for a tinfoil hat and build a bunker? No. Are all conspiracy theorists kooks? Also no. Like so much in life, the truth seems to lie somewhere in the middle. Everything in moderation. Is anything in this book true? Yes. Is all of it true? Almost certainly not.

If nothing else, it's all pretty entertaining.

I'm not afriad! They can't stop me!! I'll get the TRUTH out, no matter what!!

CONSPIRACY RUNDOWN

PLAUSIBILITY:

5/10. Someone's made conspiracy nuts look nuts. But maybe they did it to themselves.

HIGH STRANGENESS:

2/10. Aside from mind-control rays affecting one out of every thirty Americans, this isn't all that strange.

CONSPIRACY CHECKLIST:
- ☑ Illuminati
- ☐ The Freemasons
- ☑ CIA/intelligence community/the military
- ☑ Aliens
- ☐ The occult
- ☐ The Mafia

FOR MORE INFORMATION:

The Big Book of Conspiracies by Doug Moench

ON THE WEB:

Conspiracy Theorist Essay: www.rense.com/general61/dwe.htm

Index of kooky websites: www.crank.net

CONSPIRACY INVESTIGATOR SEARCH TERMS:

conspiracy nuts, crackpots, insolitology, Time Cube, no planes, disinformation

BE CAREFUL!!! You can find out the truth!!!!!! I DID!
And now I'm not safe!!! I've got to go on the run!!

Go into hiding!! You can DO WHAT I DID!
Be ONE of us. Not Them. Don't let Them fool you!!!!!

And always look behind you.

THEY'RE OUT THERE!!!!!!!!!!!

APPENDIX
BUILD YOUR OWN CONSPIRACY THEORY

After reading all about various theories, and perhaps even getting a brief insight into what it is like to be a conspiracy theorist, you might want to try your hand at creating your own conspiracy theory. You could spend months devoted to research, or you could just use the simple system presented here.

On the following pages you'll find four categories, labeled Subject A, Subject B, Means, and Goal. Choose randomly from these lists to pull together what you need to get to the heart of your conspiracy theory. You can put them together like this: "[Subject A], working in conjunction with [Subject B], is using [Means] to [Goal]"

Thus, one might create a theory that states that, "The CIA, working in conjunction with the Nazis in Antarctica, is utilizing mind-controlled assassins to take control of the world!" or, even more fun, "The military, working in conjunction with PETA, is utilizing eBay to find Osama Bin Laden!"

Alternatively, you can create your conspiracy this way: "[Subject A] uses [Means] to [Goal]." This method is more straightforward and leads to slightly more realistic (but less humorous) conspiracy theories such as "The Illuminati uses HAARP to control our minds!"

Roll dice to make your conspiracy theory associations random. Pull out the dice from Monopoly or Yahtzee or some other game, roll three of them, and count down the various lists. If you've got access to some of those funny polyhedral dice like those used in Dungeons & Dragons, you can generate numbers more precisely using "percentile dice" generating numbers from 1–100 and ignoring results that are too high. Alternatively, you can go to *www.randomnumbergenerator.com* and generate exact random numbers for each category. If you do, you'll need to know that there are 43 entries for Subject A, 51 entries for Subject B, 63 entries for Means, and 40 entries for Goal.

See how easy that is? Now you just need a tinfoil hat and a rambling website and you'll be ready to go.

SUBJECT A

The Illuminati

The Freemasons

The CIA

The FBI

The Office of Naval Intelligence

The military

The Mafia

A satanic cult

George Bush (either one)

Bill Clinton

Hillary Clinton

Aliens (Zeta Reticulans)

Reptilian alien shape-shifters

Al-Qaeda

The Knights Templar

The Trilateral Commission

Disciples of Alistair Crowley

The Mormons

The Nazis in South America

The United Nations

The New World Order

The Vatican

NASA

The Merovingians

The Church of Scientology

A popular author

Council on Foreign Relations

Skull and Bones

The Priory of Sion

The P2 Lodge

Big Oil

The Unabomber

Greenpeace

The cultural elite

Islamic extremists

Secret refugees from Jonestown

A lone nut

The Solar Temple

The media

The Bilderberg Group

Big Tobacco

Right-wing militia groups

MJ 12/Aquarius

SUBJECT B

The Boy Scouts of America

The Rosicrucians

The descendants of Christ

David Icke

CIA psychics

J-Rod

The ghost of Leonardo da Vinci

Bigfoot

Larry King

The ACLU

The Men in Black

Satan himself

Hollywood

The police

American Idol winners, past and present

The Process Church

Charles Manson

A Jim Morrison double

British royalty

The Rockefellers

The Nazis in Antarctica

The NSA

Vapid celebrities

Congress

The Supreme Court

The Octopus

The woman in the polka dot dress

The real Lee Harvey Oswald

The Shriners

The Elks Club

The Fraternal Order of Water Buffalo

Harry Potter fans

The Ancient Egyptians

Terrorists

Hippies

College Republicans

The NRA

The Communists

The anti-Communists

The Dogon

O. J. Simpson

The Walt Disney Corporation

The Kennedys

PETA

Wall Street moguls

Professional sports stars

Trekkies

Starbucks

Buddhists

Illegal immigrants

The gunmen from the grassy knoll

MEANS

The Dead Sea Scrolls

Disinformation

Mind-control implants

LSD

Hypnosis

The Internet

An atomic bomb

UFOs

Mind-controlled assassins

Secret underground bases

Rock music

Reverse-engineered
alien technology

Secrets developed by
Nicolai Tesla

Secrets developed by
Wilhelm Reich

Secrets developed by
the Nazis

CO2 emissions

Fluoride in the water

Nutra-Sweet

The artwork of Leonardo
da Vinci

The works of Shakespeare

Unmarked black helicopters

HAARP

Mind-control satellites

Cell phones

Conspiracy theorists

Informational pamphlets

The power of positive
thinking

Tinfoil hats

The secrets of
Rennes-le-Château

Secret codes in the
dollar bill

Ancient secrets
from Atlantis

The number 23

Deep-cover agents

Subliminal advertising

Magic bullets

Carefully engineered lies

Slave labor

Microwaves

Endangered species

The face on Mars

Legislation

Frivolous lawsuits

TV evangelists

A giant pyramid

Comic books

Low-frequency radio waves

Claims made by Princess
Diana

Prayer

Chemtrails

Good old American
know-how

Video games

Richard Nixon's secret tapes

Ultrasonic transmissions

Renaissance fairs

The Zapruder film

Krlll

Editorial cartoons

Genetically modified
super-soldiers

Voodoo

eBay

Vril energy

Steroids

Fear tactics

GOAL

Reveal the truth about
flying saucers!

Control our minds!

Take away our freedoms!

Take over the world!

Find the Lindberg baby!

Find Osama Bin Laden!

Build a moon base!

End global warming!

Fake his/her/their own
death(s)!

Take control of the illegal
drug trade!

Institute a new worldwide
religion!

Bring Elvis back from
the grave!

Find a cure for the common
cold!

Learn the secrets of
antigravity technology!

Build a time machine!

Devalue the dollar!

Make a killing in the
stock market!

Get girls!

Assassinate the president!

Colonize Mars!

Bring glory to their master,
Satan!

Make millions!

Become world famous!

Destroy [Subject A]!

Stage a military coup!

Ban books!

Win the War on Drugs!

Cover up the fake
moon landing!

Take over the
entertainment industry!

Undermine the morals
of America!

Blow up Mount Rushmore!

Cover up the truth behind
[Means]!

Melt the polar ice caps!

Communicate with
extraterrestrials!

Learn the secrets of
[Subject B]!

Travel to the center of
the Earth!

Frame a congressman!

Kidnap the First Lady!

Cover up all their hideous
crimes!

Write a book about
conspiracies!

SELECTED BIBLIOGRAPHY

Addison, Charles G. *The History of the Knights Templars*. (Kempton, IL: Adventures Unlimited Press, 1997)

Allen, Gary. *None Dare Call It Conspiracy*. (Rossmoor, CA: Concord Press, 1972)

Baigent, Michael and Richard Leigh. *The Temple and the Lodge*. (New York, NY: Arcade Publishing, 1989)

Baigent, Michael, Richard Leigh and Henry Lincoln. *Holy Blood, Holy Grail*. (New York, NY: Dell Publishing, 1993)

Barrett, David V. *Secret Societies*. (London, England: Blandford, 1999)

Berlitz, Charles and William L. Moore. *The Roswell Incident*. (New York, NY: Berkley, 1988)

Botham, Neil. *The Murder of Princess Diana*. (New York, NY: Pinnacle Books, 2004)

Carter, John. *Sex and Rockets: The Occult World of Jack Parsons*. (Venice, CA: Feral House, 1999)

Clarke, James, W. *On Being Mad or Merely Angry: John W. Hinckley Jr. and Other Dangerous People*. (Princeton, NJ: Princeton University Press, 1990)

Coleman, John. *The Conspirator's Hierarchy: The Committee of 300* (Petaluma, CA: Global Insights, 2006)

Cooper, William. *Behold a Pale Horse*. (Flagstaff, AZ: Light Technology Publications, 1991)

Daraul, Arkon. *A History of Secret Societies*. (Secaucus, NJ: Citadel Press, 1997)

DiEugenio, James, ed. *The Assassinations: Probe Magazine on JFK, MLK, RFK and Malcolm X*. (Portland, OR: Feral House, 2003)

Estulin, Daniel. *The True Story of the Bilderberg Group*. (Walterville, OR: Trine Day, 2007)

Fanthorpe, Lionel and Patricia. *Secrets of Rennes le Chateau*. (York Beach, ME: Samuel Weiser, 1992)

Farren, Mick. *Conspiracies, Lies, and Hidden Agendas*. (Los Angeles, CA: Renaissance Books, 1999)

Fetzer, James H. *The 9/11 Conspiracy*. (Chicago, IL: Open Court, 2007)

Fuller, John G. *The Interrupted Journey*. (New York, NY: Berkley, 1966)

Garrison, Jim. *On the Trail of the Assassins*. (New York, NY: Sheridan Square Press, 1988)

Grant, Kenneth. *Outer Gateways*. (London, England: Skoob Books, 1994)

Griffin, David Ray. *The New Pearl Harbor*. (Northampton, MA: Interlink, 2004)

Hesemann, Michael, Philip Mantle, and Bob Shell. *Beyond Roswell: The Alien Autopsy Film, Area 51, & the U.S. Government Coverup of UFOs*. (Emeryville, CA: Marlowe & Company, 1998)

Hieronimus, Robert. *America's Secret Destiny*. (Rochester, VT: Destiny Books, 1989)

Hoagland, Richard C. *Dark Mission: The Secret History of NASA*. (Portland, OR: Feral House, 2007)

Howard, Michael. *The Occult Conspiracy*. (Rochester, VT: Destiny Books, 1989)

Hynek, J. Allen. *The Hynek UFO Report*. (New York, NY: Barnes & Noble, 1997)

Hynek, J. Allen. *The UFO Experience*. (New York, NY: Ballantine, 1972)

Icke, David. *The David Icke Guide to the Global Conspiracy*. (Nashville, TN: Associated Publishers Group, 2007)

Isreal, Lee. *Kilgallen*. (New York, NY: Delcorte Press, 1979)

Jackson, Devon. *Conspiranoia*. (New York, NY: Penguin, 2000)

Jones, Jack. *Let Me Take You Down: Inside the Mind of Mark David Chapman, the Man Who Killed John Lennon*. (New York, NY: Villard Books, 1992)

Jones, Penn. *Forgive My Grief*. (Midlothian, TX: Midlothian Mirror Press, 1966)

Kaiser, Robert Blair. *"RFK Must Die!"* (New York, NY: E. P. Dutton & Co., 1970)

Kaysing, Bill and Randy Reid. *We Never Went to the Moon: America's Thirty Billion Dollar Swindle*. (Pomeroy, WA: Health Research, 1976)

Keel, John. *The Mothman Prophecies*. (Lilburn, GA: IllumiNet Press, 1991)

Keith, Jim. *Black Helicopters Over America: Strikeforce for the New World Order*. (Lilburn, GA: IllumiNet Press, 1994)

Keith, Jim. *Black Helicopters 2: The Endgame Strategy*. (Lilburn, GA: IllumiNet Press, 1997)

Keith, Jim. *Casebook on Alternative 3*. (Lilburn, GA: IllumiNet Press, 1994)

Keith, Jim. *Casebook on the Men in Black*. (Lilburn, GA: IllumiNet Press, 1997)

Keith, Jim. *Mind Control, World Control*. (Kempton, IL: Adventures Unlimited Press, 1997)

Keith, Jim, ed. *Secret and Suppressed: Banned Ideas and Hidden History*. (Portland, OR: Feral House, 1993)

Lane, Mark. *Plausible Denial*. (New York, NY: Thunder's Mouth Press, 1991)

Levy, Joel. *The Little Book of Conspiracies*. (New York, NY: Thunder's Mouth Press, 2005)

Lindsey, Hal. *The Late, Great Planet Earth*. (New York, NY: Bantam, 1973)

Manchester, William. *The Death of a President*. (New York, NY: BBS Publishing Corporation, 1996)

Manning, Jeane and Nick Begich. *Angels Don't Play This HAARP*. (Anchorage, AK: Earthpulse Press, 1995)

Marchetti, Victor and John D. Marks. *The CIA and the Cult of Intelligence*. (New York, NY: Alfred A. Knopf, 1974)

McGowan, David. *Programmed to Kill: The Politics of Serial Murder*. (Bloomington, IL: iUniverse, Inc, 2004)

Moench, Doug. *The Big Book of Conspiracies*. (New York, NY: Paradox Press, 1995)

National Insecurity Council. *It's a Conspiracy!* (Berkeley, CA: EarthWorks Press, 1992)

Payson, Seth. *Proof of the Illuminati*. (Arlington, VA: Invisible College Press, LLC, 2003)

Pepper, Bill. *An Act of State: the Execution of Martin Luther King*. (New York, NY: Verso, 2003)

Perloff, James. *The Shadows of Power: The Council on Foreign Relations and the American Decline*. (Boston, MA: Western Islands, 1988)

Piccard, George. *Liquid Conspiracy*. (Kempton, IL: Adventures Unlimited Press, 1999)

Picknett, Lynn and Clive Prince. *The Templar Revelation*. (London, England: Corgi Books, 1997)

Pope, Nick. *Open Skies, Closed Minds*. (New York, NY: Dell, 1998)

Posner, Gerald. *Killing the Dream: James Earl Ray and the Assassination of Martin Luther King, Jr.* (Arlington Heights IL: Harvest Books, 1994)

Randle, Kevin D. and Donald R. Schmitt. *The Truth About the UFO Crash at Roswell*. (New York, NY: Avon, 1994)

Randles, Jenny. *The Truth Behind Men in Black*. (New York, NY: St. Martin's Press, 1997)

Randles, Jenny. *The UFO Conspiracy: The First Forty Years*. (New York, NY: Barnes & Noble, 1987)

Raschke, Carl A. *Painted Black*. (San Francisco, CA: Harper & Row, 1990)

Reese, Mary Ellen. *General Reinhard Gehlen: The CIA Connection*. (Fairfax, VA: George Mason University Press, 1990)

Roberts, Craig and John Armstrong. *JFK: The Dead Witnesses* (Locust Grove, OK: Consolidated Press International, 1995)

Robertson, Pat. *The New World Order*. (Nashville, TN: W Publishing Group, 1991)

de Sede, Gerard. *The Accursed Treasure of Rennes-le-Chateau*. (Salem, OR: DEK Publishing, 2001)

Schlafly, Phyllis. *A Choice, Not an Echo*. (Alton, IL: Pere Marquette Press, 1964)

Simpson, Christopher. *Blowback: America's Recruitment of Nazis and Its Effects on the Cold War*. (New York, NY: Weidenfeld and Nicholson, 1988)

Sklar, D. *The Nazis and the Occult*. (New York, NY: Dorset Press, 1977)

Sora, Steven. *The Lost Treasure of the Knights Templar*. (Rochester, VT: Destiny Books, 1999)

Still, William T. *New World Order: The Ancient Plan of Secret Societies*. (Lafayette, LA: Huntington House, 1990)

Suster, Gerald. *Hitler: Black Magician*. (London, England: Skoob Books, 1996)

Temple, Robert K. G. *The Sirius Mystery*. (Rochester, VT: Destiny Books, 1987)

Terry, Maury. *The Ultimate Evil: The Truth About the Cult Murders: Son of Sam & Beyond*. (New York, NY: Barnes & Noble, 1999)

Thomas, Kenn and Jim Keith. *The Octopus: Secret Government and the Death of Danny Casolaro*. (Portland, OR: Feral House, 1996)

Thomas, Kenn and Lincoln Lawrence. *Mind Control, Oswald, and JFK*. (Kempton, IL: Adventures Unlimited Press, 1997)

Tuckett, Kate, ed. *The A to Z of Conspiracy Theories*. (Chichester, England: Summersdale, 1998)

Turner, William and Jonn Christian. *The Assassination of Robert F. Kennedy*. (New York, NY: Thunder's Mouth Press, 1993)

Vankin, Jonathan and John Whalen. *The 80 Greatest Conspiracies of All Time*. (Secaucus, NJ: Citadel Press, 2004)

Waldron, Lamar and Thom Harman. *Ultimate Sacrifice: John and Robert Kennedy, the Plan for a Coup in Cuba, and the Murder of JFK*. (New York, NY: Carroll & Graf, 2005)

Wallace-Murphy, Tim and Marilyn Hopkins. *Rosslyn: Guardian of the Secrets of the Holy Grail*. (Boston, MA: Element Books, 1999)

Wilgus, Neal. *The Illuminoids*. (Santa Fe, NM: Sun Publishing, 1978)

Wilson, Robert Anton. *Cosmic Trigger: Final Secret of the Illuminati*. (Tempe, AZ: New Falcon Publications, 1996)

Wilson, Robert Anton. *Everything Is Under Control*. (New York, NY: Harper, 1998)

Wilson, Robert Anton. *The Illuminati Papers*. (Berkeley, CA: Ronin Publishing, 1997)

Wolfe, Donald H. *The Assassination of Marilyn Monroe*. (Eureka, CA: Firebird, 1999)

INDEX

ABOUT THE AUTHOR

Monte Cook has worked as a professional editor and writer for twenty years, with well over a hundred credits to his name. Most of his work has been with role-playing games and fiction. He helped create the third edition of Dungeons & Dragons, among many other games, including one called Dark Matter, a game where the players take on the roles of investigators of conspiracies and the paranormal.

A graduate of the Clarion West Science Fiction and Fantasy Writer's Workshop, Monte has published a number of short stories and four novels. His second novel, *Of Aged Angels*, dealt with such conspiratorial themes as the Knights Templar, the secret bloodline of Jesus, aliens, JFK, Marilyn Monroe, Jim Morrison, and the Holy Grail, to name just a few.

He currently resides in southeastern Wisconsin with his wife, Sue, and their Welsh corgi.